# Scaling the Ivory Tower

# Scaling the Ivory Tower

## STORIES FROM WOMEN IN BUSINESS SCHOOL FACULTIES

Edited by
### Dianne Cyr and Blaize Horner Reich

Foreword by Denise M. Rousseau

Westport, Connecticut
London

**Library of Congress Cataloging-in-Publication Data**

Scaling the ivory tower : stories from women in business school
   faculties / edited by Dianne Cyr and Blaize Horner Reich ; foreword
   by Denise M. Rousseau.
      p.   cm.
   Includes index.
   ISBN 0–275–95085–9 (alk. paper).—ISBN 0–275–95673–3 (pbk.)
      1. Business schools—United States—Faculty.   2. Women college
   teachers—United States.   3. College teachers—Tenure—United
   States.   I. Cyr, Dianne J.   II. Reich, Blaize Horner.
   HF1131.S3   1996
   331.4'8165'0071173—dc20          95–45416

British Library Cataloguing in Publication Data is available.

Library of Congress Catalog Card Number: 95–45416
ISBN: 0–275–95085–9
      0–275–95673–3 (pbk.)

First published in 1996

Praeger Publishers, 88 Post Road West, Westport, CT 06881
An imprint of Greenwood Publishing Group, Inc.

Printed in the United States of America

The paper used in this book complies with the
Permanent Paper Standard issued by the National
Information Standards Organization (Z39.48–1984).

10   9   8   7   6   5   4   3   2   1

*To the women who have opened their lives to us: reexamining their past, revealing their wins and their losses, as they scale the ivory tower.*

# Contents

# Foreword

The stories in this book are not a history. The authors give few dates and do not particularly name names. These are narratives, to be read to appreciate the personal choices, trade-offs, risks, and chances that unfold as one builds a career in increasingly competitive academic organizations. The *Oxford English Dictionary* offers many definitions of a "story," but one is particularly pertinent to this book: these stories capture "an existence worthy of record." These authors and their stories help us understand ourselves, whether female or male—as academic scholars, administrators, teachers, and institution builders.

It was not until the 1970s that women, particularly North American women, had access to academia in large numbers—as graduate students and faculty members. Now we have had more than twenty years of experience. Even the most senior among us is still in the middle of her story. As such, this is the first time that a set of stories could be collected. Women in academia are popular subjects of novels, but these novels are often mysteries centering on a struggle with mixed motives and moral conflicts, such as Dorothy Sayer's *Gaudy Night* or Amanda Cross's *Death in a Tenured Position*. Stories about the lives of real women academics are rarely written. This book is a welcome exception.

Overall, the women who tell us their stories are achieving success. Several factors replay throughout these stories and provide some sense of the context in which these women live. Unfolding from the following chapters are lessons about achieving excellence and balancing life goals, and about the forms of support required by the contributors at both personal and professional levels. There is much to learn from their successes and struggles. The women who have contributed to this volume have taken us into their confidence. We can repay their trust by working to understand their experiences.

Denise M. Rousseau
Professor, H. John Heinz III School of
Public Policy and Management
Carnegie Mellon University

# Introduction

*Life begets life. Energy creates energy. It is by spending oneself that one becomes rich.*

—Sarah Bernhardt, 1844–1923

## A PERSONAL STORY

This book is about women academics in university business faculties. Each contributor presents a first-person account of her experiences related to career decisions and choices. This collection of stories reflects the challenges, rewards, inconsistencies, support systems, highs, and lows on a path chosen. In many instances, these stories critique how decisions were made and why. Key issues and choice points are of particular focus, and the contributors seek to describe the *processes* that have contributed to their professional as well as personal development. For these women who have opted to "scale the ivory tower," the tales also involve other significant individuals or groups within each contributor's personal frame of reference. Parts of the journey have been travelled with significant support from others; parts have been more solitary. By virtue of being female, the path is generally strewn with more brambles and boulders than is usually the case for male counterparts. Expectations are different. Achieving life's balance poses unique difficulties.

Unlike previous books that have addressed the topic of women in an academic setting, this volume is based on real and contemporary stories. We are able to learn from each woman's personal experiences and from her wisdom. As such, this book will serve as a chronicle of experiences relevant to academics in a wide range of disciplines and country locations, Ph.D. students who seek a better understanding of the choices to be made as part of their future, and individuals who are contemplating a career in a university setting.

## ACADEMIA IN THREE PHASES

This book documents the experiences and insights of women academics who are at different stages in their career development. Three contributors are in the early (pre-tenure) stage of their careers, three are mid-career women with established professional directions, and three women were chosen because they were felt to have left a long-term and continuing impact on their chosen field of interest.

As editors, we provided the contributors with an outline of issues to consider in their respective chapters, with the caveat that creative license was to be encouraged and respected. We realized that each woman would have a different emphasis to her story—a different setting based on context and personal parameters. We also acknowledged that life is not linear and that each story would "spiral" to incorporate decisions or events related to both the past, present, and, in some cases, the future. As such, the chapter outline was a guide to "jog your memory and to provide some consistency between the stories of all of the participants." We added, "please elaborate on the points that make sense for you and add others that are unique to you." We wanted our participants to focus on personal decisions or choice points in their stories. For this reason, we suggested that dates, published works, or other specific references were less relevant than in other forms of academic writing. Reflection supersedes documentation.

In the following table, we have detailed the topics that the contributors were asked to consider. Although the chapter guideposts provided were similar across all three career groups, we added some variation to reflect the stage of career development. For example, early-career women were likely to focus more on issues related to completing the dissertation and landing the first job. Mid-career women were likely to be concerned with attaining tenure and moving into a post-tenure research or administrative agenda. Finally, our more senior academics were be able to elaborate more on their role as leaders in the field.

To aid the reader in making comparisons across the nine chronicles, we have provided summary sections at the end of each career phase (i.e., early-career, mid-career, and more senior academics). The summary includes a brief snapshot of each contributor, recurrent themes, interesting issues or challenges, and the lessons learned from their collective experiences. At the conclusion of the book, we provide a further summary outlining key themes and issues across all the women contributors.

**Topics Used as a Guideline for the Chapters**

| Early-Career Women | Mid-Career Women | Leaders in the Field |
|---|---|---|
| Career before Grad School | Choosing to Enter Academia | Choosing to Enter Academia |
| Choosing to Enter Academia | The Choice of Research Topic or Methodology for the Dissertation | Choosing the First Academic Position |
| Choice of School and Discipline | Choosing the First Academic Position | Developing a Post-Ph.D. Research Agenda |
| Journey through the Course Work | Developing a Post-Ph.D. Research Agenda | Teaching in the Pre-Tenure Years |
| Journey through the Course Work | Teaching in the Pre-Tenure Years | Choosing Other Pre-Tenure Professional Activities: Administration, Journals, Consulting |
| From Proposal to Defense | Choosing Other Pre-Tenure Professional Activities: Administration, Journals, Consulting | Balancing It All |
| Choosing the First Academic Position | Balancing It All | Preparing for Tenure |
| The First Couple of Years | Preparing for Tenure | The Tenure Process |
| Transition from the Ph.D. Thesis to a Research Program | The Tenure Process | Post-Tenure Energy |
| Publishing Your First Article(s) | The Tenure Process | Leading the Field |
| Teaching in the Early Years | Looking Ahead . . . Options for the Future | Looking Ahead . . . Options for the Future |
| Keeping Your Balance | | |
| Preparing for Tenure | | |

## EMERGING THEMES

Although the nine stories are based on individual experiences, certain themes emerged that suggest lessons for all readers, both male and female. These themes are reflections of the characteristics and requirements of high achievers who aim to excel in their professional and personal lives. The themes include:

1. *Serendipity*—The role of chance events and the need to seize opportunities that are fortuitously presented are apparent in these stories. In many instances, the life path is not rational or planned, but spontaneous and unexpected.

2. *Personal Mastery*—These women have all deliberately set out to excel and to challenge themselves in the development of excellence. They go beyond their own strengths to achieve levels of performance even higher than they themselves anticipated. Persistence and organization are the keys.

3. *The Female Dilemma*—Along the path of life, certain events may affect women more than men. These include the birth and rearing of children, deferring careers to those of their partners or spouses, and dealing with career situations when being female may have negative consequences.

4. *Support Systems*—Each woman has a source of support in her endeavors. Support is usually provided by a husband or other family member, or through mentors or networks of colleagues.

5. *Periods of Stress*—High levels of anxiety are exhibited at certain periods in the career cycle and at certain points on the career path. Stress is particularly related to completing the dissertation, obtaining a first position, and gaining tenure, for example.

6. *Achieving Balance*—Trying to create a balance, or in some cases an integration, in life events is important to our contributors. Each struggles in some way with the creation of an equilibrium between work and family, or between teaching, research, and administrative duties.

These themes serve as the linking pins in each story and provide us with information about the requirements of success in academic careers. Their variability is indicative of the wide spectrum of choices and the vast assortment of opportunities and challenges that are part of the academic territory.

## THE CONTRIBUTORS

Our group of contributors was chosen based upon either personal associations and/or an assessment of individuals who are representative of a career stage. We had an enthusiastic response from those women who were contacted to participate in this project. In fact, of the women we initially approached to write a chapter for this volume, all accepted except one. Despite huge work loads, each has allotted valuable time to a task that is not part of the set of accomplishments on the official tenure track tally.

The participants represent a broad range of academic disciplines including international management, organizational behavior, management information systems, strategy, marketing, and finance. Collectively, they embody a wide band of academic experience at various stages of the academic career sequence. In addition, they are a diverse group due to family background, marital status, or level of child care responsibilities. Our contributors, by career stage and in alphabetical order, include:

### Early-Career Women

Yolande E. Chan is an assistant professor specializing in management information systems at Queen's University in Kingston, Ontario. She has undergraduate and graduate degrees from MIT, and is a Rhodes Scholar. Prior to turning to academia, Yolande had a brief but successful career with Andersen Consulting. Yolande is married, and has a three-year-old son.

June N. P. Francis is an assistant professor of international marketing at Simon Fraser University in Burnaby, British Columbia. Similar to Yolande, she worked in the private sector as a marketing manager for Procter & Gamble before turning to academic pursuits. June is married and has three children. Due to go up for tenure evaluation shortly, she has been plagued by a neck injury that has necessitated a lengthy leave of absence from the university.

Marlene K. Puffer is currently an assistant professor in finance at the University of Toronto. She finished her undergraduate degree at age eighteen and then spent the next ten years completing her master's degree and Ph.D. She has been active as a role model for female students in finance and has participated on a task force to examine the status of women in her faculty. In the near future, she plans to take a leave of absence from her post to consult full-time in private industry. Marlene is single with no children.

### Mid-Career Women

Cynthia M. Beath is an associate professor of management information sciences at Southern Methodist University, Dallas, Texas, who has just received tenure. Prior to her current appointment, she was on the faculties of the University of Minnesota and UCLA. She recently completed a sabbatical as a Fulbright scholar in Bangkok and is now poised to continue a project on software sourcing. Cynthia is involved in a long-term relationship and has no children.

Sheila M. Puffer is an associate professor specializing in Russian management at Northeastern University in Boston. Sister to Marlene, she has a long-standing love of languages and travel. Fluent in French and Russian and also speaking Spanish and German, she was part of the ground-breaking Harvard research project into management practices in the former Soviet Union. Recently granted tenure, Sheila receives ongoing support from her husband as they raise two young children.

Carolyne F. Smart is an associate professor at Simon Fraser University.

Turning her energies to administration, she is active in making changes in the Faculty of Business as the associate dean. She was the first woman in the business faculty to receive tenure and to hold an administrative position. Carolyne is married with no children.

### Leaders in Their Field

Janice M. Beyer is a professor at the University of Texas in Austin. She has been the editor of some of the most preeminent journals in the business field (e.g., *Administrative Science Quarterly* and *Academy of Management Journal*) and is the past president of the Academy of Management. Now single, Janice has two grown daughters.

Karlene H. Roberts is a professor at the University of California at Berkeley. Her research interests have taken her where no other woman has previously tread—studying how accidents might occur aboard U.S. Navy aircraft carriers. She has been active as an editor and has served on the Academy of Management's board of governors. Karlene is divorced and has a son.

Mary Ann Von Glinow has recently joined the faculty of Florida International University in Miami as a professor of management and international business. In the last five years, she has authored six books as well as numerous journal articles. Mary Ann is the current president of the Academy of Management and is active as a consultant to multinational corporations. Married with no children, she and her husband sustain a commuting relationship between New York and Florida.

In the context of these rich and diverse backgrounds, let the journey begin.

# I

# Early-Career Women

# 1

# "Going the Extra Mile"

## *Yolande E. Chan*

*ad astra per aspera (to the stars through difficulty)*

My old high school motto—*ad astra per aspera*—could be my personal motto. It's not so much that I aspire to reach the stars. I know that the admiration of others can be fickle. But the achievements in my life have come largely as a result of hard work, perseverance, and prayer. As I have responded to work demands and other career challenges, I have struggled to keep my balance and avoid the pitfall described so well by Charles Swindoll: In the process of making a living, how easy it is to forget the value of making a life.

I am currently an assistant professor at Queen's University in Kingston, Canada. I conduct research at the School of Business on the alignment of information systems (IS) strategy and business strategy, the structure of the IS organization, and the business performance impacts of IS. I also teach IS analysis and design and IS strategy to undergraduate, M.B.A., and Ph.D. students. I was hired primarily because of my potential as a researcher but, in my three plus years at the school, I've pursued a more *balanced*, but perhaps riskier, approach than pure research: excellence in research, teaching, and administration.

I have tried earnestly to remember my priorities and to make choices that have *not* involved the sacrifice of my values, family life, or health. I have made giving time to the important people in my life a priority. This includes my husband, Michael, a physician who is extremely supportive of me personally and professionally. Another important person in my life is my son, Jonathan, who is three years old. A very big part of who we are as individuals and as a family revolves around our Christian faith. We are members of St. James Anglican Church, located on the university campus. To a lesser extent, our family activity also centers around sports. We jog, play tennis, cycle, and enjoy long walks together.

## CAREER BEFORE GRADUATE SCHOOL

I am of African and European heritage and was born in Kingston, Jamaica. There I attended two of the best schools in the country—Immaculate Conception High School (ICHS) and Campion College. Both are Roman Catholic schools (Franciscan and Jesuit respectively). I was the valedictorian of my graduating ICHS class and head girl at Campion College. At the end of my high school education, I won scholarships to Cornell, Harvard, MIT, Yale, and University of the West Indies. The Franciscan sisters at ICHS who knew me well recommended that I go to MIT because of my strong science and math orientation. I deliberated and prayed and went to MIT.

I graduated from MIT with a bachelor's degree in electrical engineering and a master's degree in electrical engineering and computer science. At the time, the vast majority of my instructors and fellow students were male. I seriously considered working toward a Ph.D. in electrical engineering and computer science but eventually rejected the idea. I didn't like what I saw around me—a number of colleagues who basically lived at the university, in poor health, unapproachable, and lost in the game of advancement. There was little evidence of balance in their lives.

I thought about what I could do with the bachelor's and master's degrees. I didn't see myself programming or building circuit boards for the rest of my life. I enjoy working with people, not just machinery. But to transfer my skills to a business setting and be able to manage people in the Computer Science area, I needed an M.B.A.

I also needed a rest. While at MIT, I had been involved in a large number of extracurricular activities. Also, because I was on a four-year undergraduate scholarship but wanted to obtain my master's at MIT, I had completed the six-year bachelor's and master's degree program requirements in four years. By the time I graduated, I could have written a book on time management techniques! However, my coveted rest did not materialize because, during my final year at MIT, with some prompting from family and colleagues, I applied for a Rhodes Scholarship to study management at Oxford University. I suspect that I am not the only Rhodes Scholar who, on hearing the good news, sighed wearily instead of celebrating.

At that time, Oxford did not offer an M.B.A. program. It did offer an M.Phil. in management studies, a rigorous two-year program that emphasizes the *theory* of management. The M.Phil. involves a thesis (as had both my MIT bachelor's and master's programs) that provided excellent practice for the later Ph.D. dissertation. Even more unique than the thesis is the primary method of teaching—small group tutorials in which students present and defend essays they create based on their review of assigned literature. The M.Phil. helped me learn to synthesize material, write well, and argue well—skills that proved useful for me later in academia.

It was during the M.Phil. program that I met and married my husband, also a Rhodes Scholar studying at Oxford. After completing our studies, my husband and I traveled to Canada, where he would complete his four-year residency in psychiatry. I joined the Toronto office of Andersen Consulting, where I worked as a management information systems (MIS) consultant and was eventually promoted to manager. MIS consulting made use of my early university training in engineering and computer science and the later training in management. It seemed to be the logical ''join'' of the two disciplines.

Being a woman did not limit my opportunities at Andersen. My client engagements were numerous and varied. In terms of skills and experience gained, my four years with Andersen were probably equivalent to double that time in a traditional MIS department. When I left, I was enjoying consulting and supervising project teams. I was also beginning to make a generous salary (not something I generally associate with doctoral studies and academia). But what I didn't enjoy was the office culture, which seemed to suggest that a dedicated consultant would consistently give work a higher priority than family life. For instance, I regularly put in sixty-plus-hour work weeks. I was also constantly traveling. I couldn't see how to reconcile my desire to raise children with my absence from home and rapid accumulation of frequent flyer points. I realized that I had to bid goodbye to my talented colleagues at Andersen.

## CHOOSING TO ENTER ACADEMIA

My experience at Oxford had convinced me that academia could be consistent with living a well-rounded life. Many of the faculty and students had been female, and the faculty I'd worked with had been more approachable and more concerned about the individual student as a ''whole'' person than at MIT. I had also come to realize that to fulfill all my goals I really needed a career that would allow me to choose my own hours, work from home sometimes, and *not* always be on the road. The university offered these benefits.

I took the time to read *What Color Is Your Parachute?* and to reflect on my goals, strengths, and weaknesses. I briefly considered being a stay-at-home mom. After all, my mother, who is very talented and has won several scholarships, gave up her ambitions to stay home as a full-time mother of four. However, she has at no time suggested that I do the same. I am the third child in a family of high achievers. My father is an attorney-at-law who, even after his "retirement," continues to practice. He exemplifies his own personal motto: Work hard; people who succeed are those who use every moment of their time. Two of my siblings are Cambridge University graduates; all three are professionals (a doctor, a veterinary surgeon, and a lawyer), and all three have doctorates in addition to their professional qualifications. Somehow, staying at home full-time didn't seem to be the only answer!

## CHOICE OF SCHOOL AND DISCIPLINE

By then, Michael and I were Canadian immigrants, but I hadn't done any of my academic training in Canada. Unless I got to know the Canadian faculty and university system, I was not going to be able to "plug into" the Canadian academic network after I obtained my doctorate.

My Andersen colleagues' high praise for Western's M.B.A. program, clearly considered to be one of the best in Canada, convinced me to look into a Ph.D. there. I visited the school and met with the chair of the Ph.D. program, faculty, and several Ph.D. candidates. I was impressed by the comprehensive and thorough Ph.D. course work. It suited my pragmatic orientation while providing rigorous research preparation. I only sent off one Ph.D. program application—to Western—a practice I do not generally recommend. In my case, however, I was still employed by Andersen Consulting and was prepared to explore career opportunities outside academia. I would not have been at a loss if the application had been rejected. Needless to say, though, I was delighted to hear that my application to study MIS at Western had been accepted. While I pursued my doctoral studies, Michael practiced psychiatry at a nearby hospital.

## JOURNEY THROUGH COURSE WORK

Western is known as a "case" school, which means that, like Harvard or the University of Virginia, it emphasizes top quality teaching, using business cases. However, in its Ph.D. program, the emphasis is on research. It was soon made clear to me that progress within most top-tier academic institutions largely depends on *research* excellence and output.

I had initially been attracted to academia because of the flexibility in work hours and the opportunity to teach and mentor students. At Western, however, I discovered the other half of academic work—the wonder and delight of well-crafted research. The courses that most influenced me were the compulsory research methodology and statistics courses, which enlarged my vision of methodological and analytical rigor; the compulsory business policy and international business courses, which sparked a keen interest in business strategy and heavily influenced my later choice of an interdisciplinary dissertation topic; and, of course, the MIS courses.

During the first year, I took the maximum allowable Ph.D. course load; I expected a lot of myself and wished to "go the extra mile," no matter what path I followed. I combined the course work of the second year with my preparation for the MIS comprehensive exams. After passing my comprehensives, I focused on my dissertation proposal and successfully defended it in the early part of my third year.

Because only a few Ph.D. candidates were generally admitted each year at Western, a certain degree of competitiveness was fostered, no doubt to spur candidates to give their best to their studies. Although I possibly achieved more than I might have otherwise, I found that the competition somewhat diminished my enjoyment of the program. Certainly, it dissipated any illusions of the "ivory tower" of pure academia. Obtaining a Ph.D. in business administration sometimes involved working with people who were as aggressive as anyone I had dealt with as a consultant.

Even though office space was shared and sometimes noisy, I found it helpful to go in to work at Western daily, even after the structured course work had ended. This fostered a healthy routine and a sense of useful activity and progress, while avoiding the potentially damaging isolation described by some Ph.D. candidates. Not having any children at the time, I found it possible to work late into the evening; during the week, I sometimes ate the majority of my meals at the business school. Although my husband and I would have enjoyed having more time together in the evenings, both of us felt we could manage this short-term sacrifice. We agreed it was important that I complete the Ph.D. program well, and on a timely basis.

## CHOICE OF DISSERTATION RESEARCH TOPIC
## AND METHODOLOGY

Toward the end of my second year in the Ph.D. program, I tried for months to come up with a topic that was of interest to both my advisor and myself. As I mentioned earlier, I had developed a keen interest in business strategy as a result of being exposed to business policy and international business courses in the Ph.D. program. In my view, IS strategy lies at the intersection of the management of information systems and business strategy. This was the area I wished to study. At that time, my advisor was the Western Business School faculty member doing research in the area of IS strategy.

I believed that the dissertation should be of mutual interest to the student and advisor. The student has a lot at stake: the dissertation should be chosen carefully because it provides an opportunity to develop unique competencies in a new area. Also, the student will likely work in this area for many years after graduation. However, the faculty member cannot be expected to invest much time in research that is of marginal interest. I wanted to avoid a situation where I found it difficult to get faculty input and feedback.

The dissertation topics I suggested to my advisor were clearly influenced by my work as an MIS consultant. They addressed issues that the clients of Andersen Consulting had been trying to resolve, such as the management of technological change. Unfortunately, however, this is a broad topic area, and I could tell my advisor wasn't really interested. I also thought about studying the justification of information technology investments. Again, I was interested but the potential advisor was not. I finally saw a gleam of interest one day when, using a blackboard to sketch out the details, I suggested some possible MIS extensions to an earlier study on business strategy. We eventually agreed on the thesis topic "Business Strategy, Information Systems Strategy, and Strategic Fit: Measurement and Performance Impacts."

Strangely enough, I had not identified the topic as a result of the MIS literature searches I had undertaken. Rather, I'd stumbled across an article on the dissertation subject while doing a directed readings course with a business policy professor. When I wasn't looking for a dissertation topic, I found one!

I next drafted a research proposal, a modified version that was submitted to an external granting agency. The funds received were used for the dissertation study and related research activities. The proposal was also submitted to research competitions organized separately by the Marketing Science Institute and the Center for Telecommunications Management. I was heartened about my choice of topic when the research proposal tied for first place in both of these competitions.

My proposal required me to conduct a survey to quantitatively assess relationships among the constructs of interest (business strategy, information systems strategy, strategic fit, information systems performance, and business performance). The timing for such a study was good—my statistical skills were probably at their peak, and two members of the dissertation committee had exceptionally strong statistical skills.

One drawback to a survey approach was that some of the constructs were "messy" and ill-defined. It could have been argued that in-depth case studies would have been better. But I had read everything I could find on the constructs of interest; I now wanted to develop instruments to measure them and test the relationships between them. In-depth case studies would not support instrument validation and the empirical testing of links between constructs. I also realized that I couldn't do everything in one dissertation. I decided to leave the in-depth case studies to others and/or to carry them out myself at a later time.

The decision about what methodology to use was not politically sensitive. Case studies and survey approaches were both considered defensible at Western. In any event, by the time I formally defended the research proposal, I had made sure that all potential and confirmed members of my dissertation committee had seen multiple versions of the proposal. I wanted neither to provide nor receive any surprises at the proposal defense. I was fortunate enough to be able to incorporate, and defend, a multi-disciplinary research perspective. On the committee, in addition to two MIS professors, were a research methodologist, a business policy expert, and a statistician.

## FROM PROPOSAL DEFENSE TO DISSERTATION DEFENSE

The dissertation research activities were challenging. Over one thousand companies had to be surveyed, with four persons in each company providing data. Up to five reminder postcards, letters, questionnaire packages, and phone calls were directed to companies that had not returned completed questionnaires. A PC database was established and maintained to track the status of our contacts with the companies. A research associate and several part-time research assistants were employed to assist with the survey administration.

By this time, Michael and I were expecting our first child. We had been married for several years but had postponed having children until I could lessen the pace of my life and devote more time to raising a family. Although life was not yet quiet, I was getting older and there was a limit to how long we could delay having children.

For the first time, I worked mostly out of home, away from the research assistants. I found it a challenge to keep the quality of phone interviews and correspondence high, while staying on schedule, tracking and controlling expenses, collecting and examining the data received, and keeping the project team's morale high.

I don't think I was ever in danger of becoming an "ABD" (all but dissertation). This probably had as much to do with my tenacity as with the student-oriented Western Business School culture, an experienced and accessible supervisor, and a committee that was prepared to review early drafts of the dissertation document on a timely basis.

The closest I may have come to "ABD-dom" was the day I discovered that the data we had painstakingly gathered couldn't be analyzed. I could not see why the Partial Least Squares (PLS) analyses I was trying to run kept generating cryptic error messages. I tried various versions of the software to no avail. Months passed, and I agonized over the problem. Finally, a faculty member at the University of Calgary heard of my dilemma at a local conference. He suggested that I might be encountering a model size problem. That is, the research model might be too big to be analyzed by the software I had access to at Western. He volunteered to run my PLS routines using his more powerful version. Without any syntactical changes, the code that hadn't run for several months at Western, ran flawlessly at Calgary! I was immensely relieved to find myself back in business—largely because of the kindness of a stranger.

In the Ph.D. program, I enjoyed several successes in the form of prestigious student and research awards, fellowships, and scholarships. However, there were also several stresses. Two months into my doctoral studies, my father was seriously burned in a near-fatal fire. Later, I painfully witnessed the health of a friend break down as she strove to excel in her Ph.D. studies. I also watched another friend, a faculty member at a North American business school, leave the school because she felt that the treatment of women professionals was unsatisfactory; her story was disillusioning. At times, I found it difficult to work closely and network with colleagues who were mostly male. Michael, family and friends in Jamaica, Canada, the United States, and Britain, and the local Anglican community provided continual support and encouragement throughout these years.

## CHOOSING THE FIRST ACADEMIC JOB

In the fall of my third year in the Ph.D. program, I got an electronic mail message from an MIS faculty member at Queen's University about a job opening. Was I interested in applying? I certainly was. As mentioned earlier, Michael and I had elected to make our home in Canada. Michael wished to practice medicine in Ontario. Queen's is an excellent Canadian university, based in Ontario. It has one of the top MIS departments in the country.

When I visited Queen's to be interviewed and make a formal research presentation, I was "sold" on the university. I was impressed with the research program office at the School of Business and the support provided to new faculty to permit them to make rapid research progress. This includes internal competitions for teaching releases and access to research assistants and research funds. I was also impressed with the dean's office and the plans outlined for the School of Business. I was struck by the track records of, and rapport shared by, my MIS colleagues. The school's awareness of and support for women's issues was another important factor. I wanted to be part of the team. When I received a formal offer from the university, I had a real sense that it was the right opportunity for my family and me. Michael had also investigated job opportunities in the area, and they were promising.

Looking back, I can see that I've never been comfortable with a "shotgun" approach to anything, including job applications. I believe in focused, quality (not quantity) communications. That was why I did not go through the customary annual conference placement activities. Admittedly, I might have had to eventually if I hadn't been fortunate enough to be approaching the completion of my Ph.D. studies at a time when there were still several job opportunities at good universities.

Today, I am pleased with my university affiliation, colleagues, and research support. If I had to do it all over, I'd still say a resounding "yes" to Queen's.

## THE FIRST COUPLE OF YEARS

When I accepted the Queen's job offer, my dissertation data were still being gathered and had yet to be analyzed. In addition, my son Jonathan was born just six weeks before we moved to Kingston and a mere three months before I began teaching at the university. I decided to continue to nurse Jonathan even after I began teaching and elected to work out of home as much as possible. All this made for a challenging start to my Queen's career.

### Research

Keeping up the momentum of the dissertation research, while staying on top of child care and teaching responsibilities, was hard but not impossible. On the work front, electronic mail, telephones, fax machines, couriers, cars, and planes all enabled me to stay in touch with my advisor and other members of the Western Business School dissertation committee. On the home front, we were fortunate to have Michael's mother living with us for two years after Jonathan was born. My mother-in-law helped look after Jonathan during regular work hours, but I tried not to ask for assistance in the evenings. Despite the slight loss of privacy and the discipline it took to remain Jonathan's primary caregiver, the help I received from Michael's mother was invaluable. Today, Jonathan is happy, well-adjusted, and secure as he attends day care.

After the first teaching year had ended and summer had arrived, my balancing act became more manageable. But I recall many weeks when my work days ended at 2:00 A.M. while the rest of the household slept soundly. With the assistance of a patient and supportive advisor, an editor who reviewed the dissertation manuscript, and an army of secretaries, I finally submitted the dissertation in time to meet the summer term deadline. The timing was so tight that I couldn't courier the copies of the manuscript. Michael and I drove to Western (a five-hour journey in each direction) in order to submit them on schedule. I successfully defended the dissertation in September of that year and graduated from Western shortly thereafter, exhausted.

Of course, I was pleased when the dissertation tied for first place in the annual International Conference on Information Systems Doctoral Dissertation Competition a year later. I'd certainly given the research every ounce of energy I could while trying to maintain my commitment to a balanced home life.


### Teaching

The teaching load at Queen's University is four semester-long courses per academic year. However, faculty are able to obtain a limited number of teaching releases through internal School of Business competitions. I have been fortunate enough to receive at least one course release each year since my arrival at Queen's.

I have been also fortunate in my teaching responsibilities. Although I have had several courses to prepare, they were *not* courses no one else wanted to teach. On the contrary, the dean's office and my MIS colleagues have asked me about my course preferences and largely respected them.

I have been comfortable in the classroom, having decided early on to focus on student needs and not their impressions of me; I have concentrated on conveying my enthusiasm for MIS and explaining the subject matter clearly. In addition, I have felt prepared. While at Western, I'd used every opportunity I could to improve my teaching skills by acting as a course assistant, giving guest lectures, and taking optional teaching methods and case teaching courses.

For the first two years at Queen's, I scheduled a mid-term appointment with each of my students to ensure they knew where they stood in their class, were able to ask questions about course content, and could provide suggestions for course improvements. I designed these meetings to encourage more reserved class members and provide opportunities to get to know them better. My hope was that, as a result, they would be more confident and would participate more fully in class.

From my perspective, these meetings were taxing. One hundred and twenty interviews over a three-week period combined with the usual teaching and research responsibilities were, to say the least, draining. But they set the tone for a committed, high-performance class. My own effort made it reasonable for me to expect a lot from my students. In an ideal world, I would have continued this practice. But the world isn't ideal, and this past year, with a particularly demanding research project under way, I could not schedule formal student interviews. I did, however, allot class time for large group discussions to receive student feedback and address questions on course content.

My efforts to put a lot into my teaching did not go unnoticed. In my third year, I was one of three School of Business faculty members nominated to receive the Commerce Teaching Excellence Award. I was even more pleased to be nominated for, and to receive, the Professor-Student Life Award. This award is given by the final year undergraduate class to the School of Business professor who has contributed most to the student life of the class over the students' four years in the Bachelor of Commerce program.

### Administration

Ideally, I should have avoided administrative duties in the early stages of my academic career. However, during my first three years at Queen's opportunities arose that I didn't want to miss. These included a seat on a committee to review academic standards at the School of Business and a chance to assist with, and eventually chair, the research ethics committee at the school. I have also served on the computing committee, an appropriate contribution for an MIS professor. As a Rhodes Scholar and Queen's National Scholar, I have sat on Queen's candidate review committees for Rhodes Scholarships and Chancellor's Scholarships.

Over the years, I have also been a reviewer for several journals and conferences. Being a reviewer has been sobering but helpful. Many journal editors share comments with other reviewers so they can get feedback on their own work. I have tried to be supportive, and yet have witnessed researchers young and old, hopeful and well-established, being torn apart by their peers. I've found that although at times I may be more critical of articles I review than my peers, my final adjudications (revise and resubmit, generally) tend to be kinder than those of other reviewers (rejection with less feedback). Sometimes I've wondered about our "academy." Why do we seem more ready to reject, than to salvage the good in, the papers we critique? However, the time I have given to the peer review process has given me knowledge and experience critical to my own academic success. I have learned: Whatever is worth doing, is worth doing well; it is important to take the time to submit only polished, well-crafted work. I have also learned not to be overly disheartened by the criticisms my publications receive and not to take these criticisms personally.

## PUBLISHING THE FIRST ARTICLE(S)

At Western Business School, Ph.D. candidates are encouraged to publish articles while they are students. As a result, when I left Western, I already had some articles on my curriculum vita. However, my Western training was oriented to practitioners, so I published mainly for this audience, in journals devoted to their interests (a practice I do not, in general, recommend early in one's academic career). I realized that in order to succeed as an academic, my next few publications would have to be in top MIS research journals.

Accomplishing this goal has taken me longer than I had hoped. This is partly because I took on the position and teaching responsibilities of an assistant professor without first completing my Ph.D. (again, a practice I do not recommend; the overall Ph.D. and faculty workload can be onerous). I also introduced delays by choosing to write working papers for internal circulation and peer review before I submitted finished products to journals; this is because I preferred quality to quantity journal submissions. I was also working with co-authors whose input and feedback sometimes came at particularly busy times for me, and vice-versa. Finally, the peer review processes at the journals themselves are lengthy. The net result has been that today, three years after I joined Queen's as an assistant professor, my key dissertation articles still are in the "pipelines" of top research journals. This is despite the fact that my vita is full of peer-reviewed, practitioner-oriented journal articles, conference proceedings, book chapters, and industry publications.

## TRANSITION FROM THE PH.D. THESIS TO
## A RESEARCH PROGRAM

The transition from the Ph.D. dissertation to a research program also had its challenges. For example, one question that I had to address was to what extent I should continue to work with my dissertation advisor and other members of the dissertation committee. This question resolved itself in the end, because the advisor and committee members were quite busy with their own ongoing research commitments. I was pleased that this situation gave me an opportunity to spread my own wings.

While I was at Western, Ph.D. candidate involvement in grant writing was encouraged, so I was not unfamiliar with or intimidated by the grant application process. I submitted a research proposal to the Social Sciences and Humanities Research Council of Canada (SSHRCC). The research was designed to address many of the "limitations" and "suggestions for future research" described in my dissertation document. The research constructs were the same as those in the dissertation study. However, the questions raised and the methodology used (case studies) were quite different. The SSHRCC application was successful.

Much of my second summer at Queen's was spent planning and organizing the case research. I even employed a research associate to assist with this work. But before the study could get underway, it had to be halted because of some more good news! Another research grant application that I'd submitted to the advanced practices council (an elite group of chief information officers) of the Society for Information Management (SIM) International had been successful. I was delighted because SIM is the largest group of MIS professionals worldwide.

Fortunately, the SSHRCC research, which addressed the dissertation constructs via different approaches, and the SIM research, which added new but related constructs to those investigated in the dissertation, were complementary. Thus, after some changes to the team and schedule, both projects got under way. Since then, I have been able to work in an area (IS strategy and structure) that interests me immensely and is professionally satisfying. I believe that my research is relevant to both academic and practitioner communities.

The only drawback has been that, because the grant application process has been so successful, to this day I remain exceedingly busy carrying out *new* research. The SIM-funded research, in particular, has involved a series of studies, presentations, and reports. As a result, it has been very difficult to take the time to document fully, and publish, "old" (i.e., dissertation) research.

## FINDING THE BALANCE

Trying to achieve balance has always been a struggle in my life. Excellence in one domain only (e.g., research) is not what I am all about. I do not plan to work flat-out, with a narrow research focus, until I am tenured and able to pursue a more balanced approach to academia. Because I believe that patterns, once established, are not easily broken, I'm determined to continue to move toward a balanced lifestyle now and not postpone this until after the tenure decision. Once I am tenured, there will be other pressures such as becoming a full professor.

Because the number of hours that I can devote to research each day is limited, I have tried to "stretch" that time and achieve more by working with, and through, others. Most of my research funds have been used to fund part-time associates, assistants, and students. These arrangements have not always been successful. Despite my time constraints, I have poured a lot of energy into research and insisted on maintaining high standards; no doubt, I have been difficult to work for because I've demanded a lot in terms of commitment and quality.

I have tried to be a trustworthy researcher who cares about the whole person, not just the intellect, and the whole research team, not just what's in it for me. At times, my Christian principles (e.g., look out for weaker team members) and my business training (e.g., replace the weaker members) have suggested different courses of action. Occasionally, an assistant has mistaken Christian compassion for weakness and sought to take advantage of that compassion.

I have learned to value integrity as much as talent. I pay as much attention to the personal traits of assistants as I do to their academic preparation and ability. Difficult issues involving egos, idea ownership, article authorship, travel, overtime, and monetary remuneration have had to be resolved with more than one assistant. Nonetheless, in my view, the "pros" of research assistance have outweighed the "cons."

I have also tried to carry out joint research with colleagues at other universities, and I hope eventually to carry out joint research with other MIS faculty at Queen's. I have learned that it is important to identify faculty who are interested in similar research areas and have the same work ethic.

Maintaining a healthy balance represents an ongoing struggle. Frequently, it means that I must say no to interesting research, teaching, and administrative opportunities. I keep reminding myself: the good is ever the enemy of the best. To achieve balance, I have had to set up some guidelines. I try to leave the university each evening by a certain hour and not bring work home. I also try to do very little work on weekends. This represents a drastic change from my lifestyle prior to the defense of my dissertation. I find this schedule hard to stick to, but my family and my health are worth it.

When I'm at the university, I use time management techniques to make the most of each day. For example, I try to be organized and focused, set daily goals, address the most important items first whenever possible, leave mail and messages until the times in the day when I'm tired and unable to be creative, and close my office door when I'm writing. Despite these precautions, my in-basket appears infinite. I am peaceful, however, when each day I prioritize the in-basket entries and tackle them with all the energy I possess.

The result? I work hard and yet am healthy and enjoy a full life. In other words, in the long term, despite the glamour and wealth associated with other professions (e.g., consulting) that I am also qualified to practice, I'll probably still *want* to stay in academia. If my financial situation permits, I do not wish to combine academia with consulting early in my career. Each day only has only so many hours. Time spent consulting would be time not spent documenting research, preparing classes, or enjoying my family.

## PREPARING FOR TENURE

Am I worried about getting tenure, that is, a long-term academic niche? Yes and no. I am not sure what tenure really provides today. I have witnessed very talented academics denied tenure and realize this can happen to the best of people. In addition, I have learned that tenured professors can be "let go" if university budget cuts are required. In keeping with today's business realities, I have always just tried to be "marketable." I would like to think that tenure or no tenure, contract or no contract, the university with which I am affiliated will always find that they are getting *more* return on their investment in me than they bargained for. In fact, I'd like their main concern to be that I might go somewhere else. Thus, if *my* main concern ever became how to stay, I would think it was already time to leave.

Despite this, I have no desire to uproot my husband and son so that I may find employment at another university. I have no desire to go through the financial and emotional hardship often associated with seeking new employment. Still, obtaining tenure is not my goal. Being true to myself and others, giving of my best always, and balancing all the desires and demands of my life—this is what I'm about. Each day, I recall William Shakespeare's words: To thine own self be true.

## CONCLUSION

I have not found that success comes easily in academia. However, I have never wished to have an easy life, just an excellent one. I have learned that when the workload seems unbearable, difficulties insurmountable, and balance impossible, I need to listen to my heart and my head. With my head, I can often identify ways to meet the challenges. With my heart, I can discern which challenges really need to be met. I live my life intensely, but I enjoy it and approach my career in such a way that:

> In the process of making a living, I remember the value of shaping lives — my family's, colleagues', students', friends'.

# 2

# "Keeping the Balance"

## June N. P. Francis

*Never look back . . . there may be somebody gaining on you.*
—Satchel Page, baseball great

Reflection on the milestones that explain the route one has taken is rid-
dled with revision and reconstruction. It is difficult to determine which
factors were responsible for the turns taken. Yet I welcome this opportunity, early in my career, to reflect on my experience and to cast a light
down the tunnel of the future. I hope this look backwards will not con-
firm Satchel Page's fear but will instead provide some valuable insights.

As an assistant professor at Simon Fraser University in Burnaby, British Columbia, Canada, I am at the great crossroads of an academic career
as I approach tenure. On a more personal note, I am married with three
children aged three, nine, and fourteen. On a daily basis, my husband
and I wrestle with trying to balance the demands of toilet training, teen-
age tantrums, and missing library books against more adult pursuits in
our professional lives. But of course we wouldn't miss it for the world.

## MY CAREER BEFORE GRADUATE SCHOOL

### The Early Years

I believe my decision to enter academia later in life was a result of
family and cultural influences in my childhood and young adulthood. I
was born in the mid-1950s in colonial Jamaica. The runt of the litter, I
was the seventh child following behind two brothers and four sisters.

My mother, from a rural background, did not achieve a very high level of formal academic training, but from my earliest recollections, chided us to put great emphasis on academic achievement. She was particularly concerned that her daughters achieve the independence that she thought would come from excelling academically. A woman with strong Christian ideals, she placed great emphasis on using one's God-given talent to its fullest extent. She made it possible for us to concentrate on school work by providing emotional support and shielding us from the everyday demands of life. We did very little housework. I have often mused that she gave us no alternatives but to develop careers for ourselves, as we were ill-equipped to be housewives.

My father was a self-made man who, through home schooling by his mother and self-education, rose to become one of the first black journalists in Jamaica. He attempted to start a newspaper with the famous Marcus Garvey (a black folk hero) and was active in developing an indigenous journalistic tradition. By the time he had to retire (in his fifties, due to eye problems), he had become the chief sub-editor of the major daily newspaper in Jamaica.

The most significant milestone in the schooling of a Jamaican occurs very early in life. We were all expected by the age of eleven to write an exam that determined the academic stream each of us would take. Those among us who excelled were put in the academic-oriented stream and attended the "better" high schools. Failure, on the other hand, relegated one to the more vocational or the less academically oriented schools. I passed this common entrance examination, as was expected, and attended Ardenne High School along with three of my sisters.

Being the seventh child, I was expected to follow in the scholastic footsteps of my siblings. At school, I was constantly referred to as "a Francis" child, with a strong inference that I was clearly expected to excel. Strong academic performance was taken for granted, and as a child I understood this intuitively. My "best friend" and I competed each year to see who would gain the title of top student in our high school class.

Race was a critical influence on the path one took in Colonial Jamaica. People of European decent occupied positions of power and commanded most of the wealth. On the other hand, the population that was of African or mixed decent had few routes available for upward mobility. Entry into one of the professions was the route most often taken for raising or maintaining one's social and economic position. Therefore, if a child demonstrated academic aptitude, he or she was strongly encouraged to do well. This attitude remains in post-Colonial Jamaica, as well.

The quality of schooling one received was also determined by academic performance. Academic institutions including elementary schools, the "better" high schools and, during my school days, universities were free or relatively low fee for most students. Academic merit therefore became the primary basis on which one entered the better "institutions."

The school system, being of the British tradition, encouraged specialization, and I was channeled into a science stream quite early on. I had excelled during my high school years in the science-oriented subjects and simply continued along this path when entering college. When I enrolled in the University of the West Indies for my undergraduate work, I gave little thought to my options and automatically took courses in the natural sciences. Reinforcing this path was the fact that one of my sisters, who preceded me at the University of the West Indies, was pursuing a medical degree. I simply followed in her footsteps and undertook natural sciences as a stepping stone to entering medical school.

It wasn't long before I started to question the wisdom of this decision. After being exposed to the liberal arts and social sciences by my university peers, I was motivated to move away from the specialization of the pre-medical stream. By the time I graduated from the University of the West Indies, I had entered four different faculties. Beginning with the faculty of natural sciences, then the faculty of arts, followed by the faculty of social sciences, I finally graduated from the faculty of management studies.

There were three factors associated with my undergraduate degree that I believe influenced the future course of my career. The first is that I failed my freshman year at the University of the West Indies. My first year at college was spent enjoying the new-found social liberties, and I paid little attention to my university courses. My attendance at classes was sporadic. My attention to assignments was almost nonexistent. While it came as no surprise to my friends, it was a great shock to me that I had failed. Due to the good graces of the institution, students were allowed to write supplemental examinations during their first year. That summer, I shamefully spent my time studying and explaining my apparent demise to friends and family. Although I finally completed my first year, the experience left an indelible mark. Failure was so distasteful to me that I never wanted to experience it again. From my second year on, attention to my academic work increased dramatically, and I truly became intrigued by learning. I eventually graduated from the university with first class honors, a distinction very few students achieved.

The second formative experience of my undergraduate years was a passing comment made by a faculty member's wife. At a graduation party, she suggested that given my achievements I was now expected to do graduate work. Often, the last thing one has on one's mind when completing an undergraduate degree is pursuing a graduate career. My retort was that I had no intentions of continuing my academic work. But her words planted the very first thoughts about pursuing graduate work.

The third factor is my migration to Canada. Graduation from the Uni-

versity of West Indies brought me to a decision point. Having just graduated with a degree in management studies, I was offered employment
with various organizations in Jamaica. However, the political upheaval
in Jamaica caused me much concern. Because my parents had migrated
to Toronto along with two of my sisters, I had a similar opportunity. I
was also romantically involved with someone who was pursuing a Ph.D.
in Toronto at that time. He encouraged me to consider graduate work,
which led me to writing the admissions tests required for entry into a
graduate school of management.

I immigrated to Toronto the summer after my graduation, without
ever holding a full-time job in Jamaica. Immediately upon moving to
Canada, I entered a graduate program at York University to pursue a
master's degree in business administration. With some luck and a lot of
persistence, I was able to complete the degree in twelve months. However, my experiences at York University had a lasting effect on later
decisions that I would make. First of all, having migrated to a country
with a climate quite dissimilar from the warm tropics that I was used
to, I had a very difficult time adjusting. I wondered about the wisdom
of leaving the warm climate of Jamaica in favor of one that did not
appear habitable. However, with time, I got wrapped up in graduate
work and began to integrate into my new environment. While I never
learned to tolerate, let alone enjoy, an Eastern Canadian winter, as winter
melted into spring, I began to truly explore the metropolis of Toronto
and dropped any immediate concerns about remaining in Canada. It was
during this time that I met my future husband, a Canadian.

When one examines the past, there are seminal experiences. During
my studies at York University, two such experiences gave me a flavor
of the difficulties of living and working in a different culture. In one of
my specialty courses, a senior professor chose to punish me academically
for what I have come to believe was personal bias. Using my parents'
approach to adversity as a model, I challenged his right to do so. The
appeal went to the highest levels of the university, resulting in the acceptance of my challenge and an upgrade of my mark.

My culture clash with elements of Canadian society has had its humorous side as well. My future employer, Procter & Gamble, used a
"knowledge" test as one of the criteria for its selection process. The test
was very culture specific, asking such detailed questions as, "Who was
Conrad Black?" (a prominent Canadian industrialist). Only being in Canada for five months at the time I knew very few Canadianisms. The
company interview followed similarly, with one of the executives going
so far as to ask me what was my first language—to which I answered
Russian. To the company's credit, they decided their culture-specific test
wasn't relevant and they could use a Russian-speaking (comedienne)
brand assistant.

My decision to join Procter & Gamble to pursue a career in marketing management was not without its difficulties. At that time, a job with Procter & Gamble was perceived to be one of the most desirable jobs a marketing graduate could land. Simultaneously, however, I was offered a job with C.U.S.O. (the Canadian University Student Organization—a foreign outreach arm of Canadian aid to developing regions) to go to Papua New Guinea and take up a challenging assignment to help develop a communications system for public health information. This forced me to make a decision that seemed more like a clash of values and ideals than a choice between jobs. On the one hand, Procter & Gamble certainly offered an unparalleled opportunity to enter corporate Canada. On the other hand, public service in an environment like Papua New Guinea seemed a much more meritorious service. I eventually took the conservative route and entered corporate Canada. While this decision opened many successful avenues for advancement, I have often regretted not taking the riskier, but "worthier" route. I believe my later return to academics was partially an attempt to return to a "nobler" pursuit.

As a brand assistant at Procter & Gamble in Toronto, the business world embraced me with full force. The company promotes only from within. Each year it goes to campuses seeking "bright lights" from across Canada to begin their careers in competition for the next lofty step of brand manager. We were all "keeners," excited about joining Procter & Gamble. Although the company exacted many hours of our time, in return we learned a lot about marketing and the corporate world. In the course of my "real life" education, I oversaw the production of my first radio and TV commercials, was allowed to defend the brand's budget, and was schooled in the workings of corporate Canada. "Procter" expected us to be good writers, and so my business school writing was subjected to enormous scrutiny and correction, and I learned the tedious art of editing. I feel this experience was one of the most positive of my entire career and still use many of the fundamental principles that I learned at Procter.

It was a heady time, as Procter & Gamble employees like myself were constantly bombarded with job offers from many competitive firms by virtue of being employees of this marketing giant. I did not spend a long time with Procter, as the winters in Toronto seemed to get worse or I became more intolerant of them. When the Clorox Company of Canada, then located in Vancouver, British Columbia, offered me a significant salary increase and an attractive lifestyle improvement away from the winters of Toronto, I grabbed the opportunity. Vancouver offered a climate and a location that was more reminiscent of home, at least in so far as Canada could offer.

On moving to Vancouver, a slower paced business environment, and a much smaller company, I immediately experienced some letdowns from the higher paced Toronto business culture. However, Clorox provided a wider scope of responsibility, and I became a brand manager (being fully in charge of a brand). Later, I was given responsibility for new products which provided exposure to top management in our international operations. However, the scope for advancement appeared quite limited. I started to wonder whether the Vancouver environment, which was clearly the lifestyle decision that I made, was the appropriate choice for a career in marketing. I realized that my packaged goods marketing background did not have as much application in Vancouver as it did in Toronto. I contemplated switching to a new discipline or moving into a new type of company. This was when I began to seriously think about an academic career.

## ENTERING ACADEMIA

On reflection, the comment made earlier in my life by the faculty member's wife that I would somehow pursue more advance academic studies kept re-surfacing from my subconscious. While the master's program in business was demanding, I had found it quite applied and not intellectually stimulating. The notion of pursuing more "academic" knowledge in its own right was becoming more and more attractive to me, and I started pursuing various academic courses simply for the fun of it.

One precipitous event quickly crystallized the idea of pursuing further graduate work. One Easter weekend, I suggested to my husband that we go to the University of Washington in Seattle to get some information about its graduate program. I arrived on Good Friday to find an almost deserted university. By a stroke of luck, the Ph.D. program director in the business school was there. He indicated that while the deadline for application to the Ph.D. program had passed some months before, that very morning one of the accepted candidates had declined his or her space. As such, the space was available. After interviewing me about my academic background, my score on the graduate test (GMAT), and my professional experience, he strongly urged me to apply immediately; if my credentials proved out, it looked very good for acceptance.

My husband and I then spent many hours discussing the merits of pursuing a Ph.D., as we had not done so previously. I realized then that my desire to complete graduate work was strongly motivated by a sense that I had not completed my academic journey. It was not so much motivated by a desire to become a professor, I was more interested in the academic process. Our considerations revolved around the process not the outcome. Would I get the kind of experience that I was looking for? Could we afford to do this? With Seattle over a three-hour drive from our home, what impact would this have on our relationship? My husband was well-placed in Vancouver in a senior position, and we agreed to consider only alternatives that fit both our goals. We decided this was as good a time as any for just such a move.

Yet many uncertainties remained. My career in marketing was just beginning, and it appeared as if there were many unexploited opportunities in the corporate world. While many opportunities for progressing in package goods may not have been available, there were options for going into crown corporations and other industries. It should be clear, however, that I had made no decision about the kind of career that I would pursue after the Ph.D. program. Call it a stroke of luck or call it fate, the University of Washington was the only graduate program I applied to, as application deadlines for most other schools had passed. And the location was ideal, since either of us could commute between Seattle and Vancouver on weekends.

On reflection, I realize that I undertook doctoral work with far too little knowledge. I researched the reputation of the school as a whole, but only later did I come to fully appreciate the large number of questions that one should ask. A crucial factor in selecting a graduate school ought to be some understanding of the research focus and productivity of the graduate faculty. A look at the publication record of the various faculty members not only gives indications of the faculty's focus of research and research productivity but provides insights into the research paradigm that's dominant. I think it is critical to be part of an environment that is active in research. This gives hands-on research experience prior to the dissertation stage and provides opportunities for mentorship. Making contact with a prospective faculty supervisor is also a very good idea. It generates commitment by the faculty member to the student early on in the student's program and allows for a more focused choice of courses and direction to one's work. Discussions with current graduate school students are always a good source of inside information.

The choice of career after graduate school should also be carefully considered. I did not realize that faculty members would discount any future path that did not involve an academic career in a recognized research institution. My early expectation was that my career alternatives would remain open and leave me the opportunity to return to industry or enter consulting and/or academics. As such, it was quite shocking to me when I arrived and realized that I would not be taken seriously if I did not espouse a single-minded interest in academia. Therefore, an important consideration is to determine whether the research focus of the faculty is largely pure research or whether more applied research with greater relevance to the business or professional practice will be tolerated and valued. Another important issue in the choice of a graduate program includes the track record of the program. Has the institution had the experience to educate and graduate, in a timely manner, a large number of students, and have these students been placed in reputable institutions or companies? A small class may seem like an opportunity for hands-on teaching but, in my experience, it lacks the critical mass to allow faculty to mount specific courses and seminars designed particularly for Ph.D. students.

## THE JOURNEY THROUGH THE COURSE WORK

### Choosing Course Work

In my graduate program at the University of Washington, Ph.D. students were required to determine their major area of study prior to acceptance in the program. I was accepted as a marketing major. The core courses were, therefore, largely pre-determined as marketing seminars. However, I was required to select two minor areas of study to support my research orientation.

There were two schools of research in my department—the behavioral school and the more quantitative school. Each had a different approach to research and clearly valued its own work more highly than the other. I elected to do econometrics as a minor area, partly because I felt it gave me the necessary credibility to demonstrate that I was a serious "researcher" in the making. Image management was particularly important, as I had come from industry and was not yet considered a sure-bet to make a "serious" academic. Many of my choices of course work were made to validate my academic orientation.

On the other hand, I did undertake socio-cultural anthropology as my second minor. This was immediately suspected in the business school as an attempt to find an easy minor area, not subject to academic rigors. I found the courses stimulating, rigorous, and intellectually expanding. The field of study would later prove to be vital to my dissertation research, and I learned the importance of being self-directed and sticking to my own research ideals.

I maintained a very high grade point average throughout my course work and won respect from my faculty members and peers. Most of the course work required tremendous devotion in time and energy, but I think it is critical to maintain high standards. There are three factors that contributed to my timely and high level of achievement in my doctoral course work.

One, and perhaps most important, was the support and camaraderie of my fellow doctoral students. I was fortunate to enter the marketing doctoral program with two other women with whom I maintained a close friendship. We shared information; we advised each other; we shared all of our academic resources. These friendships proved particularly important during preparation for my comprehensive exam.

The second factor that contributed to my maintaining a high standard in the doctoral course work was that I totally immersed myself in the program. From Monday to Friday, I was away from my husband and hence free to enjoy all facets of student life. I have always been grateful for this isolation from family ties, because it allowed me to be involved, not only in the course work but also in the social life of the Ph.D. program. Later on, this proved to be tremendously important for sustaining me through the thesis work.

The third reason was that my husband was enormously supportive of my need to be away from home and cocooned me from most of the requirements of everyday living. With no children yet, we exquisitely enjoyed our weekends together, while I was left free to spend most of the work week concentrating on my doctoral work. In the end, I finished my course work within the scheduled time and wrote my comprehensive exam at the end of this two-year period.

My biggest mistake during the course work stage was that I didn't identify a dissertation topic and select an appropriate supervisory committee early on. I could have more wisely chosen course projects that contributed toward my thesis and fostered relationships with faculty members that would have furthered my progress. My advice, therefore, is for Ph.D. students to define their thesis direction as early on in the process as is feasible. It is inordinately important to foster a relationship with a supervisory committee and to draw on the wisdom, contacts, and experience of this supervisory committee rather than attempt to go it alone. Without sounding Machiavellian, I think it is important to recognize that at any level in a professional school, a win-win relationship between students and faculty can be beneficial to all.

### The Comprehensive Examination

I found the comprehensive examination to be inordinately stressful. There weren't enough previous classes of Ph.D. marketing students to allow us to go by earlier examinations. We were the first cohort that was going to be examined together. As such, we were operating with an ill-defined set of expectations and recognized that what was done before would be no indicator of the kind of exam we could expect. However, we decided early on that we would study together. We shared all information and worked cooperatively to the point of outlining a study schedule. We reviewed these topics together on a weekly basis as we approached the exam. We discussed potential questions, and we gained one another's trust to the extent that we could assign specific topics for each of us to prepare and share with the others.

The marketing comprehensive examination lasted for six hours and stretched us to our very limits. We believed the most important principle was to demonstrate we were capable of making the transition from student to researcher. As such, we attempted to look at the material in a holistic manner. We sought to recognize the theoretical "tenets" of the materials, to pay attention to the philosophy of science, to understand the inter-connectedness between the areas of our study, and to make sure that we were methodologically quite well-educated. We did not simply study the details of the course but tried to recognize that our job was to demonstrate that we had reached the intellectual maturity required of prospective future researchers. Fortunately, we all passed and progressed to the ABD (all but dissertation) stage.

## THE CHOICE OF RESEARCH TOPIC

Choosing the research topic for my dissertation was an extremely agonizing and difficult process. I was plagued by having too many interests and changed my research topic at least four times before finally selecting one that was meaningful to me on a very personal level. Before going into the details on my topic, it is important to discuss a few life changes that occurred over this period of time and the influence they had on my dissertation research years. The summer after I completed my doctoral comprehensive exam and achieved my official status of "ABD" was not a very fruitful one for me. The ABD designation belies the fact that the dissertation is perhaps the most significant aspect of one's doctoral program.

Because I had not selected a topic prior to the completion of my course work, my objective that summer was to find a dissertation topic and to begin work on it. My dissertation advisor was selected and had agreed to serve on the basis of recommendations about me by his faculty colleagues, since he had been away from the university during my course work. The result was that we were unfamiliar with each other on both a personal and professional level. He was definitely the most suitable faculty person for assisting me on my dissertation, but we had to establish our working relationship. In retrospect, I now see the challenge he had in dealing with someone who had so much uncertainty as to her dissertation direction.

My life also took a turn during the upcoming fall that was unanticipated. During the summer, I was diagnosed with severe endometriosis and was given the news that I was probably infertile. I was therefore quite torn much of the summer by simultaneously trying to deal with this medical occurrence and the selection of a doctoral topic. In the fall, after much medical consultation, I elected to have surgery performed in Seattle to help relieve the symptoms of this painful condition. The surgery was scheduled and absorbed much of my energies and time. While awaiting the surgery, I found out that I had in fact become pregnant. This pregnancy was miscarried later on that fall. However, in January I became pregnant again with my first child. This significantly changed and disrupted my Ph.D. progress and direction.

I have come to realize that society's attempt to "equalize" careers for males and females has been at a price. Having a miscarriage, a surprisingly common experience, or having a successful pregnancy results in tremendous physical and emotional changes. To treat these as non-events or to minimize their effects on the person's career/work is grossly inappropriate. Ironically, I also shared some of these philosophies that placed little importance on pregnancy before undergoing my metamorphosis. I now recognize that these very human hiatuses may be interruptive to careers but need not be long-standing. Similar to sabbaticals, they can provide time for rejuvenation or redirection that culminates in more positive efforts. I had not specifically planned this change in advance but welcomed it given that I had faced the prospects of infertility. However, this not only distracted my attention during an important phase of my educational progress but also, I believe, distracted my committee from the major focus of my work.

I spent the first year after my comprehensives gravitating between various dissertation topics. I was advised at different points to simply take on the topic of my advisor and pursue one of his research directions. I knew this would not be satisfying to me. I really wanted my own research topic to fulfill a number of criteria. The first was that I wanted my research to be relevant to professional practice in some way. The importance of this criterion stemmed largely from my work experience and the need I had to somehow incorporate it into my academic life. The second criterion was that my research had to be international or cross-cultural. During my doctoral work, I had come to seriously question the cross-cultural validity and application of many of the marketing and business principles that were so commonly accepted in North America as being universally true. I met tremendous resistance to this notion. It may seem difficult to understand now, but international marketing and international business at that time did not enjoy the popularity they do now. The third criterion was that the work had to reflect my individual contributions and personal stamp.

It took four different forays into various areas to find a research topic that was international, had business relevance, and represented something that was personally important and hence would give me the energy to be fascinated and passionate about my work. These three criteria have continued to guide the kind of research that I do, and they were critical in helping me through the arduous task of completing my dissertation research.

My dissertation research was entitled "When in Rome" and subtitled "The Effect of Cultural Adaptation on Inter-cultural Business Negotiation." It was motivated primarily by my own personal observation and experience. At that time, inter-cultural research was enjoying a tremendous amount of popularity in the area of comparative work. Through reading and thinking, I came to question whether or not the advice from this work was really appropriate in a business setting. Specifically, I got curious about what the appropriate response to cultural differences in business negotiation ought to be.

Most scholars and business pundits of the day recommended, implicitly or explicitly, a strategy of adapting to the foreign culture in inter-cultural business negotiations. I thought that while this advice seemed on the surface to make sense, it was questionable on further scrutiny. I do confess that the initial hypothesis was derived simply from my own personal experience. You see, being Jamaican, people have always attempted to welcome me by showing that they understand my culture. For example, typically somebody will see me and say "mon" or indicate in some way that he or she was adapting to my Jamaican culture. I always found this terribly offensive, although I recognized that most of the attempts to adapt were well-meaning. For one, these people usually adapted on very stereotypical perceptions, ways that communicated some form of contempt for my culture. Secondly, attempts at adaptation usually indicated to me that they thought they could somehow bridge the cultural gap with very trivial or superficial methods.

Based on this intuitive approach, I then searched the literature to see what kinds of theories and research had been undertaken on this whole area of inter-cultural adaptation. Much of my research's theoretical underpinning came from work in European social-psychology on inter-group behavior. I then married that to research in our own North American social-psychology. I had to be personally responsible for the theoretical development, as I had very few precedents from which to build. It was the kind of work that I had been seeking.

The research followed a very simple design but was quite complicated in execution. My hypotheses centered around the effects of Japanese business people attempting to adapt to American culture. I was testing the main hypothesis that a moderate level of adaptation had a positive effect on the trustworthiness and the likeability of business people. This thesis went against the then conventional wisdom that going native or extensively adapting would be beneficial to both how trustworthy business people were perceived and to whether or not they would be liked. I further hypothesized that no adaptation at all would probably not affect how trustworthy people appeared but would in turn affect whether they would be liked or not. I hypothesized low levels of liking for people who did not adapt.

To execute this research, I conducted an experiment in which M.B.A. student subjects were each presented with a scenario of one of three conditions. The scenario either depicted Japanese businessmen who behaved in stereotypical Japanese style, with a moderate adaptation to American culture, or with a substantial adaptation to American culture. This was also replicated using Korean businessmen.

While I initially proposed using a script, my committee exhorted me to use a videotape of the encounter. I was reluctant to do this for what I believed to be sound methodological reasons. However, I went ahead and produced three, thirty-minute-long videos based on my dissertation. I hired actresses, actors, and producers and, with the help of a video technician at UBC, produced this video for my research. I did this while working on my written script design simply to save time. I decided that arguing with my committee would be inappropriate without providing some proof. In effect, what I did was to work on both methodologies simultaneously. Without even seeing the video, my committee decided on the written script. While the video production cost me both in time and money, I believe my willingness to pursue my committee's directions made them more receptive to my ideas.

Conducting the study was one of the most fulfilling research experiences that I have had. This was partially because it represented academic entrepreneurship. The research direction needed a lot of championing and reflected my personal direction. My committee chairman was extremely skilled, and I drew very heavily on the support of committee members; one committee member, in particular, supported me through the periods where my chairman was away.

I spent over three years completing my Ph.D. dissertation. This moderately long period of time resulted from a number of factors. First of all, as I previously mentioned, the birth of my first son went a long way to derailing my focus. I had not fully anticipated the impact his birth would have on my life. After his birth, my priorities changed enormously. For the first time, there was inordinate competition for my time, for my emotion, and for my energies. Secondly, within a year of my son's birth, my husband and I adopted a daughter who came to us when she was six years old. This event had a tremendous impact on our lives and my ability to expeditiously finish my dissertation.

At the same time, I had returned to live in Vancouver and taken a job as a visiting professor, further distracting me from my research. While I was strongly advised not to move away from my home university base and definitely not to take a visiting job, I proceeded to do both. Primarily, this was done because I needed to be close to my children and felt that the trade-off was appropriate. There is no doubt that distance from my home university was a source of significant distraction, and at times I doubted that I would finish this dissertation. In addition to all of these, I became more and more absorbed by the day-to-day realities around me.

To further complicate my life, but consistent with the continuing thread of my varied interests, my husband and I and another couple undertook a hugely successful entrepreneurial venture during World Expo 86, an international fair that was being hosted by Vancouver. We wrote a guide book to the fair as a small business venture that blossomed into a profitable and personally rewarding experience.

Fresh from our first successful entrepreneurial effort, we decided to organize a multi-cultural carnival. This idea was an outgrowth of our common interests in other cultures and the rich mosaic of cultures living in Greater Vancouver. While we were unable to duplicate our initial financial success with this project, we did gain tremendous insights into the cultural nuances and political processes within our community.

However, while I profited from and enjoyed my entreprenurial digressions, I became extremely desirous of seeing the end to my thesis. It became very clear that I would seriously disappoint myself if I did not. I was still waffling about the direction my life would take but knew that completion of my dissertation was a very necessary personal step, even if it was not a very necessary professional one. During the last twelve months of my Ph.D. program, I made a new commitment to follow through with my dissertation. I cocooned myself from as many obligations as I could. I had just two priorities—my children and my dissertation. Even my husband was ignored in attempt to refocus my energy. I went so far as to forgo direct involvement in another venture into the realm of entrepreneurial publishing. Although I would help formulate marketing and production strategy, I had to remain in Canada while my husband and our partners traveled to Australia to fashion a guide book for Brisbane's World Expo 88. Given the excitement we all experienced from our first venture and the prospect of visiting Australia, this was no small sacrifice. I would work through the night, to avoid distractions, and in the early morning and late evening. My husband was drawn in often to prepare charts and attend to any details he could. I remember the night before I handed in my final draft. He stayed up all night long with me, attending to the last-minute details that always emerge. Without sleep, we piled our children in the car and drove to Seattle with this most prized object—my dissertation. By the time I handed it in, my three-year-old son turned to me and exclaimed, "Mom, promise me you will never do another 'dithertation' again." I was delighted to make this promise, of course.

## PREPARING FOR THE DEFENSE

I had immersed myself so completely in the dissertation that I didn't think there was a question that could stump me. However, there was one risk I feared. I knew the limitations of my dissertation so completely that these loomed large in my mind. I became so obsessed with minutiae that I had to spend time drawing back from the dissertation and looking at the "big picture." I had to remind myself that no one else knew the details I did and so were unlikely to ask these minor details. To calm myself, I prepared defensible responses to all possible questions—even those very unlikely ones. Needless to say, the eventual defense was far from the nightmare I had imagined. I was proud of the research and its findings. I was so in love with what I had accomplished, that I believe my presentation was infectious. My committee was congenial and the questions, while taxing, were all anticipated. Nonetheless, when I was asked to leave the room to await the verdict, I could hardly breathe. It seemed all my years of work had come down to this moment. When I was congratulated and given very minor changes to make, I felt such relief that a vivid memory of the moment remains with me.

In terms of some of the lessons learned, I realize now that the decision to leave the residence of the university and move away from my committee was a risky one. However, given that I needed to spend time with my children, I still believe it was the right decision. Clearly, having a family made the context of my life very different. I have since had a lot more distractions. I also realize now that it was very important for me to embrace a research direction that impassioned me. Actually, it consumed me. I continue to test my theory every time I am in an intercultural situation. I recognize that to chart one's own course is a very difficult and risky route. It requires more self-direction, and the potential benefits are less secure; while I don't advocate this as the most efficient route, I believe it was the most appropriate route for me.

### Choosing the First Academic Job

When I decided to finish my dissertation, I was in the employ of the University of British Columbia on a limited term contract. Over the years, I had been contacted by many academic institutions outside of Vancouver who were interested in talking to me about job prospects. I had, while pregnant with my first child, officially gone on the market and in fact interviewed after my doctoral consortium at the major recruiting conference for marketing graduates. After my son was born, I immediately withdrew from the job market and suspended making any tough academic decisions. Suddenly, the choice of a career was no longer one to be made by me and my husband in isolation but involved choices affecting my children.

When I was nearing the end of my dissertation, I started to seriously consider my job prospects. We were content with our lifestyle and enjoyed Vancouver immensely. However, the job prospects appeared to be far more attractive in the United States and in Eastern Canada. Some tough choices had to be made.

Simon Fraser University happened to be in the market at the same time for an academic position in my area of study. To my good fortune, this university was a remarkably good choice for an academic career. To assure myself that I wasn't simply interviewing with Simon Fraser because of its location, my husband and I went through the usual rigors of comparing my alternatives. We went through the pros and cons of various aspects of the job: the school's reputation, size, openness to research approaches, support for teaching, and offering salary. Investigating the school, I found a good fit between the institution and myself. For one thing, I was looking for a school that would give me some latitude in terms of pursuing research in international marketing. Simon Fraser is relatively liberal in terms of allowing young faculty to define one's research orientation as long as he or she remains productive. The university had recently acquired a downtown campus, and that was attractive to me in terms of exposure to professional students. It had newly started a center for inter-cultural studies, which was an incredibly attractive resource given the support this would offer my research. The student body was well mixed in age and socio-demographic characteristics, which was personally appealing. I also found the colleagues with whom I interviewed to be open, collegial, and research oriented.

In sum, I felt that this was the environment in which my research would flourish. On the downside, compared to salaries that were quoted to me by various institutions "back East and down South," Simon Fraser's seemed relatively low.

### The First Couple of Years

I had big plans for my first years at Simon Fraser. I was going to follow the straight and narrow path to achieving tenure. I would simply focus on my research, attend to teaching as my second priority, and stay clear of every administrative job that was not mandatory. From the very beginning, I found it difficult to adhere to this ideal. First of all, after spending so many years being a student, I wanted to make a contribution in other areas of my life. It was a tremendous temptation to get involved in every aspect of the institution, which of course meant administrative work. I found the first year, in particular, very exhilarating but at times overwhelming. I had the good fortune to have the support of senior colleagues who helped me resist the temptation to sway from my narrow path. I found them receptive in the "West Coast" kind of a way. They were willing to help and were supportive, but they were not intrusive. They received me as an equal. However, it was difficult to find the research time I had hoped for during those first years.

## Transition from the Ph.D. Thesis to a Research Program

It is sometimes very difficult to make the transition from being a Ph.D. student to taking on the responsibility of one's own academic career. This transition is perhaps easier for people who have had mentors in their Ph.D. program. I was not so fortunate. My main advisor was no longer in close proximity. Without a mentor to guide me, I had to take full responsibility for my academic research productivity. I was extremely fortunate to have colleagues who, from the very outset, took on this role and advised me to submit at least one article out of my dissertation as soon as possible. Senior colleagues made themselves available to read my manuscript and gave extremely detailed responses to my work. They suggested that the tone I set would initially be very important not only in terms of how I was viewed but in helping me establish a balance between teaching, researching, and administrative responsibilities. One of my committee members also proved to be an extremely valuable resource, as she helped read my work and guide my early priorities.

At first, I was quite embarrassed to submit an initial article to my colleagues' scrutiny. To my relief, they were quite positive in their responses, although an enormous amount of work was clearly needed to bring it to publishable form. The involvement of my colleagues was invaluable in getting me over that initial fear of submitting my work to public scrutiny and of being reviewed in academic journals.

In the late spring of my first year at SFU, I submitted an article from my dissertation to a top-tier journal in my discipline—a shotgun approach. Although this strategy had some risk, I felt it was important to establish myself as a serious academic. I was extremely fortunate. My article was positively reviewed, although I needed to make moderate revisions. I was relieved, of course, because I had been told how difficult it would be to gain acceptance by a top-tier journal. The article was eventually accepted after two more revisions.

At the same time as this work was being reviewed, I initiated an article with two senior colleagues, one at Simon Fraser and the other at the University of British Columbia. Never having really worked cooperatively with others before on an article, I looked forward to being exposed to their thinking. The result was another article published in a top-tier journal. Although we struggled with this article and had several difficult moments, the process taught me the necessity of tremendous perseverance in academic pursuits. My colleagues, with their greater experience in the research process, were able to take a long-term view. They felt the article was of sufficient caliber to publish in a top-tier journal and recommended against going the quick route of getting it in a second- or third-tier journal. Their advice obviously paid off for me; both of these articles were in inter-cultural negotiations.

As often happens, I became bored with my dissertation topic and started looking at some new research directions. This led to a number of forays into research areas that were less familiar to me. I embarked on a data collection spree that somewhat distracted me from the main goal of producing articles. My varied interests, while serving to fuel my academic bent, caused me to become distracted to more short-term objectives. I collected data for some six studies but found it difficult to find the time to complete individual articles. Subsequently, I have decided to concentrate on fewer areas to accomplish my publication goals.

### Research Grants

I have always seemed able to secure research grants throughout my academic career. In my master's and Ph.D. programs I received financial assistance. Initially at Simon Fraser I was able to secure two small grants that were available to new faculty. I used these grants to launch a study on the export performance of information technology firms in British Columbia. This allowed me to cover the kind of incidental expenses associated with field studies as opposed to laboratory research. More recently, I decided to apply for grants to fund larger research projects and was able to secure an SSHRC (Social Science and Humanities Research Council) grant that I believe will be invaluable for sustaining the productivity of my current research direction.

Working with students can be mutually beneficial. SFU does not have a Ph.D. program in business administration, so it is more difficult to make these arrangements. I have, however, worked with both graduate and undergraduate students in ways that provide mentorship for them and contribute in some way, however small, to my research. For example, I have worked quite closely with a former undergraduate student on my recent work on information technology. His position as research assistant provided him with needed exposure for the job market and gave me invaluable research support.

### Teaching

Prior to joining Simon Fraser University, I had taught during my years of course work at the University of Washington and during the completion of my thesis as a visiting professor at the University of British Columbia. Although teaching presented some initial challenges such as getting to know the students at Simon Fraser and fitting into their teaching structure, I felt reasonably well-prepared for the task. In my very first year, I had some initial feelings of resentment about the amount of time I spent teaching. I had to continually remind myself of the value of teaching in order to cope with my emerging resentment. Simon Fraser, while stressing research over teaching, has always put a significant emphasis on teaching. I was surprised at how many good teachers there were, since I was led to believe that universities placed very little emphasis on teaching.

Simon Fraser's business school has only recently introduced mechanisms to aid new teachers. At the time that I started, there was very little institutional support, training, and mentoring for teachers. This, of course, is not unusual for academic institutions, but I believe this trend is changing. We are seeing an increasing emphasis on teaching as political reality dictates that students are satisfied in order for institutions to attract public support.

I believe we continually need to find more efficient and effective ways of delivering our pedagogy to students. My teaching has evolved to incorporate audio-visual and computer supports. I have increasingly become disenchanted with lecturing as a way of delivering materials. Experimential exercises, discussion, projects, interaction with the real world through guest lecturers, field trips, etc. are vital to students gaining a real understanding of business administration. I have also come to value the knowledge that students bring to bear in the classroom; this being particularly evident in my international courses. I have students of many nationalities who provide valuable insights, and I ensure there is time for student input.

### Administrative Involvement

In my experience, the most valuable committee for an untenured faculty member to sit on, is the tenure faculty committee. I had the privilege of serving on this committee for two years and observing the criteria used to evaluate candidates for tenure. This has helped me set priorities.

In my first year, I was assigned to a high-profile hiring committee. I gained a lot of insight into SFU, as hiring decisions often reveal much about the dynamics and priorities of an institution. Subsequent to this, I served on various faculty-level committees including other hiring committees and a research committee. In addition, I served on a search committee at the university level for a senior administrative post, also a valuable learning experience. I have ventured far afield unto committees that are the type senior faculty warn against. For example, I sat on an ad hoc committee for designing a new graduate program. Although I cannot say my membership was strategic, I enjoyed this committee and got exposed to interesting people across the university and in the wider community.

## A Personal Note

My first years also saw many changes in my personal life. These conflicted greatly with my academic ambitions. First of all, I suffered a second miscarriage. I then became pregnant for the fourth time and delivered my second son. I had a very tiring pregnancy and slow recovery from childbirth. I was away on maternity leave for five months, and both my pregnancies disrupted my research program quite significantly. Simon Fraser University has a very forward thinking maternity policy that allows tenure-track faculty to extend by one year one's tenure clock in the event of an adoption or birth of a child. Without this policy, I am unsure if I would have continued toward tenure with optimism.

At this time, my family was struck by a tragedy. My second oldest sister, who had been fighting the ravages of breast cancer, succumbed. It is hard to describe the impact such a death has on the whole family. My parents have had to cope with the loss of their child. I have lost a dear and close sister with whom I had shared many experiences. I have yet to come to peace with this loss.

More recently, I was involved in a car accident and sustained quite extensive neck injuries. This has severely constrained my ability to conduct research, teach, and perform my administrative responsibilities. As of this writing, I am still suffering the effects of these injuries.

## Keeping the Balance

Keeping the balance between research, teaching, and administrative work at school is one thing; keeping the balance between all that and one's private life is much more difficult. I had anticipated that the flexibility of academia was an advantage: having flexible working hours, being able to work at home, getting up at two in the morning if so desired, would all make the situation easier. However, I now believe that keeping the balance between one's private life and one's work life is extraordinarily difficult. Our family, with two working parents, is continuously in turmoil over the setting of priorities. Our children now run the gambit from "teenage-hood to toddler-hood" creating enormous demands on both myself and my husband. We are pragmatic in some ways and buy time wherever possible. For example, we invested in a full-time nanny to relieve us of much of the day-to-day chores and activities. We have lowered our standards about housekeeping to more manageable levels. We are presently involved in a lot fewer social activities than we would like to be. However, with tenure pending and with a young family and the challenges they present, we believe this is the best and most rewarding approach.

Beyond one's private life, other opportunities are presented for consulting, being involved as a volunteer in one's community, sporting activities, and for political involvement that have to be balanced. At my pre-tenure stage, I have had to limit most opportunities outside of the very essential. My health concern has also significantly narrowed my playing field.

On the other hand, I have always had strong religious convictions as a practicing Christian. I have never valued my achievements simply on career success alone. So while my career is very important to me, I view my life in much broader terms and will endeavor to try and keep balance among the various aspects of my life.

## Preparation for Tenure

The preparation for tenure predated my joining Simon Fraser University. The quality of my dissertation and, therefore, the ability to publish from it was certainly the initial step in preparing for tenure. It clearly allowed me, as a new faculty member, to have some current research that could be published. Even more lucrative would have been publications done with committees or peers prior to assuming an academic position. In terms of tenure, I have not focused so much on the long term as on the short term. I have tried to structure my semester in such a way that I can at least pay some attention to research while teaching. I believe that it is critical to do the best one can do on a daily basis, rather than be overwhelmed by looking down the road and wondering how on earth it's going to be possible to produce the number of publications required for tenure. As with other institutions, the target for making tenure continues to move and become more demanding. I am also focusing more specifically on getting articles published rather than starting new ventures. Achieving tenure will bring great relief, allowing me to move on to a new phase in my career. With the wind of tenure behind me, I can move to more policy-oriented research with greater scope than current endeavors. I remain excited by the challenge of teaching in a changing environment and anticipate greater involvement in the administrative life of the university.

# 3

# "Finding My Place"

## Marlene K. Puffer

*College professor—someone who talks in other people's sleep.*
—Bergen Evans

### WHERE AM I NOW?

I am an assistant professor of finance at the University of Toronto, where I also completed my bachelor's and master's degrees in economics. I teach advanced undergraduates and second-year M.B.A. students as well as Ph.D. students for the first time this year. Most of my teaching involves international finance, but I have taught introductory finance, corporate finance, special topics, and empirical methods. My research focus is mainly in the area of empirical international financial markets and foreign exchange risk management. I try to keep my administrative duties to a minimum, although with so few women on our faculty (there is a grand total of four tenure-stream women on a faculty of approximately fifty people), committee work is unavoidable. The most eye-opening committee was the Task Force on the Status of Women in the Faculty of Management. More on that later.

I am actively involved with students, spending a lot of time counseling undergraduates about potential career paths and graduate school, M.B.A. students about course selection and job offers, and Ph.D. students about courses, research, and the job market in my new role as advisor to Ph.D. finance students. Given the shortage of role models in the academic and financial worlds, I try to pay particular attention to female students.

I sit on the board of advisors of the local committee of an international student group called AISEC, the International Association of Students in Economics and Commerce. I was actively involved in the group when I was an undergraduate here, and was lucky enough to work in France for two months during the summer of 1983 as part of AISEC's international job exchange program. At the time, I felt that faculty involvement would improve the organization greatly. When I returned to the university as a faculty member, I volunteered to get involved.

This year I accepted a position as chair of the finance committee of an arts, athletics, and recreation center on campus. Despite my efforts to minimize committee work, I see this as an opportunity to serve the wider university community rather than only my own department. Since the committee oversees a multimillion dollar budget, it is also valuable practical financial experience that should have positive spillovers into teaching.

My consulting career is in its infancy. I recently started working with a consulting firm, advising corporations on strategic management of foreign exchange, interest rates, and commodity price risk. I am enjoying the opportunity of applying some of the concepts I teach to real business problems. This experience also provides credibility demanded by M.B.A. students in light of my purely academic career path.

I am thirty years old, recently separated from my husband, with no children. When I'm not in my office, I can usually be found in the kitchen cooking up a storm, having fun with my niece and nephew, in the gym (on the stationary bike with the *Economist* or the *Financial Post* in front of me, of course!), in the swimming pool, on the squash court, or speed-walking outside when the weather isn't beastly. Since I injured my back and developed some other medical problems, I had to make fitness a priority to remain pain free. I love to travel and I do as much of it as possible, usually at least partly for professional reasons. For example, one year's trip consisted of two weeks teaching at the Academy for the National Economy in Moscow, followed by two weeks traveling in Turkey and Greece.

## HOW DID I GET HERE? THE ALLURE OF ACADEMIA

My father is a successful businessman, but he did not graduate from high school. He has an exceptional work ethic, but the only school he thinks is worth attending is the "school of hard knocks." My mother attended business college and was a homemaker for many years before she went back to work in various secretarial positions. I am the youngest of four children and feel lucky to be endowed with good genes. You can refer to my eldest sister Sheila's chapter in this book for her story. When I started college, she had completed her B.A. in linguistics, was working for the Canadian government and doing her M.B.A. part time. My brother completed his Bachelor of Commerce degree and is a successful "computer geek" (these are "his" words). My other sister is more artistically than academically inclined. My siblings had always excelled in school, so by the time I came along, solid academic performance was implicitly anticipated. There was very little explicit pressure, but I grew up sensing that I had to live up to high expectations. Although I assumed my parents were proud of my academic ability and achievements, they were generally downplayed, and there was little encouragement or recognition.

I was fortunate to have had a guidance counselor and two math teachers in high school who recognized my potential and did everything they could to get me into a university three years ahead of schedule. I suspect that I would have been very bored had I stayed in high school the usual amount of time, and I hate to imagine the sort of trouble in which I might have found myself. Upon graduating from high school third in my class (behind the top student by a tiny margin, as I recall) at the tender age of fifteen, I was disappointed that the universities offered only a small entrance scholarship with no renewable component. I had been proud of my grades in high school, and the lack of recognition contributed to recurring motivational problems and a relaxed attitude toward grades in college. It no longer seemed worthwhile to strive for those extra few points that make the difference between a B+ and an A−, or an A− and an A. I was more interested in learning what caught my interest in my own way. I assumed that entrance scholarships were the end of the road as far as scholastic awards are concerned.

I was never told that outstanding performance nevertheless had the potential for monetary awards. Nor was I told, until at least my third year of college, that excellent performance in undergraduate courses could result in substantial scholarships for graduate study. Had I been properly armed with this information, I might have been more ambitious and opened up even more opportunities for myself. I don't know why I didn't figure this out on my own! Luckily, my parents provided financial support through my undergraduate and master's degrees, and I performed well enough in important courses to obtain generous financial support from the university for Ph.D. studies.

When I started at the university I did not have a career mapped out for myself, but I had a vague inkling that I would eventually go to graduate school. Having been hit by a wanderlust at an early age (we moved several times when I was young, which I thought was great), I knew that my career would have to allow me to travel, either for purposes of the career itself, or for allowing adequate vacation time so I could investigate the world on my own. I had no idea at that stage that academia fits the bill. All my first-year professors were older men with sawdust personalities who looked like they spent all their time locked up in their offices with their noses buried in books, never seeing the light of day and never talking to anyone outside their field. With that impression of academic life, no wonder it didn't occur to me as a potential career!

In my first year at the university, my interest in mathematics was accompanied by a passion for languages. I enrolled in two theoretical mathematics courses, and I studied French, Russian, and philosophy. I remember having a counseling session at my college before I selected courses. When I told the counselor that I planned to take the most difficult real analysis and abstract algebra courses, she was surprised and questioned my choice without providing any useful information. Despite her response, I took the courses. I wonder whether a male student would have faced the same reaction?

Very early in my first year, I discovered that the counselor's hesitation about the math courses I had selected had some merit. The math courses did not spark my interest, and I had a hard time recognizing the purpose of some of the lectures and problems we were solving. The professors were not very highly motivating. I dropped the algebra course and eventually completed the real analysis course with a rather dismal performance. I knew that I had hit my mathematical "wall" and did not have enough appreciation of the beauty of high level math for its own sake. What I really wanted was to use math as a tool to understand some aspects of the real world. I apparently belonged to the lowly category of "applied mathematicians" rather than "pure mathematicians." This was a big shock to me, since I had always been excited by math and it had always come very easily to me. I began to doubt my own abilities, and my self-esteem started a rollercoaster ride that had ups and downs throughout the rest of my studies.

I chose less theoretical math courses for the following year and set about looking for an application for math. I was disappointed by the lack of guidance and advice available at the university. At the suggestion of some friends, I took a summer economics course and got hooked. The quantitative nature of the field appealed to me, and I really enjoyed my newfound ability to understand the nightly newscast and the technical articles in the newspaper. I was fascinated by the usefulness and seemingly infinite applications of basic economic principles in everyday life. I also liked the idea that I was studying something that might actually be useful if I wanted to get a job (I think I could hear my father's voice echoing in the caverns of my brain the same way my brother and sister had).

In my second year, I decided to combine my interest in economics with my interest in language and international issues. I enrolled in the international relations program, which combines economics, languages, history, and political science. However, two weeks into the first semester, I took another unexpected turn. I dropped the boring political science course and, since I was enjoying my macroeconomics course so much, decided to take microeconomics as well. The snowball kept rolling from there. Scheduling reasons dictated that to take microeconomics, I had to drop European history, which I wasn't enjoying anyway since it just didn't seem to have any structure or logic. This left another hole in the schedule, which I filled with a statistics course. Suddenly I became an economics specialist with a language minor.

The professor who taught the second semester of my statistics course turned out to be a major influence in my academic career and in every dimension of my life. He noticed my interest in statistics above and beyond the boundaries of the course and suggested that I consider graduate school. He was a natural mentor. He was a real contrast to my first year professors—he was handsome, in his early thirties and talked a lot about the interesting traveling he did for academic reasons and about the opportunities academia provides to meet people and to continually be learning something new. Suddenly the idea of an academic career seemed much more appealing! Beginning in the summer after my second year, I worked for him as a research assistant, which provided a great opportunity to learn about empirical research methods and academic life in general. I chose my courses over the next two years with graduate studies in economics in mind, but I wasn't completely committed to the idea.

My enjoyment of, and generally good performance in, the relatively difficult quantitative courses was not without its traumas. For example, I was so stressed out at the first midterm in econometrics in the third year, that I walked out of the exam early without handing it in. I felt overwhelmed by the amount and difficulty of the material and did not feel adequately prepared. My mind went completely blank during the exam. I was devastated, dropped the course that day and thought I might try it again the following year. What I hadn't counted on was my mentor's reaction the next day. He was understanding about the stress I was going through, but he was adamant that I continue in the course that year because it was important for the research work I was doing for him. I didn't have the guts to tell him that I had already dropped the course. Panic set in once again. I soon found out that I was not the only student who panicked during the exam and that the grading scheme for the course was changed so the test could be eliminated from the final grade. After a large dish of ice cream at my favorite ice cream parlor, I traipsed back into my college registrar's office to "undrop" the course. Mission accomplished. To my amazement, I got an A.

In addition to the occasional panic attack, my motivational problems reared their ugly heads when professors or the subject matter just didn't spark my interest. I graduated with a mixed transcript, with A's in some of the most difficult courses and poorer grades in others. When motivation was low for course work, I immersed myself in research assistance work, AISEC activities, yoga classes, dance classes, or squash.

## THE DOCTORAL DILEMMA

In my fourth year I wanted to continue to study econometrics, which necessitated taking Ph.D.-level courses. Several faculty members suggested that I take a finance course, since the academic job market for finance specialists was heating up. I took introductory finance in the M.B.A. program and really enjoyed it. In the middle of my fourth year, when applications for Ph.D. programs were supposed to be submitted, I was still only eighteen years old and not yet ready to commit to a Ph.D. However, the idea of getting a "real" job didn't appeal to me either. Entry-level positions just seemed too tedious and life in the business world too full of constraints. I hated the thought of a boss telling me how to spend my time, and I wanted to continue to be able to think about whatever caught my interest. I didn't have any brainstorms about other career paths that offered the travel opportunities and flexibility of academia. Interesting jobs in economics or business that seemed likely to capture my interest in the long run required graduate study. Like many undergrads at the university, I decided to stay for one more year to test the waters in the master's program in economics. I tossed around the idea of doing an M.B.A. afterwards (was that my father's voice again?). Gradually, the idea of a Ph.D. became more appealing, so when I enrolled in the master's program in economics I took the core courses in the economics Ph.D. program. I also took more finance courses in the business school.

During my master's year, I applied to some of the best American business schools for admission to their Ph.D. programs in finance. I was concerned about my chances of admission with financial aid because my transcript was mixed. However, my choice of courses prepared me very well for a Ph.D. program in finance compared to most students, and my two years of experience as a research assistant was valuable. Fortunately, I impressed a few faculty members who apparently wrote strong letters for me, and I think the kicker was that I did very well on the GMAT and GRE exams. I sought advice from faculty in the economics department and in the faculty of management about the relative strengths and weaknesses of various programs, obtained as many catalogues as possible, and phoned most of the schools to talk to their faculty directly. I was accepted by several good schools but with less financial aid than a more consistent transcript might have generated. I chose the school that made me the best offer of financial support because it also has a relatively small, high-quality program with a quantitative and empirical emphasis. It also had good placement of graduates on the academic job market and at the school. The location of the school within a few hours' drive from home was also important, since by this time I was romantically involved with my mentor who had a tenured position.

The idea of staying at the same institution or in Canada for my Ph.D. did not even cross my mind. I think it is extremely important to change schools for graduate work. It was particularly critical for me, since I had some interest in being on the faculty of my home institution after completing my degree. Changing schools is important for personal and professional development, even if there is a short-term cost in terms of personal relationships. It is unfortunate that for many people, women in particular, relationships form a major constraint. If the long-term goal is a faculty position in the city you are currently living in, the best route to take is to leave the city in the short term to get a Ph.D. and cross your fingers that schools in the city will be hiring when you are on the market. Spousal job considerations often rule this out. If you stay in the city to get your Ph.D., it is unlikely that the school where you obtained your degree will hire you fresh out of the program. If you don't have geographical flexibility when job hunting, chances are high that you settle for a position at a school that is of lower caliber than your qualifications or for a non-tenure stream contract position, possibly with greater teaching duties. Both choices make success in the academic world more challenging.

It was obvious that I should go to the best feasible school to open as many doors as possible upon completing the Ph.D. program. Living in different cities from my future husband seemed like a small price to pay. We had general plans to jointly look for jobs when I completed my degree. We would face the constraints of finding two jobs in the same city, but we were flexible about location.

As it turned out, a visiting appointment in the economics department at my school became available, so for my first year in the Ph.D. program we lived together. However, the next year he moved back home, so I took the three-hour drive most weekends during my second year of course work and throughout the following year. We were married in the summer between my third and fourth years in the program, and the following academic year, my husband was on sabbatical and visited different American schools. I spent alternating two-week periods at school and visiting where he was. I took a couple of months off in the spring that year to accompany him on a trip to Asia, where he taught an econometrics course. I spent another year after that commuting on weekends.

Course work and comprehensive exams generally went smoothly since I was well prepared. My performance was a bit more consistent than it had been as an undergraduate, but still had its ups and downs. Despite strong performance in previous econometrics courses and feeling fairly confident about the material, I had another traumatic econometrics exam.

My car broke down on a snowy day on the way to the final exam, so I arrived about twenty minutes late. I panicked, never regained my concentration, and failed the exam. Doubts about my ability in the area resurged. Luckily, the experience didn't repeat itself to the same degree during the econometrics comprehensive exam. The thesis stage was another story.

## DISSERTATION DRAMA

The philosophy at the business school where I did my Ph.D. is that it is extremely important that students come up with their own research idea. Very little guidance is offered at that stage, and I did not take an optimal path toward thesis completion. My search for a thesis topic was long and frustrating. The Ph.D. program is well structured; after completing comprehensive exams in June of the second year, the remainder of the summer is dedicated to writing a required research paper. Unfortunately, not everyone is lucky enough to choose a topic that develops into a thesis. I was one of the unlucky ones. My second-year paper was a modification of a recently published paper on liquidity and asset returns, but the modification was minor and did not lend itself easily to further extension. My next two topics were also dead ends. I wrote a paper on whether industry explains the abnormal returns of small firms in January, but the data did not cooperate to yield an interesting conclusion. I also started a paper on dividends and asset returns that did not pan out. I learned the hard way what I now relay to Ph.D. students: a good empirical research topic is one where the question is interesting, no matter whether the data support or refute your hypothesis.

After several dead ends, I started to consider the idea of a topic in international finance, which had been of vague interest since my days as an undergraduate. Many business schools were starting to "internationalize" their programs and were recruiting junior faculty specifically in the area of international finance. I attended a lot of conferences to try to stimulate ideas and gain exposure in the profession. Finally, I found a research area by accident. I attended an econometrics conference where a few finance papers were being presented. One was on volatility "spillovers" in foreign exchange markets around the world. It struck me that a natural extension was to volatility in international equity markets. The idea generated interest among the faculty, so I obtained data as quickly as possible and wrote a first draft of a paper. Unfortunately, someone beat me to the punch. I became aware of a very similar working paper that was quickly accepted for publication in a top journal. I had to dream up a new twist.

I wrote a related paper on the effect of Saturday trading in Tokyo on weekend volatility of the New York stock market that was an extension of a paper written by two faculty members. The results were met with some interest, but the paper was viewed as a candidate for one chapter of a thesis at best. By this time, I was tired and discouraged and several months elapsed without progress. One faculty member, who was a potential member of my thesis committee, counseled me to consider giving up on the thesis and look for a job in the financial community. I was infuriated, since he insinuated that I did not have the ability to complete the Ph.D. I knew I had the ability, it was motivation and creativity that were problematic.

Based on a casual comment by another faculty member, I decided that rather than investigating volatility spillovers in general, I would examine the international financial market response to a specific piece of information: U.S. monthly trade announcements. The econometric methodology was much simpler than what I had suggested before, but the economic issues were much more interesting. I also examined determinants of cross-sectional differences across industries in the stock return response to trade news and foreign exchange movements on trade announcement days. Once my thesis topic was selected, progress was somewhat easier.

My advice to students on how to avoid the frustrations of searching for a thesis topic is to start the search even before they start the program! It is never too early to start reading at least the abstracts of recent articles in top academic journals and those geared toward practitioners and start to understand what kinds of research questions are of interest to both academics and the business community. One piece of advice I remember getting from faculty that I now pass on to students is to regularly read the business press including newspapers, popular magazines like *Business Week, Forbes,* and the *Economist,* and more specialized magazines specific to the field of interest. Research topics can easily arise from current topics in the financial press. Once you have an interesting question, devising a way to answer it is relatively easy.

One mistake I made was to choose my thesis advisor before finalizing a topic, since working as his research assistant gave me insight into his econometrics skills, research interests, and personality. He seemed like the best match for me. Unfortunately, I ended up selecting a topic that was outside his area of expertise, which introduced complications. Luckily another professor, whose work is closely related to mine, joined the faculty late in my thesis progress and agreed to serve on my committee. Another drawback was that I was the first student whose thesis my primary advisor had chaired. This fact made him a bit more demanding and hesitant to offer detailed advice. Communication with my chair was not always perfect, and commuting didn't help. There is something to be said for having an experienced advisor . . . my advisor and I both learned about the process together. Despite the drawbacks, my chair was very supportive and patient, and I couldn't have finished the degree without him. In hindsight, I should have gathered more information from students further along in the program about selecting an advisor and about how to obtain guidance and feedback.

I now advise students to select an experienced chair and set up regular meetings, whether the professor suggests it or not. I recommend that even at the earliest stages of searching for a thesis topic, that the student write down ideas and provide a short document for the advisor to read before each meeting. Notes should be taken during the meeting, written up by the student, and circulated back to the professor to ensure agreement about what was said. There are too many instances of miscommunication where students fruitlessly follow what they believe to be the advice of the professor, only to discover that the professor meant something different. I also suggest that students set a weekly schedule and keep a brief written summary of each paper they read to develop the habit of recording ideas in written form and to make it easy to remember the essentials of each paper. I remind students that they don't need to know absolutely everything about the literature to begin work on a thesis and encourage them to stop reading and start writing. I also suggest that they spend as much time as possible on campus interacting with faculty and other students. Working in isolation increases the danger of getting unnecessarily discouraged. Sharing frustrations with other students reduces the stress level.

The long search process took a tremendous emotional toll, and I found it very difficult to keep motivated. I read a lot of journal articles and attended conferences to learn about the most recent research but had trouble coming up with ideas that seemed adequate for a thesis. I fell into the trap of believing that a thesis had to be a major new development that seemed to be unattainable, when in fact a relatively small idea or extension of existing work is all that is required. I had expected to make rapid progress through the Ph.D. program, and failing to quickly get through the topic search phase was extremely discouraging. I have witnessed many students falling into the same hole and have watched their self-esteem plummet as mine did. I think the problem is that most Ph.D. students' identities are too wrapped up in the degree. Anything less than ideal progress stirs up feelings of inadequacy and failure that further hamper progress. Students too easily lose sight of the fact that they are bright, capable people who have many opportunities available outside academia. The most successful Ph.D. students seem to be those who maintain the perspective that the Ph.D. is not the most important thing in life!

The emotional rollercoaster during my topic search was partly associated with being torn between dedication to my own career and my relationship. My husband was very encouraging, but since he had taken only a few short months to complete his dissertation fifteen years earlier, I had underlying feelings that anything less than a similar performance would be a big disappointment to him, and to me. I set high standards for myself but still feel that I don't always live up to my fullest potential. Being unable to live up to such high standards made me repeatedly question whether I had chosen the right path, but it was difficult to talk to anyone about it. I knew that fundamentally I had the ability to complete a thesis, so I perceived my difficulty in finding a topic to be a major flaw in my personality. My husband was also continually tempting me with exciting travel opportunities. We both felt the need to spend time together, and I did all the commuting which reduced my interaction with students and faculty. The continual change of scene was disruptive for me and made it difficult to stay focused. Without frequent deadlines to meet or exams to study for, I was easily distracted at the thesis stage by other demands such as working as a teaching and research assistant. I still seem to be easily distracted from long-term projects when shorter term projects, with more immediate payoffs, require attention.

## PROPOSAL, DEFENSE, PROFESSOR!

My thesis topic jelled in the summer after my fifth year in the program, and I went on the job market in the fall of that year. For my sixth year as a Ph.D. student, my husband and I were living in the United States where he had a visiting appointment. I was treated as a visiting doctoral student for the year, so I had an office and access to all the university facilities but basically worked on my own. I went back to my university a few times that year. We both looked for jobs, hoping to find two jobs in the same city, which is much easier said than done. We had a few opportunities but were constrained by the limited number of schools hiring junior faculty in finance and by the even smaller number of schools interested in hiring a senior econometrician. Given our preference for big city life, it was not too surprising that once I had an offer, we decided to return to Canada where my husband was already tenured.

I thought I would propose my dissertation in the spring of my first year of teaching full time, but it was not until the fall of the following year that I managed to accomplish that. The formal thesis proposal generally happens after completion of the majority of the work on the thesis. The delay was due to heavy teaching demands, work on another paper that was eventually published, anxiety, and difficulty getting advice from my committee. It is never easy to get feedback from advisors when you are in a different city. I wish I had been more confident and more assertive. Bombarding my committee with new drafts more frequently rather than worrying about every little detail before sending a new draft would have helped.

The proposal is the major stumbling block, and it went fairly smoothly. The remaining work did not seem particularly onerous, but communication with my advisors was not perfect and my confidence and motivation were not high enough to push for a timely defense. The changes that were made to the last two or three drafts were minor, and there was no good reason for them taking as long as they did. I finally scheduled my defense in the spring of my third year of teaching. The timing of the defense turned out to be fateful. A week before the defense, which was scheduled for a Monday, my father had a severe stroke while he was golfing in Florida. Luckily I was only teaching on Tuesdays that term, so on Wednesday I went to Florida and helped my mother with arrangements to fly my father home to Calgary, then I caught a flight on Sunday, and defended on Monday. Needless to say, my preparation and concentration were not at their peak. Fortunately, the defense went well and the final draft of the thesis was accepted a week later. The following week I had a terrific party. The doctor was finally in!

## TEACHING

The transition from being an undergraduate student to being a faculty member at the same institution was a fairly smooth one. My new colleagues and those who had previously been my professors have treated me with respect and have lent a helping hand when ever needed. There have been a few awkward and amusing moments associated with the relative novelty of having a woman lurking where so few have lurked before. Thoughts of one incident still make me smile. One Friday afternoon after the finance workshop guest speaker, a few faculty were on their way out for the customary beer. Ordinarily I would join in but that particular day I had other plans. I was chatting in the hall with two of the male faculty who were going out, when a non-finance colleague passed by. He heard me say that I would not be joining them and remarked in a jovial tone, "What's the matter . . . aren't you one of the boys?" I interpreted the remark with humor as it was intended, made an appropriate retort, and thought nothing of it. The timing was impeccable. The next day, the news of the Anita Hill/Clarence Thomas incident broke and everyone was glued to their televisions for the weekend thinking about issues of sexual harassment on the job. Well, Monday morning, to my astonishment, my colleague traipsed into my office with his tail between his legs and apologized profusely for his remark! It amazed me that something so trivial that hadn't phased me in the least could have made him feel so sheepish! I was touched that he was so sensitive to the issues and did my best to convince him that no offense had been taken. We had a good laugh about it.

I was very surprised at the total absence of any sort of formal orientation for new faculty either at the university level or within the Faculty of Management. After I arrived, I had an appointment with the personnel office to discuss benefits and was given a campus map, a calendar, a handbook, and a key to an office. That was it. I had no information about the organizational chart or governance of the faculty. I can remember getting a memo early in my first year addressed to "all members of Faculty Council" announcing the time and agenda for a meeting. I wondered why I had received the memo, but it never even occurred to me to attend. The day after the meeting, one of my colleagues asked why I had not attended the Faculty Council meeting. I was puzzled and said that I didn't realize that I was supposed to have attended. Little did I know that every faculty member is automatically a member of Faculty Council. Any major policy changes within the faculty are formulated by smaller committees but are eventually approved by Faculty Council. This is completely different from the governance of the economics department with which I was more familiar. Judging by meetings I have attended since, I didn't miss much by not attending that first one!

It took a lot of initiative on my part to get settled in. I sought out the appropriate people and asked a lot of questions. I can only imagine how isolated and frustrated I would have felt had I not been in familiar territory. I think there should be a more formal orientation policy for new faculty. In the absence of that, I now do whatever I can to make new faculty feel welcome and to help guide them through the administrative maze.

It amazes me that despite the fact that most Ph.D. students pursue academic careers, Ph.D. programs generally provide no training on teaching methods, although our university recently started offering such a course for Ph.D. students. Somehow, we are expected to magically learn to teach by watching and by gaining experience as teaching assistants grading papers and giving tutorials. Teaching an introductory course where the syllabus is chosen by someone else and the lectures closely follow the textbook is relatively easy to do without any guidance or experience. However, planning a new course from scratch and structuring lectures and choosing topics, textbooks, and grading schemes, is an onerous task for a fresh Ph.D. I had to do both. I was fortunate to be able to warm up on undergraduates in the fall before facing M.B.A. students in international finance in the spring. I was also lucky to have a helpful colleague who had taught the course for many years. In fact, I had taken M.B.A. international finance from him six years earlier when I was working on my master's in economics! He was always available for a chat about what topics to cover, how to convey particular ideas, or whatever problems arose. Another colleague from whom I had taken introductory finance was also available with words of wisdom when needed.

The only time that teaching really made me nervous was on my first day. The course was international finance for fourth-year undergraduates. The location was a dreary classroom in the main building on campus for undergraduate arts and science classes. I was twenty-six years old and felt the necessity to somehow avoid looking like a student, so despite my hatred of business attire, I put on a suit (unlike most of my male colleagues, I still do most of the time for teaching). I can still remember the looks on the faces of the students in the front row when I walked in the room and they realized that I was the professor. Shock and amazement buzzed through the room. Many of them had never had a female professor or a professor under the age of forty, let alone both wrapped up in one! I knew I had to establish control and respect, so I immediately launched into a discussion of how difficult the course would be and how hard the students would have to work. This seemed to convince the students to take the course and me seriously. I still use this strategy during the first class each term, although it is less necessary now since my reputation precedes me. The second class is more fun than the first!

The next semester, I faced my first class of part-time M.B.A. students in international finance. I was a bit anxious since I have no work experience in finance, but some of the students had substantial work experience in fields directly related to the course. For example, I knew there was a foreign exchange trader in the class. I decided that to cope with the situation, I would use the students to my advantage. Rather than trying to appear as the expert on everything, I ask questions to draw out the students' expertise. The more experienced students are a joy to have in class, and I have learned a lot from them since they generally contribute their practical knowledge freely and appreciate learning the theory behind the work they had previously been doing by the seat of their pants.

The exception was last term when I taught corporate finance for the first time to part-time M.B.A. students. The dreaded student from hell appeared. His sole purpose each class seemed to be to undermine me and to contradict whatever I had to say, just for the sheer fun of it. Unfortunately, he got under my skin. I spent more time than necessary preparing for each class, just to protect myself from his assault, since I was not feeling confident about my institutional knowledge in the area. His strength was in citing specific examples of companies and their situations that appeared to contradict theory. At first I felt obligated to give his comments serious consideration despite his arrogant attitude and obviously deliberate attempt to get my goat, but I eventually realized that he was not as brilliant as he thought himself to be. I couldn't argue with his facts since I was not always aware of the particular firms. This made me uncomfortable, and he knew it and played on it. I had to come up with another way to challenge him and shut him up, since most of his comments were not useful to the other students. Despite the rest of the class being on my side in this battle, it was not until near the end of the semester that I managed to put him in his place and regain the upper hand. When he made some inane comment about a specific company that appeared to contradict what I had just stated, I said something to the effect that his comment was irrelevant to the question at hand and contributed nothing to the discussion. The rest of the class let out a small cheer, and he kept his mouth shut after that. No one will be able to get to me that way again!

## COMMITTEE WORK

Until last year, there were no tenured women at the Faculty of Management. Last year, two women were granted tenure. Out of approximately fifty faculty, there are only four women, including me, in tenure stream positions. The small numbers along with a few incidents prompted the dean to strike a task force to examine the status of women in the faculty. Despite the general policy that junior faculty should be spared committee work, I was asked to sit on the committee in my first year. The apparent logic was that there should be at least one female faculty member on the committee and, not surprisingly, the other female faculty were all tied up on other major committees. I felt in no position to turn down the dean's request and was curious about the committee's agenda.

The committee consisted of approximately twenty people: students, staff, faculty, and representatives of the business community. I found it quite amusing that I was chosen for this particular committee. No one knew anything about my views on "women's issues," and I think the committee was surprised by them. It has never occurred to me that my gender is a help or a hindrance in anything I want to do with my life, and it seems to me that having that attitude is virtually a self-fulfilling prophecy. I have very little patience for the "women have been victims through the ages, so we need special treatment now to make up for it" attitude. However, there were a lot of subtle issues to which I had never devoted much thought, and the committee forced me to face them head on.

I remember thinking at the first meeting that there was no way that we would be able to reach any consensus on the issues, given the extreme points of view that were represented in the room. I found myself agreeing more closely with the men than with most of the women. It was fascinating to watch the committee gradually meet in the middle ground on most issues. Those who automatically believed that the same problems facing women in the business world must be present in the academic environment discovered that we are lucky to face fewer difficulties. Those who believed there were no problems whatsoever associated with gender in the faculty had their eyes opened. For example, numerous incidents of demeaning remarks and offensive language used by male professors in the classroom were described by students in focus group discussions. One professor on the committee, who thought women had no reason to complain, seemed genuinely surprised to learn that his language was annoying to women and rather humbly vowed to change his behavior. I don't know whether he has changed, but awareness is half the battle.

Among other issues, the committee sparked my interest in the relative lack of female participation in class discussion. I find it difficult to draw out the women in the room, despite trying to create a relaxed atmosphere where students feel comfortable expressing their opinions and asking questions without having the professor jump down their throat. The difficulty often persists even when the women are at the top of the class in terms of ability. There is a noticeable improvement when the proportion of women in the class is relatively higher; a certain comfort level is generated by greater numbers of women. Unfortunately, the proportion of women in our M.B.A. program has stagnated at around 35 to 40 percent, and the proportion in finance classes is even lower. Aside from increasing the number of women in the program and encouraging them to take the quantitative finance courses, we were unable to come up with ideas on how to improve their participation.

I had a good chuckle when I was chosen to write up the subcommittee recommendations on maternity policy. I am the only female faculty member without children! I suppose that gave me a relatively neutral attitude about the policies. It was interesting to think about the issues, since two of my friends from graduate school were pregnant at the time. One was at a Canadian university with quite generous maternity policies, and the other was at a U.S. state school with stingy policies. The contrasting treatment they received opened my eyes to the importance of formulating a policy for teaching relief that does not depend on the timing of the birth during the school year.

I also sat on the subcommittee on tenure and promotion. I think the ideas we came up with are important and summarize my feelings on committee work, so let me present a brief excerpt, beginning with a recommendation on women and committees:

The selection criteria for membership on committees should be gender neutral. Ensuring representation of women on committees should only be done when gender is explicitly relevant to the agenda of the committee. When there is a perceived need for women on a committee, the Faculty should investigate whether women from other Faculties, students, or alumni might be appropriate rather than focusing only on female members of the Faculty of Management.

If committee work continues to significantly affect women more than men, rather than forcing women to take time away from research to serve on committees, it seems more reasonable to allow teaching relief. Unfortunately this implies that women would be slightly less visible to students, but until the number of women on faculty is greatly increased, representation of women on committees requires some trade-offs. Teaching credit of at least the equivalent of one semester course should be granted to untenured tenure-stream faculty for committee work.

To attempt to increase the presence of women as role models in the classroom we add the following recommendation: Women should be sought out as guest lecturers.

The task force report contained thirty-two recommendations in total. It has been over two years since the report was completed, and we now have a different dean. It was well received, but implementation seems unlikely in light of the other priorities on the current dean's agenda. I had a meeting with the new dean about the report soon after he took office and offered many suggestions about implementation, but they were largely ignored. Having put so much energy into the report, it is frustrating to see it sitting on the back burner. However, I am reluctant to take any further follow-up action since it could be very time consuming. I don't view it as my responsibility just because I am female, and I don't want to be viewed as an activist on this issue. I make my own small contribution by inviting female guest lecturers whenever possible and being visible and available to students. I have sat on many committees since this first one, and although I feel I have made some valuable contributions, the difficulties of instigating change at this institution are becoming a bit discouraging and disappointing.

## PUBLISHING AND PREPARING FOR TENURE

The day I found out my first article was accepted for publication, I was grinning from ear to ear. It was during my first year teaching, and I really needed the positive reinforcement to keep me going on my thesis struggle. The article was a short piece on the effect of trading in Tokyo on volatility in the New York stock market. I wrote the first draft when I was refining my thesis topic, but the article did not end up being part of my thesis. My thesis advisors were not encouraging about it, so I felt vindicated to see it in print.

The struggle with my thesis has had the fortunate benefit of buying me time on the tenure clock. The clock started ticking after I received my degree, so I still have about four years to prepare. I am sick of the sight of my thesis, so it has been another battle to get it published. One article has been accepted at a good journal, but another one or two pieces still need work before they can be submitted. I decided to motivate the revisions by planning to submit one of the pieces to a conference in San Diego in a few months. If a trip to California doesn't motivate me to revise, nothing will! Meanwhile, I have several papers in a variety of areas in the pipeline, some co-authored and some on my own. Two papers have been sitting half-finished for at least a year. I still find myself easily distracted. Starting projects is relatively easy since ideas flow more easily now than when I was looking for a thesis topic, but I continue to struggle with the detailed work involved in completing projects. The difficulty in finding reliable and skilled research assistants makes it even more of a challenge.

I recently submitted a major grant application, which forced me to devise a more cohesive research program. I look forward to launching these new projects and am crossing my fingers that I can keep my own interest stimulated enough to see them through to completion and publication.

I certainly feel more motivated for research than I have in a long time, since the weight of the thesis is no longer sitting on my shoulders. However, I enjoy the teaching and service components of the job and have to continually fight my natural tendencies to spend too much energy in these areas. Although I still devote a lot of time to students, I have made a conscious effort to be less available for questions outside designated office hours. Our teaching load is heavy (a total of six semester courses, two hours per week for each class), and I have new preparations again this year. I will be teaching the Ph.D. course on empirical methods in finance jointly with a colleague in the spring, so I hope preparation for that course will have good synergies with research.

When my motivation for research is at a low point, I wonder whether academia is the place for me. Sometimes I think the faculty member who advised me to consider a job in the financial community might have been right. I have trouble visualizing myself as a professor in twenty or thirty years. Despite the flexibility and growth opportunities within academia, I have inklings of a need for more excitement and change. In the business world, I could take greater advantage of my people skills and the slow process of doing research that I still find frustrating might be replaced with shorter term projects with more variety and immediate payoffs. I could most likely, also increase my salary substantially. Then I think about all the constraints associated with a "real job," the loss of control over my own time, and the potential for getting stuck with routine work with less intellectual stimulation and growth. That is usually enough to get me to crack the whip and focus on research again. I remind myself that consulting is always a possibility to satisfy my business world urges. So far, I have enjoyed my taste of the consulting world.

## WHERE AM I GOING?

Life is starting fresh for me in many ways. New courses to teach both at home and abroad, innovative research directions to ponder, and life after divorce each presents its own challenge and opportunity. Writing this chapter has made me think again about people who have influenced my professional choices and has motivated me to take more action to have a positive influence on others. I have been rethinking the reasons for the relatively small numbers of female finance academics and the tiny numbers of women at my business school in any field. The answer always seems to point to the absence of role models and the tendency of girls to shy away from quantitative fields at an early age. Aside from counseling students at the undergraduate and M.B.A. levels to awaken them to career opportunities, I have made the connections to do my part to encourage girls at a much earlier stage to pursue their interest in math. I will soon start speaking at elementary and junior high schools. I hope my presence and enthusiasm is enough to motivate a few individuals to embark on as interesting a road as I have had the privilege of traveling.

## EPILOGUE

It has been seven months since I completed my chapter for this book. When I wrote it, I was already feeling ambivalent toward academia. My ambivalence has intensified. I told myself at the beginning of the academic year that if I did not get excited about research, I would have to make some changes in my life. I had hoped that putting together a major grant application would light a fire under me, since it forced me to devise a cohesive research program. However, as usual although these ideas and questions sparked my interest, the thought of the grunt work necessary to see the projects through to completion and the endless editing and rewriting required to satisfy referees for publication many months or years down the road extinguished my fire before it really got started. The reward of more publications that make small contributions to the literature, and the carrot of tenure (which yields a perpetual repeat of the process) just don't have enough allure to fan the flames. I don't value the job security and, in some ways, I view it more as a burden than a bonus. Even involvement in (unsuccessful) hiring this year and discussing the latest research with enthusiastic new Ph.D.'s didn't generate much heat.

I had made every effort over the years to be sure that academia was what I wanted. However, after separating from my husband, who is a very accomplished academic and who had been the most important mentor to me since I was eighteen years old, I realized that he was a big part of the reason why I had stuck it out, despite growing feelings that it was not the right place for me. Naturally an optimist, I focused on the good things that I liked about the marriage and academic life and put the things I didn't like on the back burner. I finally reached a point where I couldn't do that any more. Since I have made major changes in my life, my health has improved and I feel like I have finally figured out what makes me tick.

I am taking a leave of absence from the university to give the "real world" a try. I had an interesting opportunity to join a consulting firm advising corporations on risk management, but instead I have decided to dive head first into the world of investment dealers in the fixed-income area. I don't want to trade and I don't want to be a pure research analyst, but the whole spectrum between sales, structuring, capital markets, and strategy is interesting to me. My job search is in its final stages, and I hope to start work in a month or so. At this point, I think this is a permanent departure from academia, but since I haven't yet started the routine of arriving at work at 7:30 A.M., putting in long days in a stressful trading room, and learning the ropes in a new large institution, I am keeping an open mind. It is a real luxury to have the option to take a leave rather than to resign from the university. It makes the risk of diving into a whole new career a little easier to take. It is possible that working in the investment industry will generate new research ideas and enthusiasm, but I suspect it is more likely to lead to continued zeal for the investment world. I am eagerly anticipating using my problem-solving skills in different ways, meeting new people, and living day-to-day at a faster pace.

My need for new challenges and a different kind of excitement has won out for now. I had thought that I would always view the next research project as an exciting challenge and an opportunity to learn something new. Unfortunately, that positive attitude and my enjoyment of teaching are overshadowed by the absence of a sense of accomplishment arising from the publication process. There are other aspects of academic life that I won't miss. Endless unproductive committee meetings, internal politics, and general resistance to change among some faculty top the list. The things I will miss and that might lure me back are eager students challenging me in the classroom, intellectual freedom, and travel opportunities for teaching or conferences. I will continue to have contact with students through my involvement in AISEC and the finance committee at the campus arts and recreation facility, and the university president, who recently appointed me to the governing body of this same facility. The faculty is understaffed in the finance area, so even if I don't return to academia full time in a tenure track position, teaching opportunities abound. Experience in the investment world will undoubtedly be valuable in the classroom. I'm very curious to see where this new road leads.

## NOTE

This epilogue was received just before the book went to print, and so its contents are not included in the analysis and conclusions. Although we could not explicitly use this material, we believed it to be a thought-provoking piece for us all.

# 4

# Early-Career Women: The Formative Years

*Nothing in life is to be feared. It is only to be understood.*

—Marie Curie

In the preceding chapters, three women in the first few years of their academic lives give us a glimpse of their past and present. Although they are in three different disciplines—marketing, finance, and information systems—there are similarities to their stories. To summarize, we present first a "snapshot" of each contributor and then draw out the common themes.

## CONTRIBUTOR SNAPSHOTS

### Yolande E. Chan

Through hard work and focus, Yolande has achieved a great deal— undergrad and graduate degrees from MIT, a Rhodes Scholarship, a successful stint as a management consultant, and prestigious awards for teaching and research during her Ph.D. and early career as a professor. She seems to make each year count as two in terms of her output. Family expectations and role models, a steely determination to excel in all dimensions, the support of her husband, and a game plan to balance work and other priorities have contributed to her success.

Yolande has extended her original Ph.D. research, won several research grants, and is learning to create productive research teams with graduate students and research associates.

## June N. P. Francis

June is at a critical career point—poised to go up for tenure, yet hampered by a neck injury that is preventing her from teaching or concentrating on her research work. Her prognosis is for a slow recovery, and the uncertainty about her future with the university is adding stress to an already difficult situation. She has already taken advantage of the one-year tenure-clock stoppage after the birth of her third child, and she does not know how the university tenure process will deal with a prolonged illness.

June juggles a professional life with a rich family and spiritual life. Her three children are spread in ages by thirteen years. Her husband is also a professional with a career to build. Together, they face the challenges of life—their mutual support of each others' careers is very solid.

Frustrated by her current lack of momentum and tempted by the research opportunities present in her field of international marketing, she awaits the tenure process with some trepidation. Her experience as a marketing manager for Clorox and Procter & Gamble gives her a fallback position, but it would be second choice, as academia is the place where she feels she can balance a professional contribution with family life.

## Marlene K. Puffer

Fast tracked through school and finishing her undergraduate degree at nineteen, Marlene then took the next ten years to complete a master's degree and a Ph.D. in finance. Her progress was slowed for three main reasons: (1) her desire to spend time with her husband, who was tenured at another university, kept her away from her home university for many days at a time; (2) her lack of experience in the business world and some bad timing hampered her efforts to find a suitable Ph.D. dissertation topic; and (3) her motivation levels rose and fell, influenced by the first two factors and by an ambivalence about entering the academic world.

Having finished her dissertation and her first few years at the University of Toronto, Marlene was finding her place as a role model for other women students and as an advocate for girls in high school science programs. She was facing the difficult task of developing a new research stream to sustain her during the next few years. Finding that her commitment to academia was weak, she has accepted a one-year's leave of absence to enter the investment industry.

## CAREER THEMES

Although these women have very different backgrounds, family compositions, and fields of specialty, there are common themes throughout that we can use to interpret their lives and to create a deeper understanding of the challenges and rewards of early academic life. The remainder of this chapter will be organized under thematic headings.

### Personal Mastery

These women were not content to work within their areas of competence. They challenged their weaknesses, going beyond known strengths. June moved beyond her developed competence in marketing and organizational behavior to take a minor in econometrics. This difficult route was chosen to enhance her credibility in a faculty that did not value prior industry experiences. She then went on to fashion a piece of "academic entrepreneurship" rather than accept a more traditional methodology.

Yolande has a habit of setting extraordinary goals for herself. For example, she completed six years of work in four at MIT, and then took the maximum courses allowable in the Ph.D. program. In the first two years of teaching, she met with each student (there were over 100 per term) to get their full participation in the course and input about potential course changes.

Both June and Yolande have been rewarded for these instances of high intensity and hard work—June with an article in a top marketing journal, and Yolande with the School of Business Student Life Award, which recognizes her contributions to students.

### The Female Dilemma

Because of women's traditional place as supporters of their husband's career and primary caregivers of children, they face more severe roadblocks than men in their attempts to combine family and an academic career. Rules about tenure and residency were made by men for men and are slow to change.

June had the most obvious case of "female dilemma," undergoing six stress-inducing events during her Ph.D. program: testing and a diagnosis of infertility, a miscarriage, a birth, an adoption, another miscarriage, and a second birth. These events interfered with work productivity for both June and her husband, but the additional physical stress was felt by June alone, lengthening her time to finish the degree and possibly laying the foundation for her current neck problems. Although some might suggest she should have delayed having children, timing for this was narrowed down to only three choices—while acting as a marketing manager in two, fast-paced consumer-goods companies, while completing the Ph.D. program, or during the tenure-track years in her first academic job. There seemed to be no "optimal" time to build a family.

Marlene had a more intractable problem—a commuting relationship
with a husband who expected that she would travel to his place of work,
rather than he to hers. By doing all the traveling she had trouble concentrating on her studies and suffered from doubts and weakened motivation, which almost derailed the completion of her dissertation.
Separation of two people who are both pursuing academic life is an
endemic problem (as you will see in later chapters) and can derail careers
and marriages as it wears down even the best of relationships.

### Support Systems

Both Yolande and June in our early-career group developed a supportive environment for themselves, recognizing that personal willpower
is not enough to succeed and prosper. Marlene does not seem to have
an important support system and, for the most part, relies on her own
motivation and persistence for her career progress.

A striking similarity in stories told by both Yolande and June occurred
when each of the women and their families made a mad dash—a multiple hour car trip to their home university—to submit their dissertation
before the deadline. These journeys are revealing in two ways: they indicate the pace and the pressure of combining a Ph.D. with tenure-track
employment, and they symbolize the support these two women received
from their spouses in order to achieve their goals.

June seems to be the most proficient at creating a supportive environment for herself from a variety of people—peers, family, and senior faculty. In her early Ph.D. years, she and two other students formed a study
group designed to work cooperatively rather than competitively to pass
the comprehensive exams. Their support for each other transcended
course work and resulted in a successful completion for all. June's husband also supported her by recognizing her need to live full-time in
Seattle while he worked in Vancouver. Later, he shouldered many of the
day-to-day child care responsibilities and, in a terrific show of support,
worked with her throughout the night before the thesis was due. As a
junior faculty member, she benefited from the advice and help of a more
senior woman on staff. This assisted her to publish quickly out of the
thesis, and to then move on to other projects.

Yolande also has had terrific support from her family, most notably
from her mother-in-law who, for two years, lived with the family to take
care of her son during the day. Michael, Yolande's husband, has moved
twice to accommodate her career—first, to London, Ontario, to practice
psychiatry while she did her Ph.D. and second, to Kingston, Ontario,
where her tenure-track job was located. Fortunately, there were good
career opportunities for him in Kingston. Yolande, recognizing that her
efforts alone would not produce the amount of output she desired, has

used her research grant monies to develop a working support system of research associates, assistants, and secretaries.

### Expectations

Being placed in a situation where others expect you to do well can be a precursor to achievement. June, the last of seven children, was expected to do well, and mentions that her mother "chided us to put great emphasis in academic achievement. She made it possible for us to concentrate on school work by providing emotional support and shielding us from the everyday demands of life . . . we were ill-equipped to be housewives." Her siblings excelled at school, and June was expected to follow in their footsteps.

Yolande's undergraduate and graduate degrees in electrical engineering from MIT seem unusually impressive achievements until you realize that her three siblings all have professional degrees (in medicine, veterinary medicine, and law) and also have Ph.D.'s. Being third in this family meant that the high standards were already in place and she was expected and encouraged to follow suit. However, as Marlene notes in a letter to the editors: "expectations can be a burden if there is insufficient support and praise; it is possible to feel that you can never live up to the expectations."

### Achieving Balance

Like most working women and men, trying to balance academic life and family life is a difficult task. First, there is the problem of obtaining high-quality child care. Then, there is the issue of time—you want to participate actively in the family and also need to achieve the teaching and research results required at your university. Yolande seems to have created a workable solution for the first problem; June is still coping. Yolande, with one child and a live-in mother-in-law, had a solution for the first two years of her parenting. She is now relying more on day care to supplement what she and her husband can provide. June has a large family (three children) with a spread of ages from four to fourteen. She has tried a number of solutions to provide her children with good quality care and is now experimenting with a full-time nanny. It is an ongoing struggle.

Yolande's solution to the time issue is to compartmentalize her activities, and not bring work home at night or on the weekends. This is difficult, and she reports that "frequently, it means that I must say no to interesting research, teaching, and administrative opportunities. I keep reminding myself: *the good is ever the enemy of the best.*"

## Low Periods

From our study of these women's stories, it seems that there are periods of vulnerability occurring early in the academic cycle. These are times when the career can be derailed and plans are at risk. June and Marlene's stories demonstrate strikingly similar problems.

June reported a very difficult period after the comprehensive exam and before a research proposal had been finalized. As she says, "I spent the first year after my comprehensives gravitating between various dissertation topics. I was advised at different points to simply take on the topic of my advisor. . . . I knew this would not be satisfying to me. . . . I really wanted my own research topic . . ."

Marlene also reported significant problems in finding a research topic: "My search for a thesis topic was long and frustrating. . . . My second-year paper . . . did not lend itself to further extension. My next two topics were also dead ends. . . . I attended a lot of conferences to stimulate ideas. . . . Finally I found a research area by accident. . . . Unfortunately, someone beat me to the punch. . . . I was tired and discouraged and several months elapsed without progress." Both editors of this book have experienced this same dilemma and feel that this time period, after the letdown from comprehensives and before one can begin a substantial piece of research, is a demoralizing and difficult one.

While working on her thesis, June moved to Vancouver to take a tenure track position. Although this was a step she felt compelled to make to get back together with her family and to begin real work, it raised substantial difficulties in getting the thesis finalized when she was in a different city from her committee. The daily life of teaching and family subsumed the thesis work and she had to make a special effort to finish (e.g., working through the nights and only focusing energy on the thesis and children). Marlene also reported that "it is never easy to get feedback from your advisors when you are in a different city. I wish I had been more confident and more assertive."

Putting one's academic career at risk by taking a job too early may be a widespread but unreported problem. Within the past two years, the editors have seen two lecturers working far away from their committees, failing to finish on time and relinquishing the idea of a university-based academic career.

Another difficult period for both June and Marlene was after the thesis was finished and before the papers to be published were completed. Creating a productive research stream in the absence of an advisor is a significant task. June reports that she "embarked on a data collection spree that somewhat distracted me from the main goal of producing articles. I collected data for some six studies but found it difficult to find the time to complete individual articles." As a result, she made a deliberate decision to concentrate on fewer areas.

## Lessons for Others

There are lessons we can learn from these stories. This accumulated knowledge may not always help to avoid problems, but at least can teach us to expect difficulties and not to blame ourselves or lose confidence when they occur.

1. Work on defining the dissertation topic before finishing the comprehensive exams. Find a dissertation advisor early in your program. If you have no industry experience, read journals and trade press material to see what is happening in the field. Yolande also suggests that a topic should be chosen to match the interests of the advisor. In this way, you can build a good partnership during production of the research.

2. Expect problems when you move away and start teaching before completing the dissertation. Make this move only if you really must and then find ways to keep in touch with your committee in order to complete the degree expeditiously. One friend of ours was warned by her supervisor "move away and your work goes to the bottom of my pile." He was concerned for her progress, but unfortunately this is exactly what happens. Thesis advisors may feel little obligation to attend to your work if you are not there.

3. Evaluate opportunities more clearly by developing "personal objectives." This means defining what is most important for you, not for your advisor. For example, after searching for a thesis topic, June decided on some dimensions important in her work—her topic would be international and cultural and would deal with relevant issues. She also decided to find an academic job that allowed her freedom in her research work, avoiding the institutions which favor highly theoretical work over applied work.

4. Realize the need for support systems and create them if they are not already present. This is a characteristic of successful people. There are two kinds of support systems—personal (friends and family) and professional (mentors and peers). Both may be necessary at different times in your career. Learn to accept help and assistance that is offered and to seek it out when it is needed.

5. Take risks. For our early-career women, doing an innovative and excellent piece of research at the dissertation level was the first step toward tenure. For June, this strategy resulted in publishing several articles in top-tier journals. Yolande's innovative research ideas attracted a large grant, which in turn allowed the successful accomplishment of her project. Grant money is very difficult for students to obtain, and finding a topic that will attract a mentor and research money has long-term benefits.

6. Leverage your efforts. Major achievements in research need a cooperative approach. Find a strategy that will create a productive environment (e.g., research teams with students, peers, or industry partners). Being successful

will necessitate learning how to create effective teams and how to generate enough research money to keep the teams well supported.

7. Think excellence. Ensure that every piece of work submitted to a good journal is of the highest quality. One strategy for accomplishing this is to submit the drafts to peers or more senior academics for critical review before submitting them to a journal.

# II

# Mid-Career Women

# 5

# "A Good Traveler"

## Cynthia M. Beath

*A good traveler has no fixed plans and is not intent upon arriving. A good artist lets his intuition lead him wherever it wants. A good scientist has freed himself of concepts and keeps his mind open to what is.*
Lao-tzu, *Tao Te Ching*, trans. Stephen Mitchell
(New York: Harper and Row, 1988, p. 27)

**WHO I AM**

Last month there were two parties in my honor—one was to celebrate my having been granted tenure and the other was to celebrate my fiftieth birthday. Both of these are significant milestones but, strange though it may seem, neither seems like anything that I "accomplished." Being fifty is obviously not something that I caused to happen. Similarly, getting tenure, while it's something that I thought about a lot, doesn't seem like something that I caused to happen, though not for lack of trying. Rather, tenure more or less rolled into my life, along with so many other people, experiences, degrees, and many, many surprises.

Presently I am an associate professor of management information sciences (which includes information systems, or IS) at the Edwin L. Cox School of Business, Southern Methodist University. I do research on the relationship between IS professionals and their clients, in particular with respect to how they jointly manage a firm's information technology assets. I teach courses on systems development (or "reengineering" as it's currently called) and the management of information technology to undergraduates and M.B.A. students. I also teach a first-year M.B.A. core course on the global business environment. I am an associate editor for two of the top journals in my field, and I indulge in quite a lot of reviewing to sublimate my doctoral student mentoring instincts (we do not have a Ph.D. program). I am active in the two main professional societies in my field, the International Conference on Information Systems and the Organizational Communication and Information Systems Division of the Academy of Management.

I live with an artist, Denny McCoy. We share interests in food, film, sports, music, and art. Later this year, we are going to Thailand for six months, where I have a Fulbright grant to teach and do research with the IS faculty at Thammasat University in Bangkok. From Thailand, I hope to travel to Cambodia, Laos, and Viet Nam, those parts of Southeast Asia that are so much a part of my generation's history.

## ENTERING ACADEMIA

Between my early twenties and my mid-thirties, I moved up a typical career ladder in the information systems field, working as a programmer, systems analyst, manager, and consultant. At first I worked for the pay, then for the recognition my work brought me, then with a fascination for the problems of implementing and managing information technology. Even though I was always employed by large firms or a consulting company, I felt that I worked "for myself." I say this because I felt like an outsider, an oddity, a pleasant but not totally fathomable colleague—not an insider, a member of the team.

My more interesting and engaging pre-Ph.D. work was traveling the world, meandering through eighty countries on all the continents except Antarctica and all fifty states in the United States. No place, even Kinshasa, was really unpleasant. Some people, like the Fijians, were more wonderfully charming than others, but overall there was no one I was sorry to meet. There was no place that was uninteresting and no event unworthy of my time and attention.

I traveled around the world for a year in my mid-thirties. On returning to Los Angeles, I found myself at loose ends. My husband and I had decided to have children, and I was worried that the frequent traveling that consulting entailed would make it difficult for me to get pregnant. I cast about for some productive activity that would give me more flexibility to come and go and a healthier life style than consulting. As it happened, I heard about an interesting class at UCLA, where I'd gotten my M.B.A. a few years before. Now the biggest problem with taking a class at UCLA is the parking, as anyone who has been there will tell you. I knew if I was going to take this class, I was going to have to be a registered student of some kind, and hence eligible for parking. The class I was interested in was a Ph.D. seminar, so I quickly came to the conclusion that I should become a Ph.D. student in order to (1) get a parking permit so I could (2) take the class. I completed the application, requested recommendations from faculty I remembered from my M.B.A. years, and badgered the dean of the doctoral program until he admitted me, on the condition that I did not need any funding or financial support. Imagine my surprise when I discovered that the seminar entitled "Research in Information Systems," which the previous year had been all about data bases, had a new professor and a new topic like "new and interesting research in IS."

Unexpectedly, I loved the seminar and marveled at my classmates' interest in the politics and sociology of "academia." I signed up for more classes. For several years when professors asked me whether or not I would eventually "go on the market," I'd respond by saying, "I'm too old for the tenure process," meaning that I couldn't see myself working as hard as I imagined it would take to get tenure.

As it turned out, children were not in my cards. After three years of doctoral studies, I took a leave of absence, went to Japan and China for six months, and wondered where my life was going. Three years later, I was separated from my husband and finished with my Ph.D. I'm not exactly sure when I decided to pursue a career in academia, tenure track and all. It might have been when I attended my first academic conference and met the biggest crowd of fun and interesting like-minded people I could imagine. Or, it could have been when I attended a doctoral consortium and got swept up in the nuances of job search competition. More than anything else, I think it was just that I didn't stop to think of the alternatives. I liked reading, mulling, and writing. I liked my colleagues a lot. I felt good about what I did and who I was.

## EVOLVING A DISSERTATION

My dissertation topic evolved out of my continuing interest in information systems project management. My work experience had shown me that project management was a complex and poorly understood process. Most projects were tense and uncertain, and outcomes usually fell short of some desired level, for at least some participants and clients. To be sure, there were usually significant business benefits as well, but there was always the lingering feeling that these projects could be better managed.

In terms of methodology, my decision to use a field-based research design was driven in part by my work experience: I knew where I could find some project data and was comfortable asking for access to it. Perhaps more important to my choice of a field approach was that I believed that the "theories" of organizational life I was learning did not adequately explain real-world events. Many of the constructs and theories pertaining to project management seemed (and still seem) to be divorced from organizational reality. I believe that IS researchers do not have useful, meaningful constructs, and so what is needed is not theoretical refinement through better testing, improved measures, and so forth, but new perspectives of the key phenomena, such as information technology, its use, or its outcomes. To develop these perspectives, it is critical to stay close to those phenomena when conducting research, despite the so-called "perils" of fieldwork.

In the early 1980s, when I was designing and carrying out my dissertation work, my field had a paradigmatic preference for the adoption and testing of theory from what were reverently referred to as "reference disciplines" (that is, disciplines such as economics, psychology, or sociology that were more academically legitimate than information systems). The received wisdom was that "established" theory from other areas could be adopted, applied, and, ideally, extended, to explain or understand information systems problems or phenomena. In addition to adopting the theories, the methods of the adopted discipline could then also be used as a basis for rigorous scientific testing. Since, at least at UCLA, economics was at the peak of the intellectual pyramid of reference disciplines, I adopted institutional economics as my reference discipline. A relatively new theoretical area, it had few deeply established methodological procedures. This newness was both a drawback and a strength, in that it left me much to my own devices in terms of measurement. As I result, I learned more about the theory I was using and about measurement in general than I would have by using a more established theory.

I selected my dissertation advisor because I had great respect for the way he thought about research. He was relatively unfamiliar with the theory and problem area of my research, so our conversations tended to focus on "why" I was doing this or that rather than "what" I was doing. He never seemed to tell me what to do—I think he just kept asking me to explain myself until I answered with sensibility. This suited my need to work independently and, at the same time, made me feel responsible for the project. While I was a doctoral student, and for several years after I graduated, I also worked with my advisor on one of his own projects, writing a series of cases on software maintenance. On that project, particularly at the beginning, he was more willing to tell me what to do. The combination of the two assignments—the first, the dissertation project on which I worked relatively at my own risk, and the second, the software project on which I shared responsibility with an experienced researcher—gave me the confidence to work independently and a deep respect for the value of a good collaborator. Both of these seem very important in the relatively tiny IS field, in which so few faculty have the opportunity to collaborate closely with departmental colleagues.

## CHOOSING AN INSTITUTION

Choosing the location of my first position was probably the only systematic thing I have done in my entire academic career. In the fall of my last year, I identified about fifteen schools that I thought might be interesting places to work. I chose only schools that had doctoral programs and faculty that I respected and with whom I thought I might enjoy working. About ten of those schools had openings that year, so I called or wrote or got my advisor to call or write, and I managed to get interviews with all of them at the International Conference on Information Systems (ICIS), where the IS faculty market takes place. Following the conference, I accepted invitations for visits to six schools, first to the University of North Carolina to get my feet wet and then to five schools in a sort of "grand march" or "circle tour": the University of Minnesota, Harvard, MIT, New York University, and the University of Texas at Austin. All these schools had doctoral programs and fun, nice, productive IS faculties.

My husband, from whom I was actually separated, traveled with me on this tour, acting as my coach, personal trainer, and valet. He patiently sat through all the dinners and lunches, asked appropriate questions, and indicated his sincere interest in moving to Minnesota, Boston, New York, or Austin. I asked him to go because I sensed it was very important to appear to be a "normal" married woman to the various department chairs and deans. On the other hand, I also wore my favorite watch at the time, a $2.00 Gumby watch, which looked like a piece of green Play-Doh wrapped around my wrist. The Gumby watch, to my delight, provoked a great deal of conversation and reaction, which, it seemed to me, captured the culture of each institution. Where some were aghast, others were amused. The lesson I learned from my tour was that candidates should be less concerned with how they come across to the schools and more concerned with how the schools come across to them.

By the time I came home, I had an offer from Minnesota and had decided to go there. The Minnesotans were amused by the watch, I liked everyone I met, a woman was already on the faculty, and the doctoral students seemed very happy. The drawbacks were mostly geographical, but I had never been one to be constrained by geography. I accepted the job, defended, filed my dissertation on my mother's birthday, and moved to Minneapolis.

My first year at Minnesota was miserable. I was terrified in the classroom (I had never taught a single class before arriving). I missed talking to my advisor about research. I connected with almost no one in Minnesota. Trying to get out and make some friends, I went ice-skating with another new faculty member and a group of people she had met. I felt very out of place, and when a young man asked me, "Have you ever been married?" I said, "No," and then after a pause I added, "Oh . . . I forgot . . . I am married." I was homesick for everyone and everything about Los Angeles.

That summer and the next one, I left Minneapolis for Los Angeles as soon as my last class was over. I went back to my little house on Malibu beach, wrote, worked out and ate properly, made many new friends, did fun things, and then went back to Minnesota and its dark, negative climate. It seemed that organizational politics dominated every moment of every day. After three years of Minnesota, I took a leave of absence for a visiting position at UCLA.

Interestingly, UCLA turned out to be worse than Minnesota, even though it was in sunny Los Angeles. I worked hard, but got less research done. School politics—mostly the animosity of the non-IS faculty and administration for the IS faculty, the IS program and the IS doctoral students—dominated every conversation, almost exactly as it had at Minnesota. At the end of the two years, I finally settled my divorce, sold my beach house, and went back to Minnesota, ready to make a new attempt at settling down. I tried to get Denny (my favorite artist and current companion) to come, probably to save me, but he wisely stalled.

While at UCLA, I had watched a favorite colleague get chewed up and spit out by the tenure process. It was a miserable experience for me and much worse for her. Back at Minnesota, it was deja vu all over again, as another favorite colleague went through the same experience, no-holds-barred ego battery by a tenure committee. In both cases, I believed the "no" that was being voiced by the committee was directed at the department, not the individual. But the experience is life-shattering for the individual, nevertheless. By spring, I was ready to throw in the towel and go back to consulting. Even if I got tenure at Minnesota (which everyone seemed to think was assured by virtue of my gender) I would be part of a disrespected team. I would never be an insider, an institution builder. Life looked glum.

Fortunately, I am luckier than that. Two colleagues at Southern Methodist University, both of whom I'd known for years, understood my distress and saw an opportunity to fill a slot that had unexpectedly opened in their faculty. They talked me into visiting SMU while I was in Texas for another meeting. Surprisingly, I liked all the people I met, even the dean. I was suspicious that they had carefully selected the people I spoke to, but they denied it. The facility was terrific. For my talk, I chose my most outrageous piece of research, but no one seemed outraged. They said, "We think this would be a good place for you." I wasn't exactly sure what they meant at the time, but I trusted them both implicitly and took the offer.

Now that I've been at SMU for two years, I understand what they were thinking. For the first time in my career, I am an insider, not an outsider. There are at least two reasons for this. For one thing, my two senior colleagues are both chaired professors, as highly respected both in the Cox school and across the campus as they are in the IS field, both among academics and practitioners. They have both chaired important search or institutional change committees at SMU. Our department is regarded as having something to say about information technology and business, as making a contribution to the school and its future.

The second reason SMU suits me is more subtle. At SMU, the proportion of senior-to-junior faculty is about 50–50, not 90–10 as it was at Minnesota or UCLA. Thus, even as an associate professor, I am expected to take a leadership position. There are junior faculty who need mentoring, there are new programs that need shaping or reshaping, there are relationships with the other parts of the university or the business community that need attention. If the Cox school were stocked with full professors, most of these opportunities would not be available to me. I serve on the planning committee for the Cox school and SMU's women's studies council. Because SMU is a small school, I am on a first-name basis with the provost and the top information technology officer. If I weren't heading off for Thailand, I would be involved in SMU's project to reengineer its student services.

Another consequence of having a lot of junior (or otherwise new) faculty is that there is a critical mass of people who are looking to socialize with others. For some new faculty, children provide an easy entree to a new social milieu, through school and after-school activities. As a single, older woman at Minnesota, I found it hard to find a social niche among the deeply rooted, married, male senior faculty in my age group. At SMU, on the other hand, the junior or recently arrived faculty form a diverse social network that I fit into easily, and my house has often been a site for get-togethers. Moreover, the resulting social ties among the faculty seem to contribute to good relations among all the school's areas. The SMU faculty seem to work together on research projects more than the faculty at Minnesota or UCLA, but this is probably because there are no doctoral students with whom to collaborate. I do miss doctoral students. I learned so much from facilitating doctoral students and working with the very high-quality students at Minnesota and UCLA. I'm grateful to have had this experience, and I believe it contributed significantly to my development as a scholar.

Trying to extract a little advice from this, I find the following: (1) expect to be a little homesick at first if you move away from your roots, (2) go to a school where your field is well regarded by the rest of the faculty and the deans (some signs to look for—important appointments recently or currently held by senior faculty in your area; the dean's office actively involved in your recruiting; and faculty in other areas complimentary about your area), (3) go to a place where the proportion of junior faculty (or new faculty) is relatively high (as compared to the entrenched faculty) if you enjoy leadership or if you will want to make friends at school.

## A RESEARCH STREAM

My post-Ph.D. research project selection process has been relatively opportunistic. Because IS-client relationships are an integral part of information technology implementation, management, and use, there is almost no end to the possibilities for study.

I didn't publish many papers from my thesis—one article in the *ICIS Proceedings* (and also an earlier one based on the proposal there) and another in a practitioner journal. I was tired of this project and wanted to get on to new work. I am a task-oriented person, and I erroneously considered my dissertation "finished." Today, I realize some additional data analysis would have been fruitful, and I regret not giving my dissertation data more attention. During the first two years I was at Minnesota, I continued to publish several articles and a book with my advisor from the case studies on software maintenance that we had done before I left UCLA. These projects provided a reason for me to return to Los Angeles in the summer, for which I was deeply grateful. My advisor and I migrated comfortably from a supervisory to a collegial relationship. We have not worked together recently, but I believe we will at some point in the future.

In my first year at Minnesota, I was invited to join a large funded project for a proposal that was being submitted. I agreed to join principally because my share included a course reduction and extra doctoral student assistants. I listened carefully to what I was told about the project and attended several meetings to discuss the proposal, but, in truth, I understood nearly nothing about the objectives of the project and absolutely nothing about the project's deliverables or my role and obligations. As it turned out, the project gave me the stimulus and opportunity to continue work along the lines of my dissertation, exploring the application of additional theories from institutional economics to the sourcing of information services. On the down side, the project consumed hours and hours of my precious research time on issues I found uninteresting. I learned from this experience that grants or research funds are a two-edged sword: they make you structure and plan your research, but they tend to constrain what you do; they provide resources that are difficult to obtain from the university, but they obligate you to a lot of nonproductive busy work.

I believe that, in the main, research grants have limited my absolute research productivity. That is, I have produced fewer papers for the number of hours I spent on research because of the time required to write grant applications, administer or account for funds, produce interim reports, and to deal with plain old bureaucratic red tape. On the other hand, grant submission dates always get me thinking, and report deadlines keep me moving on a project that otherwise might drift to the bottom of the piles on my desk. In addition, the legitimating effect of grants is important, given that my research tends to be somewhat nontraditional. Therefore, I still apply regularly for grants to support my work.

In my experience, the key to applying for grants is to attend very carefully to the request for proposal from the grantor and respond to it as closely as possible. To do this, read the request for proposals extremely carefully and repeatedly while you are crafting your proposal. In addition, call the people at the granting agency to get more details on what they want. Ask what they are looking for. Tell them how you understand their request and listen to their response. Ask them what mistakes proposers commonly make, and how the evaluation process works. Finally, use the language of the request for proposal or the granting agency's other materials in your proposal. Consider the grantors' dilemma: the agency has some mission, but it doesn't really want to dictate the nature of the research. You can help the grantors by using your proposal to show how your work fulfills this mission.

Working with collaborators has been another important feature of my research. My co-authors all have been people who were friends first and research collaborators second. Much like grants, collaboration has its benefits and drawbacks. For me, collaboration adds a measure of effort to a project, in sorting out views, roles, or research tastes. However, it is an effort I enjoy, because I am working with a friend. Collaboration also means deadline pressure, but for me this is a benefit, not a drawback, as with the grants. Nearly all of my collaborations have been with people at other universities. Mostly, this is because the information systems field is relatively small and the people with whom I share interests are located all over the world.

## TEACHING

I was completely unprepared for teaching at Minnesota. Not only had I never taught before I walked into my first class, I had not paid much attention to the teaching process when I was a student. As I joked when I arrived at SMU and was faced with teaching in our undergraduate MIS program, I hadn't seen an undergraduate since the days when I didn't show up for my own undergraduate classes. Most of my Ph.D. classes had been seminars. Fortunately (for me), when I arrived at Minnesota, teaching was more of a hygiene factor than a differentiating factor for tenure-track faculty. That is, poor teaching, like poor hygiene, had to be corrected, but no amount of teaching prowess would substitute for even the most moderate research accomplishment. At SMU, teaching is also a hygiene factor, but the hygiene standards are much higher, since teachers and teaching are differentiators for the university. Also, there is much more institutional pressure on teaching, but there is also more institutional support. The students expect more from their courses, but they also bring more energy and interest to the classroom. Even though it is more challenging, I prefer the teaching environment at SMU.

The main consequence of my lack of teaching experience (or even teaching awareness) was not so much that I was terrible in the classroom but that I made some dumb choices about my teaching. I have frequently taken on teaching assignments that require significant preparation or course redesign, without really considering how much time that would take. Moreover, without any knowledge of adult learning, I adopted course outlines, textbooks, and teaching approaches from others without really knowing how they went together or how learning was supposed to result from what I was doing. All in all, teaching has been a struggle for me and not nearly enough fun. With the exception of doctoral students, who seem to blossom if the professor, or facilitator, gets out of their way, students remain a mystery to me.

I have learned a great deal about teaching since the early Minnesota terrors, by reading about adult learning, by talking to colleagues about what they do and what works for them, by attending a case-teaching seminar, and by team teaching with two excellent teachers while I was at UCLA. I have learned almost nothing from my teaching evaluations. The most enlightening experience by far has been to attend other teachers' classes (with both great and not-so-great teachers) or to invite colleagues to attend my classes and give me feedback. Their straightforward recounting of what they observed has been almost as helpful as their insights and suggestions. Last year, I taped my first-day class meetings, under the theory that on the first day I am the least self-aware while the students are watching my behavior closely. It took me almost the entire semester to get up the nerve to watch the tapes and, when I did, I saw myself as much more serious, more disorganized, and more difficult to follow than I expected. My conclusion is that I still have a lot to learn about teaching.

I definitely feel that being a woman influences my students' expectations about my courses. M.B.A. students or managers seem to make a judgment early in the semester about my level of authority on the material—whether I am "knowledgeable about information technology" or "professionally legitimate," or something like that—whereas, they seem to assume that authority in my male colleagues, even the most junior of them. If I "introduce" myself on the first day, describing my experiences as a manager and consultant and my emphasis on field research, and if

I back this up with frequent references to current events or inside knowledge of the practice of information technology, I can gain the students' confidence. I do feel, however, that many of my male colleagues do not have to jump through this hoop.

The other main consequence of being female is that my students expect me to be more flexible, understanding of their particular circumstances, sympathetic or empathetic, fair, and available to help them outside of class, than my male colleagues. To maintain a hard-nosed stance about deadlines or assignments, I find it helps if I appeal to their sense of fairness. To minimize the amount of time they require of me outside the class, I fix just one hour each week for office hours, but I make myself available by appointment. I frequently suggest in class that they make an appointment to come see me if they are having problems. Few actually do, unless they really need help.

## OTHER PROFESSIONAL ACTIVITIES

Minnesota junior faculty were given few administrative responsibilities, for which I was grateful; I was given to understand that "service" was not even a hygiene factor for tenure. A politically astute colleague recommended that I adopt a strategy of only doing service that reflected well on the business school or the university. I took this good advice and served on a few external search and program evaluation committees, always at the request of the dean. Women were in demand for such committees, which was a bit of a drag. On the bright side, no one seemed to expect me to do very much work. Observing the workings of these committees provided insights about academia. Hearing the committee members' opinions of the business school, which were often critical, was particularly enlightening.

At SMU, everyone, including new junior faculty, has committee assignments within the Cox school, so that everyone is involved in the school's and university's future. Of course, one reason that junior faculty have administrative responsibilities at SMU and not at Minnesota or UCLA is that there are proportionally fewer senior people to take on these jobs. An important outcome is that junior faculty at the Cox school quickly develop an understanding of how the school operates, what it values, and what problems it faces. If the time requirements are kept in check and the work is meaningful, I think this is a good approach.

Early in my career, for no particular reason that I can point to, I became an active reviewer for most of the main journals in my field. Reviewing has been time consuming, but I've found it a good way to keep abreast of developments in my field and to further develop my research design and writing skills. I quickly learned that reviewing for the top journals (and the wisest associate editors) was by far the best use of my time. The papers were better, the investment of my time contributed to more significant work (even if that work ended up being published elsewhere), and I learned more from the other reviewers' and the associate editor's reports. Reviewing taught me that papers can be improved with effort, feedback is absolutely necessary to develop work, and publication is a social process, as well as a technical one. That is, there are people at both ends of each review, and these people have egos, personalities, and foibles along with their knowledge, values, and opinions. Navigating the publication process takes effort, persistence, and luck as much as talent and good scientific results. On the downside, doing a lot of reviewing can also be intimidating. It can seem like your colleagues are accomplishing so much, being so insightful and writing so brilliantly, while your work stands still. The way I deal with this is by creating deadlines that force me to proceed with my own research.

My other professional activity, besides reviewing and editing, has been to participate in the program committee of ICIS and the Organizational Communication and Information Systems (OCIS) division of the Academy of Management. I was invited to be on the ICIS program committee one year, and I learned so much about how research is valued and met so many interesting people, that I quickly volunteered for the next year. Each year I have learned more and met more interesting people, and so I just keep volunteering. I have been a member of the program committee for ICIS for several years and will be a program co-chair for ICIS 1995, in The Netherlands.

My involvement with the Academy of Management has been more peripheral, or unofficial, but also focused on the development of junior faculty. During the summer of my second year at Minnesota, the Academy's annual meeting was to be held in Anaheim. Since I planned to be in Malibu that summer it made sense to attend the meeting. However, the Academy is a huge conference, making it hard to find other information systems faculty who are attending, so I decided to invite a cadre of junior and senior IS faculty to my house in Malibu for a junior faculty workshop prior to the conference. I prevailed on a handful of senior faculty to offer counsel, invited people who were interested in the behavioral aspects of information technology, laid in a supply of food, and invented "MIS camp." In addition to having serious talks about research, teaching, publication, and the tenure process, we played tennis, swam, walked, cooked, and drank a lot of beer and wine. A few years later, when the Academy expanded to include information systems, our MIS camp became the official junior faculty workshop for IS faculty. More than likely, the reason I was interested in developmental activities such as these is because I was slow to commit to an academic career and still needed a lot of developing!

## BALANCE

I laughed (or was it a sigh?) when I saw that the editors of this book wanted us to write about how we achieved balance between our academic and private lives. My first reaction was, "What private life?" and my second was, "What's balance?" My life is more characterized by integration than balance. That is, my social life is intertwined with my academic life, and so my private life is my academic life. I don't have another life that is distinctly separate from my experiences as a teacher, a colleague, or a researcher. Almost all my friends in Dallas are people I know from SMU. The newer faculty at SMU constitute a very social group, enjoying frequent celebrations, throwing impromptu dinners, and sharing season seats for theater, basketball, and baseball. An effort is made to include new faculty in these events, even while they are being recruited. It helps a great deal that there are now seven women among this group and that the wives of the male faculty also tend to be professionals. We have a good time.

Besides my friends on the SMU faculty, I have many pals among my IS colleagues at other schools. At the annual ICIS Women's Breakfast, which I have hosted twice, I have met many wonderful women in IS. Professional meetings, or those with colleagues on research projects, are great fun; for me one of the primary advantages of academic life is that I do so enjoy the people with whom I work.

## TENURE

I came to Southern Methodist University not with tenure but with an agreement that I would go up for tenure during my second year—that is, after the school had an opportunity to have a good look at me. I came with the confidence of the two chairs in IS and the dean, so I felt reasonably secure regarding tenure. Nevertheless, it was a stressful experience, as I believe it inevitably is. The tenure process is paradoxical in many respects—you feel completely out of control, in the sense that almost any outcome is possible, but also completely responsible, in the sense that your case is shaped by all the decisions and tradeoffs you have made. The autonomy of academia that we all love meets the arbitrariness of academia that we all hate.

My preparation for tenure began before I finished my degree, as soon as I began to see how the tenure process worked. They count papers? I submit papers. They rank papers by journals? I find out what the best journals want and concentrate my efforts there. They like grants? I apply for grants. They look at teaching ratings? I study the determinants of teaching ratings and keep my students out of the dean's office. They get letters from senior faculty? I learn which of the likely suspects think women can't do research and what the rest of them think of my work. There are more subtle issues as well: They don't respect the field's research or research paradigm, or the university doesn't respect the business school? Go to another school. They believe they're overstaffed in your area or understaffed in another area? Go to another school. There are no (or few) women in the tenured ranks? Consider going to another school.

## THE TENURE PROCESS

The tenure process at SMU is fairly simple. There are only a few steps, so there are fewer points where the process can get out of hand; on the other hand, disasters are harder to correct. In the ideal case, first the tenured faculty in the department (in my case, management information sciences) recommends the candidate, then a cross-department committee (composed of senior researchers from each department) recommends her, then the dean recommends her, then a council of the deans of SMU's seven schools recommends her, then the provost recommends her, and finally the board of trustees approves her. Denny didn't move to Dallas until the committee of deans had met. I didn't celebrate until after the board of trustees had decided.

One difficulty I faced in preparing my tenure packet was that my "record" had been built with Minnesota in mind, and SMU had somewhat different criteria. For one thing, teaching and service were more important at SMU. Their tenure packet includes teaching and service statements, not just research statements. Faculty at SMU usually include all their teaching evaluations as well as letters of commendation for the service they have performed. I had not kept all my teaching materials nor any "evidence" of my service activities. For another thing, I was more sensitive to the university-level decision than I would have been at Minnesota, although perhaps this is just because I never actually got to the point of putting a packet together there. Writing for a council of deans who are reputed to be skeptical about business school education was an unexpected wrinkle for me.

I got a lot of help in putting my tenure packet together. A colleague in finance who had been granted tenure the year before gave me his packet to use as a model. A colleague in organization behavior who knew the university well read my statements with an "SMU" eye and helped me make them more accessible to non-IS readers both within Cox and across campus. Of course, both my senior colleagues in IS gave me all possible advice. They reordered my vita, suggested things to include and helped me figure out how to present some odd items. They also helped me think about outside reviewers. I didn't contact any of the outside reviewers proposed, but some of them had agreed to write grant or program recommendations for me in the past. Some had offered to write a tenure letter for me, a gesture for which I was very grateful. In the end, I was exhausted and nervous, but I felt that I got as much help as a person could. Today I believe that what made me feel like a lifetime member of the Cox and SMU communities was the support I received as I put my tenure packet together, not the decision by the board of trustees.

But I didn't realize that at the time. I was jumpy. I worked ridiculously long hours. I agonized over my classes, knowing that the cross-department committee could examine my fall teaching ratings before they made their recommendation. I drove Denny crazy thinking and rethinking what to do about every little decision. I went to bat for every underdog in sight, even the Dallas Mavericks. My colleagues, bless them, put up with me and celebrated with me when it was over.

## LOOKING TO THE FUTURE

It is taking a while to kick in, but I think my post-tenure reaction is going to be upbeat and positive. Especially compared to the tenure experiences that many of my IS colleagues around the country have endured, mine was respectful, not abusive. As far as I know, no one nit-picked my record. If there were doubts, no one brought them to my attention. I am excited about having tenure at SMU; I am very invested in SMU's future.

As is my fashion, I don't have much of a post-tenure plan. In the short term, I am taking a sabbatical. I have a Fulbright posting to Thammasat University in Bangkok, Thailand, from October through March. I will teach in the M.B.A. program and hope to collaborate with the IS faculty in writing some descriptive cases on information technology used in Bangkok firms. My other academic objectives are quite limited. I have a lot of reading and writing I'd like to do, and I'd like to learn more about developing economies. I would like to travel in the parts of Southeast Asia that are just opening up to the West, and I am curious about how Western businesses respond to these opportunities. Since I expect to be in Thailand for only a few months, I don't anticipate starting any serious research projects.

When I return, I will continue work on a project on software sourcing that I started this summer and another project on chargeback. These projects are with colleagues at SMU and other schools. With luck, both will be funded externally. My teaching responsibilities are likely to change over time. Post-tenure, I am expected to mentor junior faculty, although I'm never sure I know what that means. My other administrative responsibilities may increase somewhat, and I am interested in securing more external funding for my IS colleagues. These objectives are quite vague and will be shaped around events such as the arrival or departure of senior faculty, changes in the university's senior administration, and developments in information technology. On a personal note, I hope to survive menopause by exercising more regularly and improving my diet.

# 6

# "Business School Professor: A 'Real' Job that Doesn't Seem Like Work"

## *Sheila M. Puffer*

"There is such a thing as being *over*educated too, you know."

The introductory quotation reflects how my dad would react every time I announced my plans to get another degree. Not having a college education themselves, my parents believed that the "school of hard knocks" that had brought them from the farm to rewarding business careers was the key to professional success and personal fulfillment. While I shared their values of developing practical skills to get a job, I was fascinated with literature, languages, and the social sciences. A career as a business school professor has turned out to be the ideal choice for me, enabling me to accomplish all my professional objectives. Although I took several detours along the way, I believe that my experiences on "the scenic route" toward an academic career have enhanced my ability to fulfill the many roles of this important profession.

## THE "SCENIC ROUTE" TO AN ACADEMIC CAREER

I actually started out where I have now ended—in a business school. Since a business degree seemed the most obvious way to be both pragmatic and academic, I spent my first year at St. Mary's University in Halifax, Nova Scotia, at age sixteen as a business student. But business seemed too dull compared to my real passion, languages and literature. Mindful of the goal of eventually getting a job, I hit upon the idea of studying to be an interpreter at the United Nations. This decision led to three luxurious years at two schools for translators and interpreters, where I learned French and Russian and expanded my knowledge and vocabulary in a wide range of courses in the humanities and social sciences.

After becoming fluent in French, I focused my energy on Russian, which the director of the school had urged me to take because it was the most challenging language offered there. This choice led to several years of study with an inspiring teacher, Dr. Bohdan Plaskacz. A gifted linguist versed in a dozen languages, he used the classroom like a stage to act out anecdotes and stories of his colorful life from peasant to professor. His imposing bearing was too much for some students, but his love of languages and life struck a chord with me. Two decades later, I dedicated the book *The Russian Management Revolution* to him, and was saddened to learn that he had died a few months before its publication.

Instead of becoming an interpreter at the U.N., I had a six-year career as a personnel administrator in the Government of Canada, as a result of a summer job that turned into a permanent position. At the National Capital Commission and the Ministry of Industry, Trade, and Commerce, I held positions as a bilingualism program officer, a staffing officer, and job classification and compensation analyst. I even went on "the hunt for red tape" at the Office for the Reduction of Paperburden (no kidding). These years provided a foundation for understanding organizational life that have served me well in my capacity as a teacher, scholar, and member of professional and university committees. I laugh when I find myself referring to this period as "when I was working." To me, in comparison, the intellectual and personal freedom of an academic career just does not seem like work.

With plans of building my career in public service, I enrolled in the part-time M.B.A. program at the University of Ottawa. I opted for a business degree rather than a master's in public administration, because I thought it would provide greater flexibility, both in terms of applying private-sector practices creatively in my job and developing business skills should I want to change my career orientation. At the university, most courses had sections taught in English or French. Indulging my love of languages, I took half my business courses in French, the only native English-speaking student to do so. My electives were in special topics in organizational behavior, as well as international business courses such as management of the multinational corporation and international comparative economics. So I was "back in business" again.

During the five seemingly endless years of the part-time M.B.A. program, I worked full time, engaged in some consulting projects, and taught "Introduction to Organizational Psychology" in French in the evening undergraduate business program. My life consisted mostly of shuttling between the office and the university, squeezing in lunchtime classes, and being on campus many evenings. At the same time my husband, Hugh, was working as a foreign service officer in the diplomatic corps and completing his Ph.D. in Russian literature. We thrived on this demanding, self-imposed schedule, feeling great satisfaction from focusing most of our energy on learning and career growth.

Toward the end of my M.B.A. program, several business school faculty encouraged me to consider getting a Ph.D. in business, something I had never considered and knew nothing about. Hugh immediately added his support. Soon I realized this was an appealing suggestion, since I had begun applying some of the concepts from my M.B.A. courses to my work life and had become interested in researching various applied behavioral and organizational issues I had encountered. Furthermore, teaching had been a very enjoyable experience—once I recovered from the terror of the first few classes.

As a next step, I decided to enroll at the University of California at Berkeley to learn rigorous research methodology from some of the leading scholars and to develop a further knowledge base for teaching courses in organizational behavior. The choice of Berkeley was actually reinforced by applying the rational decision-making model I had learned in my M.B.A. policy and decision-making course. Hugh and I had fun drawing decision trees of the universities we had visited on vacation, carefully weighing the options of each, since we recognized that this was a major decision point in our lives. Friends and family members were incredulous that we would leave our secure jobs and pensions with the intention of making a new life in the United States. Yet, we wanted to test ourselves, and we felt the challenges and opportunities there were greater than in Canada. Hugh had also realized, before I did, that diplomatic life would be too restrictive in terms of our personal interests, as well as for my opportunities for meaningful employment as a diplomatic wife.

My enrollment at Berkeley was postponed a year while Hugh and I went to Moscow on scholarships from the Soviet and Canadian governments. He wanted to use the archives there for his doctoral dissertation, and he suggested I study management. It turned out to be an excellent decision, but I felt pulled in two directions at the time. Berkeley faculty told me the year abroad would be more valuable after obtaining my Ph.D. and that they could not guarantee me the relatively rare and generous scholarship again the following year. I would also need to reapply for the doctoral program grant I had won from the Canadian government. After much discussion, I was won over by Hugh's argument that the timing was right and that a year abroad would be personally and professionally enriching for both of us.

As a result of the year in Moscow, I became the only non-Soviet citizen to graduate from an executive management development program at the Plekhanov Institute of the National Economy. Not only did I learn about

Soviet management education from a student's perspective, but I learned far more about the actual practice of management by talking with many of the 100 managers in the program on a daily basis for six months. These experiences are reported in my first article, *Inside a Soviet Management Institute*. At the same time, wanting to make the most of this unique opportunity, I worked as the Moscow representative of Canalux, a Canadian trading company. This job gave me the chance to meet with officials from various departments of the Soviet Ministry of Foreign Trade and learn how they did business in products ranging from ballpoint pens to spare parts for oil rigs.

Not surprising, the experience in Russia sparked my interest to study international business at Berkeley and write my dissertation on Russian management. However, faculty advisors persuaded me to study organizational behavior, a more developed discipline at the time. Furthermore, it was not feasible to conduct empirical research on Russian management during the Cold War of the early 1980s, so I studied organizational behavior, attended seminars and conferences in Russian studies, and took Spanish and German.

My dissertation was on altruism in organizations, a subject that had intrigued me while working for the Canadian government and later while living in the Soviet Union. Many times I had heard the phrase "that's not in my job description," and I had noticed wide variability in the extent to which people were willing to "go above and beyond the call of duty" in their jobs. Yet, I believed that voluntary prosocial or citizenship behavior was essential for keeping organizations functioning smoothly, since no job description or set of procedures could possibly cover all the situations that arise in work organizations. Altruism had a long research history in psychology, but virtually no studies had been conducted in work settings. With the guidance of my faculty advisors, I designed a study that was theoretically and methodologically rigorous and then conducted surveys and interviews with commission sales people in a dozen furniture stores in northern California. The results showed the way that various factors were related to prosocial behavior, sales performance, and noncompliant or deviant behavior. In addition, the positive correlation between prosocial behavior and sales performance was my "favorite" result, since it supported my optimistic view of human nature: top performers tend also to be big givers to others and their organizations.

The four years in California were happy and productive, and Hugh and I were reluctant to leave. For me, the doctoral program had been academically rigorous and free of politics, the students collegial, and the faculty supportive. Throughout the program, I kept my promise to myself to keep life in balance by not studying most weekends, not teaching, and taking exercise classes each quarter. Hugh spent the time writing his dissertation and received his Ph.D. from the University of Ottawa. Because of the poor academic job market in his field and the desire to give us flexibility as a dual-career couple, he then retrained and found work as a computer programmer.

Despite the attraction of the California lifestyle, we decided that I should seek a position at a major research university virtually anywhere in the United States rather than take a less prestigious job to remain in California. We spent the next four years in Buffalo, where I joined the faculty at the State University of New York. While not our first choice, we were glad to have good colleagues as well as the university's sponsorship of my green card that granted us permanent residency in the United States, a primary goal for us on the way to immigration.

Impressed by the exemplary careers of my mentors at Berkeley, Professors Barry Staw and Charles O'Reilly, my plan was to be adventurous—a high-risk strategy that easily might have made my career much shorter than I would have liked. My idea of adventure in research was to be eclectic, as well as to do interdisciplinary research. I developed several streams besides my primary focus on the relationship between motivation, prosocial behavior, and performance, including a major study of corporate performance with a colleague in accounting. Most of this research has been published. In teaching, besides core courses in organizational behavior, I ventured into new territory by developing and teaching undergraduate and graduate electives on management and the humanities that used literature to discuss management issues. Course development was funded by the Lilly Foundation through a national competition to promote innovations in teaching. My objective was to broaden students' vision and foster their creativity through literature. The idea came to me as a response to the attack on business education in the press that graduates were too narrow and unimaginative in their thinking to meet the business challenges of the 1990s. My efforts culminated in the book *Managerial Insights from Literature.*

The fourth year in Buffalo was a time of major transition. I decided to reenter the job market. Hugh and I had wanted to move to a city that offered better career possibilities for him, as well as a more cosmopolitan environment that we both favored. Boston came through in spades. Northeastern University offered me a tenure-track position in organizational behavior, and Harvard Business School hired me on contract as a member of their U.S.-Soviet research team directed by Professor Paul Lawrence. Thanks to Harvard (and *perestroika*), I was "back in the USSR," just as I had been nearly a decade earlier. This time, I was able to conduct research in enterprises as I had wanted to years before. Our binational team spent two months conducting interviews in Soviet enterprises and an additional two months in American corporations. From this research, our team published the book *Behind the Factory Walls: Decision Making in*

*Soviet and US Enterprises.* A videotape and Russian translation of the book followed. At Northeastern, I have subsequently been able to conduct an extensive program of research on Russian management, teach a range of interesting courses, and continue my professional and university service contributions.

My dad needn't worry that I will become *over*educated. My learning has just begun, and I hope to continue to share my knowledge with students and colleagues. I have had four fulfilling years at SUNY at Buffalo and another five at Northeastern in a "real" job that doesn't seem like work. With my candidacy for tenure currently under review, I look forward to the opportunity of having many more years as an academic. I took my Northeastern colleagues' advice and did not apply for tenure early because of organizational and political issues in the tenure process at the time that were unrelated to my case. While the evaluation of my record was very positive at all stages of review, I kept in mind that the tenure process can be subjective and political and that there are no guarantees until final approval by the president and the board of trustees of the university.

## TEACHING

My teaching experience at Northeastern has spanned all levels, and I have been involved in many of the programs offered in the College of Business Administration (e.g., the undergraduate, honors, and part-time M.B.A. programs, as well as management development and executive programs, including one for Soviet managers). My goal is to engage the students in the learning process, so that they will find the material meaningful and useful in their work lives. I like to innovate and try new things to keep myself sharp and spark students' interest. For instance, in a course on leadership, I had students interview and observe Chief Executive Officers (CEOs) who were members of the board of visitors of the College of Business Administration.

Another time, I developed a project in consultation with Northeastern's director of student activities, in which class members analyzed leadership in student organizations on campus. I got the idea from President Clinton's call for citizens to serve their communities. I felt that this particular project would be an opportunity for the class' students to learn about leadership by their peers and to make recommendations to these student leaders about their strengths and areas for improvement.

## RESEARCH AND PUBLICATION

My early publications spanned several research topics. One stream of research on prosocial behavior, motivation, and rewards produced four articles. Another research stream on corporate performance and CEOs resulted in two articles with a colleague in accounting. Other early publications included two articles on task characteristics, as well as two co-edited books of conference proceedings on information processing in organizations.

For the past several years, my primary goal in research and publication has been to become known as the leading Western scholar on Russian management. My main strategy has been to write and edit books, as well as a number of comprehensive overviews of various topics in Russian management. My hope is that this work will build a foundation for more specific studies in this emerging field. My co-authors and I have also published a number of empirical studies on specific issues in Russian management.

A final area of publication is materials for teaching, which includes the books *Managerial Insights from Literature* and *Management International: Cases, Readings, and Exercises,* as well as accompanying instructor's manuals. Two videotapes on Russian management were also developed for classroom use.

My approach to research and publication has been eclectic in terms of methods as well as topics. My publications have appeared in academic and practitioner journals, reflecting my objectives of advancing both theory and practice. I have used a variety of research methodologies as called for by the topic in question, ranging from case studies to various statistical techniques. I am equally comfortable working alone and with co-authors, who have included M.B.A. and doctoral students in addition to faculty members, with half my publications having been single-authored and half co-authored.

Multiple topics and co-authors comprise an inefficient publication strategy, requiring knowledge of several streams of research and coordination with various individuals. Wiser people than I, especially department chairs and deans, have pointed that out to me numerous times over the years. They also advised me to write only refereed articles for prestigious journals, avoid publishing books and teaching materials, and forget about complicated interdisciplinary research. However, I couldn't resist exploring diverse research questions and working with interesting colleagues and don't regret too much the extra work involved, now that the memories of multiple analyses and countless revisions have faded. I have gained a reputation in several areas as well as friendships with numerous co-authors.

## DOING INTERNATIONAL RESEARCH

Doing international research effectively requires, in my view, a close collaboration with colleagues from the country being studied. For the past five years, Professors Oleg Vikhanskii and Alexander Naumov of Moscow State University have provided such collaboration. To celebrate completion of our first "five-year plan," Daniel McCarthy, a professor at Northeastern, and I will be publishing a book with them of the work we have published together since 1990.

For me, the best way of working cross-culturally is to establish formal procedures, as well as strong personal relationships. For example, for the Harvard-Soviet project, we formally discussed and wrote summaries of our interpretations of each day's company interviews. We were also explicit about setting agendas and timetables for who was responsible for various activities, such as scheduling interviews and writing chapters. Most important, we kept the lines of communication open and regularly discussed our own interaction as a team. We would ask one another the reasons why one did or said certain things and got underlying assumptions into the open. Continued collaboration with Russian colleagues has greatly enriched my knowledge of Russian culture and managerial practices. In addition to the priceless rewards of friendship and collegiality, the knowledge gained from such collaboration has been very useful in designing and interpreting research studies of Russian managers.

## COLLEGE AND UNIVERSITY SERVICE

In my view, the service component of a faculty member's role requires responsiveness to requests, as well as the initiation of activities that will make a difference to the university. My long-term interest in research on the dynamics of prosocial behavior made me realize how critical the service role is for the functioning of an organization and how fragile voluntary behavior can be in the context of organizational cultures and reward systems. Further, I believe that both small and large service contributions are important in order to make the university a pleasant place in which to work and to serve students, employers, and other groups associated with the university community. In addition to serving on various committees, my primary contributions have been as a participant in initiatives on building relationships with business school faculty and students, particularly at Moscow State University, as well as with managers from Russia and the former Soviet Union. These involvements have been quite time-consuming but personally gratifying. So far, my untenured status has protected me from heavy service commitments, but I may be asked to contribute more in the future as a tenured faculty member.

## PROFESSIONAL ACTIVITY

Professional activity has taken four main forms for me: presentations at professional meetings, involvement with practitioners, committee work for the national Academy of Management, and reviewing manuscripts and grant proposals.

Dissemination of my research is a primary objective for me, and I have actively pursued opportunities to present my work to academic colleagues at professional meetings in the United States, Canada, Western and Central Europe, and Russia. In order to build my reputation, I decided to "invest in my career," as Carolyn Dexter, a prominent member of the Academy of Management, once advised me. I stretch my travel budget by piggybacking several conferences in one trip and also find rather obscure travel grants. That way, I average about five conferences or research trips a year, rather than the one or two funded by my department. Another important goal for me is to make my research known to practitioners and to learn about important business issues. Every year, I make a couple of presentations in corporations, business associations, and community service organizations.

My service to the national Academy of Management has been primarily as a member of two committees. The international programs committee's mission was to design and implement a plan for internationalizing the Academy as well as the management curriculum. The professional division review committee's charge was to analyze the process by which Academy divisions were reviewed, to review two divisions, and to develop policies for a divisional innovation award program and evaluate the first set of submissions. These assignments were interesting but quite time consuming, and I do not view them as a major focus for me. Instead, I prefer to devote my energy to teaching and research.

Reviewing manuscripts has been an ongoing activity, and I currently review several dozen a year for a wide variety of journals. In addition, the United States Information Agency appointed me to panels reviewing grant proposals to fund collaboration between business schools in the United States and the former Soviet Union. I am pleased to be a member of the editorial board of the *Academy of Management Executive* because of its mission to present important research findings to managers and students. Reviewing is one way I am able to give something back to colleagues in appreciation for the attention my manuscripts are given by other reviewers. It also keeps me current.

It is a pleasure to participate in a wide range of activities associated with teaching, research, university service, and professional involvement. Being active in all these roles gives me the satisfaction of having a balanced career and being a contributor to a fine educational institution and an important profession. Since I view scholarship as the underpinning of the other activities, I keep my research going forward by setting weekly goals, meeting deadlines for conference calls for papers, and taking on so many projects that there is always something interesting and pressing to do.

I make time for research by keeping consulting and teaching for extra compensation to a minimum and by resisting the temptation to read rather than to write. Janice Beyer, former SUNY at Buffalo colleague and past president of the Academy of Management, shaped my thinking early on about the importance of deciding between being primarily a producer or consumer of research. I decided to be a producer but made the first few years difficult for myself by writing on my own or with other untenured faculty and graduate students. Collaborating with established senior colleagues probably would have made publication easier, but it might have clouded my contributions and reduced the satisfaction of accomplishing things on my own. I wanted to test myself as well as show my gratitude to my advisors at Berkeley by using the training they had given me.

## CYCLES

One of the most gratifying aspects of this stage of my career is the cycles that have reunited me with people and activities encountered over the years. These cycles have been all the more enjoyable because they have been unexpected and have taken on a richness that comes with accumulated experience. Four cycles I will talk about relate to the very diverse and meaningful aspects of my life. These involve Russian colleagues, faculty at the University of Ottawa, Northeastern University Professor Daniel McCarthy, and my sister, Marlene.

### Russian Evolution

Living and studying in Russia for a year was a fascinating experience that left an indelible mark on my husband and me. Little did I know that my year there would eventually be followed by opportunities to analyze aspects of the demise of the centrally planned economy and the emergence of a market-oriented economy. Nor did I know that conducting research on Russian management would become so accessible and so exciting, after being told by Russians and Americans alike during the Cold War that it was a futile dissertation topic. How could I have anticipated working with former Russian colleagues on joint projects that would track the evolution of Russian management?

Professor Vitaly Ozira was the first Russian colleague who cycled back into my life, much to my surprise. He had been my faculty advisor at the Plekhanov Institute of the National Economy while I took part in the executive development program. Eight years later, we unexpectedly found ourselves colleagues on the Harvard Business School research project comparing Soviet and American management practices. Vitaly went out on a limb for me while I was at Plekhanov, in some ways more than

I realized at the time. He gave real answers to my many questions about Soviet management and society, rather than hiding behind Communist Party dogma. Ironically, he and the dean told the class of one hundred managers to feel free to talk to me, since this would probably be one of their few opportunities to be in contact with a Westerner. They also arranged for me to complete all the course and thesis requirements and become the first non-Soviet to graduate from the program. They included me in all the activities, even lectures on international communism and civil defense, as well as group exercises and social activities. While Vitaly was clearly a mentor during my initial stay in Russia, he easily transformed himself into a colleague on the Harvard-Soviet project.

## The Student as Teacher—Or the Teacher as Student?

It is enjoyable to return to one's alma mater. Recapturing the feelings of college days is nostalgic and gives us a chance to reflect on the directions in which our education has taken us. My return to the University of Ottawa two years ago was even more meaningful to me because I did so as a visiting faculty member in the M.B.A. program from which I had graduated thirteen years earlier. My unexpected teaching assignment was the result of an affiliation, unknown to me, between the University of Ottawa and Northeastern in which they had been collaborating for several years to offer summer programs in France and England. I was invited to teach a course on international human resources management compressed into three long, frigid weekends in Ottawa the following winter. It was very satisfying for me to teach a group of thirty Canadian and European students and to think about the strides that had been made in international management, and in my own career since I had sat in their place.

My decision years before to take half my M.B.A. courses in French and half in English paid off when returning to teach in the international M.B.A. program. Since all the students were fluent in English and French, as an entry requirement to the program, we created a pleasant international atmosphere by using both languages in the classroom. As in most successful teaching experiences, I felt like a student again and learned a great deal from this diverse group of students. I hope more international programs of this type are developed around the world. They make international courses a living laboratory by accentuating the reality of different cultures and requiring students to learn about and adapt to other cultures as part of the classroom environment.

## A Strategic Move

Another unexpected connection between my experiences at the University of Ottawa and Northeastern was Professor Daniel McCarthy. A

Northeastern faculty member while I was an Ottawa M.B.A. student, his book on business policy and strategy had been required reading in my program. Fifteen years later, we became colleagues and he asked me to be a collaborator on research. This turned out to be a strategic move. In addition to our own independent work, in less than four years, we jointly published six articles on various aspects of Russian management, including some with our Russian colleagues as well as Northeastern M.B.A. students.

What is the secret of our successful working relationship? We had worked with many co-authors and published a number of books and articles with them, and we continue to do so. But neither of us had published more than a couple of pieces with any one person. In my view, our effectiveness is based, primarily, on our complementary skills as well as our mutual respect for each other's goals and abilities. While my strengths included Russian management and empirical research focused primarily on organizational behavior, his spanned virtually all management disciplines. He had also published numerous practitioner articles and teaching materials with colleagues in every department at Northeastern's College of Business.

We chose managerial decision-making and authority as our first research topic because it appealed to our common interests. Ever since, our style has been to sit at the computer together, each making our contributions to the research, sometimes heatedly challenging each other's view. We both approach our work with a sense of urgency and enthusiasm, and fortunately, good humor, and make sure we even use just an hour if that is all the time available on a day we schedule for our writing.

Dan is a mentor, colleague, and friend. Last year, I audited his M.B.A. course on strategic management to catch up on the developments in the field since I had used his first book in 1976. Pack rat that I am, I located my notes from that course, and Dan and I were impressed by how strategy had advanced since that time. Taking the course again further broadened me from organizational behavior, just as the Harvard-Soviet project had done several years earlier. The "big picture" is becoming clearer and more appealing to me, and I plan to continue my research in this wider sphere of international business and strategy.

### Sister Scholars

My sister Marlene has also moved in unexpected cycles in relation to my life. I had no inkling whatsoever that she would pursue the same career as mine. And I imagine she is just as surprised that we have ended up in the same profession, both in business schools.

The fall I left home for college, Marlene started kindergarten, she being the youngest and I the oldest of four children. Those days came back to me vividly a few months ago when I unearthed a letter she had written to me that year about "Miss Pencil" and "Mr. Eraser." I got a kick out of sending it back to her recently for her thirtieth birthday. With so many years and miles separating us, we didn't have an opportunity to keep up with much more than the bare essentials of each other's lives. I can truly say that she carved her own niche and got into this profession for her own reasons. I do enjoy the fact that she took some Russian courses in college and that she joined a business school rather than an economics department, in spite of her econometrics training. Now that she is becoming established in her career, we have a chance to work together. This year, while she taught a course in Moscow, we conducted a study of Russian managers' views of international finance. Regardless of what we learn academically, the fun will be in learning about each other as sister scholars.

## FOCUS ON FAMILY

Like many people, I have had my family expand along with my career. A rich family life with a husband and two children helps me put my career in a broader perspective and keeps me from being overly obsessive about career ambitions. My husband and I have come a long way since we met at the Russian Club at the University of Ottawa and married two years later. Our avid interest in Russia has provided continuity and a focus for us for more than two decades, with the year we spent as visiting scholars in Moscow cementing our common interest in this country. My partner has strongly encouraged my efforts as well as befriended the students, faculty, and business professionals who have visited our home on many occasions. His multilingual "taxi" service between Logan Airport and our home is renowned among our Russian friends and colleagues. Hugh's genuine interest in Russia is a major reason that my professional life harmonizes with my family life.

As much as we wanted to have children, I was rather apprehensive about how the responsibilities of a family might interfere with my career. In good doctoral student style, I "researched" the issue by talking with several professional women who had families. Despite hearing stories of juggling and fatigue, on balance, I concluded that having a family was the way to go. Thank God I did. I would hate to have missed out on the experience.

During my last year of the doctoral program at Berkeley, our son, Douglas, and I "went on the job market" together. Naively, I reasoned that prospective employers would take the fact that I was eight months pregnant as a sign that I would let nothing get in the way of launching my career. That was certainly the way I viewed it and so I was rather unprepared for the surprised looks from some colleagues I met on campus interviews around the country. Despite this, my physical condition did not seem to bother the faculty at SUNY-Buffalo. Several faculty members there were new fathers and were very accepting of my condition and intent on making me feel comfortable. It was three weeks after the job interview in Buffalo that my son was born. A job offer from SUNY followed two days later.

I can't say that I would recommend going on the job market in the later stages of pregnancy. People can't help wondering how serious you are about a career when they view such a visible reminder of family responsibilities. Naturally, pregnancy complicates the employment interview by competing with one's professional qualifications for attention. Yet, given the short annual faculty hiring window, I didn't want to postpone getting hired for a year, as I had set a goal to leave Berkeley after four years. I have no idea whether my job offers were reduced, but I don't regret the decision. The additional responsibility of a new baby is also not the easy route to take at the beginning of a career. During the first year in Buffalo, I felt as though I had twins that kept me up late at night—a hungry baby and the following day's course preparation. But thanks to my husband's tremendous help as well as excellent day care, I have never felt that my career has been compromised by family responsibilities.

Over the years, Hugh has always strongly encouraged me to accept opportunities to develop my career, and he has shouldered many of the family responsibilities during my numerous absences. His decision to take a job that requires no travel has provided continuity and stability for the family while I have been away from home. Some of the most memorable incidents occurred when I was a member of the Harvard Business School research team investigating Soviet and American management practices. Our field research began just as my family and I were preparing to move from Buffalo to Boston. Hugh willingly agreed to take care of the move and the final sale of the house while I was away. The evening of the move, I received a message from home indicating that all was well. Upon arriving at our new home a few nights later, our four-year-old son Douglas excitedly met me at the door and blurted out a story of the rain, the plane, and the strain that he and his dad actually experienced in their adventurous move. The car had broken down in a severe rainstorm on the thruway, and after staying up nearly all night, they had to take an early morning flight to avoid a lawsuit from failing to appear at the house closing. All of this I had been blissfully unaware of, since Hugh felt I had enough on my mind with the intensive field research project.

The Harvard research project required spending more than four months away from home. Leaving my family for such a long period was by no means an easy decision, but my husband and I realized that this project was a unique opportunity that would launch me into the field I had wanted to pursue for so long. During the two months of interviewing at U.S. firms, Elise Walton and I were able to return home to our families most weekends, while our Russian colleagues, Alexander Naumov and Vitaly Ozira, were isolated from theirs. The tables were turned during the two months when the team worked in the Soviet Union. I sent postcards home weekly and called only once. My husband and I had agreed that would be our way of not worrying one another or being reminded of the separation.

Just as my son had accompanied me on job interviews, so my daughter-to-be traveled to Moscow with me a few years ago. Northeastern University was interested in developing exchange programs with Russian universities, and a group of faculty and administrators asked me to join the team. Again, this was an opportunity that I did not want to miss, regardless of my physical condition. Because of Russians' discomfort about the subject of pregnant working women, I downplayed my condition around them. However, my American colleagues were very accepting and supportive. For example, they rushed to open a window of our ramshackle bus in Moscow, so I could stick my head out in subfreezing temperatures and keep from being nauseated by the fumes penetrating the floorboards.

I have been extremely fortunate that my family life has supported, rather than impeded, my career objectives. Although life is rather hectic, there is always time for activities, as long as they are made priorities. For instance, regular exercise is one priority, while sleep is not. There will continue to be times when I need to make choices to take advantage of valuable professional opportunities, to enjoy important family occasions, or to fulfill obligations in either area. For instance, a sabbatical abroad is not feasible primarily because of Hugh's job. And it is not possible for me to attend every meeting at the university or event at the children's schools. But, overall, I think my family would agree that we have struck a balance that is satisfying to all of us and that should continue to work well in the future. After all, that's the way I felt on my first Mother's Day ten years ago while my husband and new baby watched me receive my Ph.D. at the Berkeley graduation ceremonies.

## THERE IS NO FINISH LINE

Yesterday, I was one of millions who watched with admiration the nearly 10,000 runners who participated in a Boston Marathon, in which records were broken in all categories. Marathons last but a few hours, yet take months, if not years, of preparation and determination to stay the course. Today, I completed my own intellectual marathon when, opening a letter from the president of Northeastern University, I read:

"It is a great pleasure for me to congratulate you upon your receiving tenure in the College of Business Administration."

Yet, as marathon runners say, there is no finish line. Sure, I have had my share of aches and pains, and stumbled a few times. But I am ready for the next challenge. On to full professor!

# 7

# "On My Terms"

## *Carolyne F. Smart*

*"Change is the only constant in life."*

I am a mid-career academic. Fourteen years have passed since I obtained my Ph.D. and entered academic life. Shortly after embarking on this journey, my career diverged from that of the "typical" faculty member, and I evolved into an academic administrator. I have spent the past six and a-half years serving in various administrative posts.

I was the first woman to hold an administrative position in my faculty and, currently, I hold the position of associate dean. It is said that I have "great potential" and that there are "many opportunities" for me as a senior university administrator. Although I may be prepared to take advantage of those opportunities, I will be selective and my choices will be made on my own terms.

My graduate training was in the field of policy analysis, and I have spent my academic career as a researcher and practitioner in the field of strategic management. When I was in an M.B.A. program, I took a course in managerial decision-making, where one of the assignments required students to develop a personal strategic plan with a ten-year horizon. While all of us had been well-versed in the techniques and processes of organizational planning, it was a near impossible task to bring the same scrutiny and rigorous analysis to bear on our own careers and lives. It was not an easy task then, and it hasn't become any easier in the eighteen years since I took that course. I plead guilty to not practicing what I preach.

My career overall has unfolded in an ad hoc incremental fashion based largely on opportunity and personal whim. And yet, if I look at specific stages (e.g., the individual "five-year" plans), some have been carefully thought-out and very strategic to achieve specific objectives. I do not profess to offer any guidance to other women who may choose the path of academic administrator. I have been the beneficiary of good fortune, serendipity, and an unconstrained personal life. I seem not to have faced the same sorts of struggles as many of my (female) colleagues nor many of the same choices. In fact, I never have thought of myself as "female" in the sense that I made distinctions between myself and my male colleagues beyond basic anatomy. My gender has never been a factor in any aspect of my career decisions. Nor have I perceived my gender to have negatively affected my career opportunities in any way. I leave it to the reader to discern commonalities.

## THE FORMATIVE YEARS

Change and flexibility are the two characteristics that have defined both my personal and professional life. Most people would perceive my formative years to have been unconventional and rather disjointed. In fact, some have marveled that I even managed to graduate from high school, never mind complete graduate work, establish a successful career, and develop into a reasonably balanced individual!

I am the only child of parents who lived an almost nomadic existence (I'm an extreme civilian version of a military brat). My father supervised the construction of high voltage power transmission lines (the large metal towers that one sees during a drive through the country). Rather than be separated from my father for long periods, my mother chose to accompany him everywhere he worked. Since transmission lines are built to carry electricity from its source, usually a remote hydroelectric dam, to its destination in the city, much of the time we lived in the bush—remote locations with few or no amenities. My childhood was spent in a succession of tents, shacks, cabins, float camps, trailers, and occasionally, even a regular house. Sometimes we lived in a city, but most of the time we lived in very small hamlets or sparsely inhabited areas. In many instances, my mother and I were the only two females among a population of male construction workers.

As a consequence of our lifestyle, my formal education could be described as rather erratic. I attended nineteen primary schools (grades 1–6), changing schools on average four times a year. Sometimes I didn't attend school at all, working at correspondence lessons instead. It was not until I was fourteen years old that I had some modest stability. I was able to attend a junior secondary school in a city for three years and a senior secondary school (albeit an unaccredited one) in a small mining town.

Somehow throughout my school years, not only did I survive academically, but I managed to excel. I always was an A student and usually academically more advanced than the students of similar age in whatever school I happened to find myself at the time. Various school administrators tried to persuade my parents to let me advance one or two grades, but this was always refused. Had I not been moving all the time, I might have been bored. Instead, I was always too busy worrying about being "that new kid" and adjusting to the social consequences of my nomadic existence to worry about boredom. I'm always amused when acquaintances agonize over the potential damage of changing their child's school once or twice in twelve years! I don't see myself as exceptional, although my experience is extreme, and I can only conclude that children are far more flexible and resilient than adults give them credit.

I did not fare as well socially as I did on the academic side. I grew up a social isolate with no friends. Often, there were no other children around and even if there were, I became very reluctant to try and establish friendships. The emotional toll of constantly being wrenched away from friends and pets (which were always left behind) was too great. Nor did I have any family other than my parents. My mother's family lived in Europe and my father was an only child whose parents lived three thousand miles away. During my formative first eleven years, I was thus very isolated. I came to rely almost completely on my own resources. My life was primarily inwardly focused—hours spent reading and amusing myself. And most of my social interactions were with adults rather than with other children.

As a consequence of my experiences, I perceive myself to be rather introverted (bordering on shy), quiet, and a loner who is uncomfortable in most social situations and public gatherings. Given my choice of an administrative career, these are characteristics I've had to work hard to overcome. On the positive side, I am extremely flexible and can adapt to almost any situation. I like people, listen to others very well, read very quickly, and can absorb and remember information easily. Most critically, I am very self-reliant.

My childhood was framed by a series of losses. Each time I moved, I lost all those things that give a child a sense of security such as friends, pets, home, and school. This has had some interesting ramifications with respect to my attitude toward my career. I've never had any fear of being fired, not getting tenure, offending people, etc. I always ask myself what's the worst thing that could happen? I could lose it all, but a series of losses has been the pattern of my life and, therefore, nothing to fear. In fact, deep inside, I probably expect losses. As a consequence, I've never given much regard to standard practice or convention either with respect to a career path or in my personal life. I've usually done what has interested me at any given time without much regard for the longer term implications, since I simply don't expect my future to be influenced much by the present. I do expect change, and this expectation has very much influenced my career choices.

## A FIRST CAREER

When I was ten years old, I remember a moment of absolute clarity when I decided on three objectives for my life: I would have a career, I would remain single, and I would be childless. Adult insight leads me to believe that I was influenced to arrive at these objectives by a very strong need for personal control in response to the constant moving about. Well, I compromised on the staying single part, but I have never wavered nor regretted my decision on the other two.

Remaining childless has freed me from the necessity of making difficult trade-offs between work and family responsibilities. I've had the luxury of doing exactly as I pleased. As to a "career," overall I have been opportunistic, not strategic. I didn't really care what I did as long as it was something interesting, fun, challenging, and economically rewarding. Although money has never been a primary criterion, it has been a constraint. I came from a poor family, and it was important to me to ensure that I could live a comfortable upper-middle-class life.

In retrospect, it's clear that I always implicitly expected that I would have three or four different careers, not just one. In large part, my career decisions have been driven by a need for change. If I remain settled too long, I become uneasy, since being settled is an uncommon state for me. And while I don't become bored, I implicitly feel lack of change is unhealthy. Consequently, I periodically feel driven to make dramatic changes in my life. So far, at least, I've confined these changes to my professional life; my personal life has remained absolutely stable.

My first career was in the private sector. After obtaining a B. Comm. in marketing, I spent eight years working as a women's wear buyer for a large department store chain. It was a glamorous, exciting, and interesting time, but after five years, the novelty of constant travel began to wear off. Although my job offered a lot of independence, I chafed at the restrictions of working in a large corporation. I also recognized that there were limited opportunities for me in retail unless I was willing to move. I have very strong location preferences for the West Coast, and I had refused on a number of occasions to take a transfer.

As I increasingly felt the need for a change, I also refused any longer to work on weekends—a rather unpopular stand when one works in the retail business! These choices concerning location and working hours did not make me popular with management and consequently greatly restricted my opportunities for advancement. I thought that being fired could be the worst thing to happen to me (and I wasn't worried about that; in fact, I probably was secretly hoping to be fired) and carried on for another few years all the while looking for another job. The trouble was that I was too highly paid and specialized and could not find another job equivalent in scope, salary, and degree of independence. I eventually decided that if I had to accept a lower salary, I might as well be really poor and return to school for graduate work.

One might think that I sabotaged my own success as a budding retail executive (perhaps deliberately so). However, I never anticipated staying in the business as long as I did. Initially, I planned to stay three to five years as a "first" job and then move on to something else. I really thought it was rather unhealthy and somehow lacking in initiative to still be in the same company eight years on. In addition, I knew when I finished my undergraduate degree that some day I would carry on my schooling to obtain an M.B.A. I knew I had the aptitude. I had written my GMAT exam and scored well, and I had excellent grades. Perhaps, more importantly, I sensed that higher credentials somehow would lead to jobs that would give me greater independence.

I did not anticipate any difficulty in gaining acceptance to graduate school. I was not motivated to do so right away, however, since I was bored with school after five years in an undergraduate business program. After spending eight years working the private sector, it seemed like an appropriate time to take up my second career as a graduate student. I knew if I delayed much longer, it would be exceedingly difficult to start over as a poor student, and the program of my choice required full-time attendance.

## GRADUATE STUDIES: FIRST STEPS ON THE PATH TO ACADEMIA

I view my return to graduate school almost as embarking on a second career, since it was a complete shift in focus, interests, and activities from my work in the private sector. I severed contact with almost all of my business associates and started all over again as a "mature student" in an M.B.A. program. I chose to return to my alma mater (locational preferences, again) and was very fortunate to know many of the faculty who remembered me from my undergraduate years. Also, a very close friend had completed his Ph.D. and returned to the school as a faculty member. We had been colleagues and friendly rivals all through our undergraduate years, and he had been encouraging me for the past eight years to leave retail and return to school. He hired me as a research assistant, gave me workspace, introduced me to faculty, and offered moral support. Since I was older than most students (six to eight years), had worked in the private sector, and had a mentor and friend within the faculty, I became unofficial "mascot" of the business school. In many ways, my experience was a replay of my childhood, in that I associated primarily with the "adults" (faculty) not with fellow students.

My unique status gave me the opportunity to learn a lot about the internal workings and politics of an academic unit. My mentor was a senior member of the department, and I worked at a desk in his office. People became used to seeing me around, and since I was not perceived to be a "typical" student, most faculty seemed to have no reservations about talking in front of me. I became the proverbial fly on the wall and, as a consequence, probably knew more about what was going on in the faculty than most faculty members. It wasn't long before my mentor's colleagues would ask me for information or give me messages for him if he was unavailable. In a sense, I became de facto a sort of administrative assistant, privy to all sorts of interesting information about people and issues. While at the time I had no intention or desire to do more than finish an M.B.A. and find a job, I gained tremendous insights into academic issues and internal university processes that have been most valuable.

Unlike many graduate students, I was not in a particular rush to finish my M.B.A. I chose to extend my program to two academic years, when I could have easily finished in one year. However, I viewed my time in graduate school as a "sabbatical" from work, and I found the entire process rather interesting and relaxing after so many years in a high stress, hectic private sector job. I enjoyed working as a research assistant and poking around in the library, and I was intrigued by the opportunity to view academic life close up.

The faculty member who supervised my master's thesis was extremely supportive and interested in my work. When he asked if I would consider pursuing Ph.D. work under his supervision and offered to provide a research fellowship, I did not at first take the offer seriously. I had never even contemplated the idea of an academic career and had absolutely no interest in teaching or in spending my time doing research. For all that, I was enjoying my "sabbatical" and really saw my interests and my place as being in industry or government—someplace where there was "action." A solitary childhood left me with no taste for a solitary career of reflection and research; and the shy, introverted child inside was horrified at the idea of teaching!

As I reflected on the offer of Ph.D. support, I became intrigued by the potential challenge. I also thought that a Ph.D. could be very useful to my future success as a management consultant. Somewhere along the way, I had decided that I wasn't really interested in returning to a line position in a large organization. (I already had turned down a position with the federal government.) I was interested in a career that gave me a certain amount of independence, and consulting seemed a good fit with my requirements and interests. It was not too much of a stretch to convince myself that a Ph.D. program was a reasonable undertaking.

In truth, I think that I simply preferred to remain a student. I was enjoying the life, and the research I had conducted for my master's thesis was very interesting. I reiterated my position of complete disinterest in an academic career. My supervisor (who by this time had turned into mentor number two) was comfortable with my position. He pointed out that since I had very strong locational preferences and was not prepared to move out of the city, the chances of my obtaining an academic position (had I wanted one) would be very small, since there was only one other university in the city. He stressed that if I were to enter a Ph.D. program with him, it would have to be for the sheer enjoyment and challenge of the process and not for any ultimate career objective. He also was of the opinion that I quite probably would make myself virtually unemployable in the private sector as well, since I would be overqualified for most middle-management positions.

This pessimistic view might have daunted another person, but in a perverse way it freed me to proceed, since I thought there would be no danger of slipping into an academic career I was convinced I didn't want! I started doctoral studies strictly for the fun of it and with no expectations that my degree would lead anywhere. I was reasonably well-supported financially, had interesting colleagues and a supportive mentor, and enjoyed working in a research unit with many projects from different disciplines. In short, I viewed my doctoral studies as a separate career, and at the end of my four or five years, I expected to find a new career that probably would be unrelated to my Ph.D. work.

I have heard horror stories from my colleagues about their miserable experiences in graduate school. Stories about overwork and exploitation, harassment, lack of funding, poor relationships with supervisors, and generally unsupportive situations. I had none of that; to the contrary, my experience was very positive. I worked very hard, but I was supported in all ways by my colleagues and family. I had the opportunity to work with extremely productive, bright researchers who were both active and prominent in their fields. Unlike my preconceptions of research as a solitary undertaking, I found it quite the opposite.

I also treated my Ph.D. program as just another job and brought the same work patterns to my studies as I had to my work in retail. I worked eight hours a day, Monday to Friday, and didn't work evenings or weekends (except in very rare exceptions). I've always kept my private and work life quite separate, and I believe that it is important to have an active life beyond one's work. I seek a balanced life by pursuing other activities in the evenings and weekends, and I resist any work encroachments on my "personal" time. I was therefore not the typical graduate student working all hours day and night in the library or office. I was a committed student, but on my terms.

I worked on a wide array of different research projects. My mentor believed strongly in the model of a collaborative research unit. At any given time, there might be three or four Ph.D. students and a number of master's students "in residence" and numerous projects ongoing with faculty colleagues. We were invited and encouraged to join projects on the basis of interest and/or expertise. There always was something interesting going on, and there were many opportunities to participate in diverse and eclectic research.

Although I was being trained as a policy analyst, this was broadly defined and highly interdisciplinary and included public policy, resource and environment policy, and business policy. Essentially I did what interested me. Since there was no expectation that I would have a traditional academic career, neither my supervisor nor I worried about shaping my program or research focus to ensure success in the job market. This did not mean, however, that my program wasn't rigorous. My supervisor had a reputation for producing excellent graduates who were productive researchers. He expected that everyone would have two or three (or more) publications before graduating. And since he was committed to the collaborative model, all his students were encouraged to engage in joint research.

In many respects, my experience in graduate school was ideal, but there were aspects that could be considered disadvantageous for success in a mainstream academic career. First, I was encouraged and trained to be very eclectic in terms of research focus. While this might be appropriate for full professors with an international reputation, an untenured assistant professor could be accused of being unfocused. Second, I was the product of a system that valued collaboration and, indeed, it was this aspect of the research process I valued and enjoyed. Joint research, however, may be viewed positively if one is a full professor but viewed suspiciously if one is junior and untenured. Third, I came from an environment where there was generous support for research in the form of grants, research assistants, secretarial support, etc. Most of us can attest that this is not the usual environment encountered by junior faculty. Finally, as a graduate student, I was single-mindedly focused on doing research. Unlike most Ph.D. students, I did not teach or act as a teaching assistant. As I had no expectation or desire for an academic career, I ignored teaching and had no experience with the demands of the second part of the academic portfolio.

My years in a Ph.D. program were happy and productive ones. As with my previous degree, I could have finished the program faster than I did but chose to extend my time to four years rather than complete it in three. I worked on many research projects other than my dissertation.

I have subsequently learned that four years is considered to be shorter than the average tenure in a Ph.D. program. However, at completion of my degree, I already had three refereed publications and other monographs. It is only in hindsight that I appreciate how well I was prepared for a career I didn't want and how successfully I was launched in that career.

For all that I enjoyed the process of research, I cared not a wit about the outcome—that is, the resulting publications. I had the extraordinary good fortune of having the first article I ever submitted (in the first year of my Ph.D. program) accepted by the top journal in my discipline. The paper was accepted outright, with only a request for minor modifications. The focus of the article was part of my dissertation research. My supervisor was interested in the topic, and at his urging we collaborated and submitted the paper. The journal editor called and said he wanted to publish our article if we could do a fast turnaround on some minor revisions. I thanked him politely and said I didn't think so, since my co-author was out of the country, and that I'd get back to him.

In retrospect, I realize that this was rather extraordinary behavior! Even more extraordinary was the amount of coaxing my supervisor had to engage in to convince me that: (1) revising was worth the effort, since a publication would look good on my vita regardless of my chosen career; (2) even though it was not his field, he would be pleased to have a publication in that particular journal; (3) one just didn't say no to the prominent editor of this journal; and (4) most people would give anything for the opportunity that had just been handed to me.

I eventually made the revisions, and the article was published four months later. As it turned out, the article became one of the seminal works in the field, and it is still cited extensively sixteen years later. I am proud of that piece of work, which eventually formed a chapter in my dissertation. I'm also thankful to my supervisor for giving me great freedom to do what I wanted but for dissuading me from doing things that limited my options. That first publication gave me a big boost along the tenure track and visibility within my discipline—and I almost prevented it from happening!

As I reflect on my great reluctance to allow publication of that first article, I attribute my behavior to an intense dislike of revealing anything of myself to strangers. I am an extremely private person and keep my thoughts, feelings, and opinions to myself, rarely sharing them even with my spouse or closest friends. The idea of "going public" with theories and opinions, as one would do in journal publication, really was quite distasteful to me. I believe that this theme contributed to my reluctance from the start to consider an academic career. While academics most often pursue their work privately, the fruits of their labor are very public indeed, and open to comment, criticism, and dispute. Many people thrive in such a situation and relish the opportunity to have a forum to express themselves. I, on the other hand, try to avoid it, and I still am uncomfortable with this aspect of my work.

## ENTERING THE ACADEMY

My third career commenced on a sunny September day fourteen years ago. I accepted a position as a visiting professor at the institution from which I had just graduated. How did a person determined not to have an academic career find herself embarking upon one? In retrospect, I think I had a very sneaky supervisor/mentor! (By this time, my husband and I had become close personal friends with him and his family.) He was aided and abetted by his wife (also an academic) and other friends and colleagues who thought if I were gradually eased into the academic life, I would eventually come around and find that I liked it. (Rather like a desensitization process for allergies!) I can only assume that other folks saw things in me that I didn't see in myself.

My mentor (by this time, department chair) offered me a visiting position in the business school. I would be expected to teach three sections of a fourth-year business strategy course. Even though the rule of "not hiring your own" prevailed at my institution, most faculty in the department were quite happy to have me stay on in a limited-term appointment. I was well-trained and had already established a good publication record, and they knew I was competent—in other words, low risk. I needed a lot of persuading before I accepted, however.

Why did I change my mind about an academic career? Ultimately, I believe it came down to a craving for independence. I resisted the idea of becoming an academic for a long time because I'm stubborn! I had been very adamant about not wanting an academic career, and I was loathe to give up that position. Also, I felt in some ways that by "retreating" to an academic life I would be admitting failure—so strong was my bias about graduate studies being a temporary respite from the private sector. I eventually agreed to accept a visiting position out of inertia (it seemed a huge task to start job hunting in the private sector), and also because I had come to appreciate the possibilities of an academic career that would allow a high degree of independence. Although I am a modest person, a realistic assessment of my situation led me to conclude that I had been quite successful as a graduate student and seemed to have an aptitude for the academic life. Somewhere along the road during the past four years, I had been evolving into an academic without really being aware of it. In truth, it was relatively easy for colleagues to persuade me to "try it for a year," adding that if I didn't like it or wasn't successful, I could still do something else. As with other major decisions in my life I thought, "Why not?"

The prospect of teaching, however, absolutely terrified me. I knew by nature that I was ill-prepared for the challenge of teaching and nothing in my graduate training had provided me with appropriate skills. Yet it was imperative to me that I perform well. The major downside risk in accepting an academic appointment was my fear that I would not be a good teacher. Like many of my sisters, I am "addicted to perfection" and avoid activities in which I cannot excel. I spent a lot of time thinking about how I could correct my perceived deficiencies with respect to teaching. The two primary weaknesses I identified were a soft, quiet voice and a lack of self-confidence—I much prefer to be in the background rather than the forefront.

I decided that deficiencies in voice, such as tonal quality, projection, breathing, and so on would be most amenable to correction. I also have a slight speech impediment that I thought could be ameliorated with concentrated effort. Thus, the summer prior to taking up my appointment I worked on my voice. I spent four months working with a speech teacher, an old-fashioned elocutionist who taught me many helpful techniques. This was a relatively expensive undertaking, but I've never regretted the investment. I don't know whether anyone even noticed a difference, but I gained some measure of control and felt much better prepared to teach my first courses.

Advance preparation paid off, and I did not embarrass myself. My teaching evaluations were above average but were obtained at the cost of great internal wear and tear. Prior to every class, I was nauseous and had severe intestinal distress. This continued for about four months before I finally settled down. To this day, I still suffer from severe "stage fright," and while most performers will say this is both normal and desirable, I seem to be afflicted with a rather extreme case. From my experience that first year, I concluded that I could be a good teacher but I would have to be very careful to take steps to ensure that the accompanying stress did not adversely affect my health. I believe strongly in the body/mind connection, so my strategy to address this stress management problem was to learn meditation and deep relaxation techniques. These seem to work for me, and I still practice them regularly. Five years ago, I added a regular yoga practice to my repertoire.

In assessing my situation four months into a term appointment, I concluded that I could deal with both the research and teaching functions that would be required by an academic career. While I wasn't enthusiastic about the prospect of entering academia, I was not completely adverse to the idea. My colleagues, mentors, and friends were strong supporters of the idea and they urged me to seek a tenure track position. I realized, in fact, that I already had entered the academy and the various incremental steps I had taken over the past five years were leading to an escalation of commitment.

Although I had admitted to myself that an academic career was not totally out of the question, it was with a distinct lack of enthusiasm that I turned my attention to searching for a tenure-track position. Search is perhaps too strong a word; in fact, my locational preferences were as strong as ever, and I had no intention of moving. Essentially, this restricted my options to one institution in my area, since I was not interested in working in the junior college system. I applied to the other university in my metropolitan area. The school of business administration had not advertised any positions nor did it even have a department or any faculty members in my discipline. I applied strictly on speculation, not expecting much to come of the application (and hoping that nothing would come of it, so deep was my ambivalence!) As things turned out, I was invited to be interviewed and to give a seminar. Shortly after the seminar, I was given a verbal offer of employment that was formalized by the university a few months later. My job search was as simple as that. The difficult part was convincing myself that I should take the job.

My mentor and friends marveled at my good luck and tried to convince me of the extraordinary opportunity that had fallen into my lap. It was extraordinary not only in the sense of meeting my locational requirements and having been achieved without much effort, but also the offer was for a salary that was slightly above market. After much consideration, I eventually decided to accept the position. My hesitation about the job and the institution had to do with the fact I would be required to make a major change in lifestyle: I would have to drive to work. I owned a car but, in my adult life, had absolutely refused to work or live in locations where I could not conveniently use public transportation. I had traveled by bus (two hours a day) throughout my years as a graduate student. The necessity to commute to work by car is a trivial issue for most people, but not for me. I do it, but I detest it to this day.

The dawn of my "third career" found me working in a profession about which I was ambivalent, at best, and at a university whose location required a most unpleasant change in my lifestyle. It was hardly an auspicious beginning for a new career. In my usual style, however, I decided to try it for awhile knowing I could always leave if I didn't like it, and being quite prepared to do so. As it turned out, I'm still at the same university fourteen years later.

## ON THE TENURE PATH

I am perhaps an extreme example of someone backing into a career without much forethought or planning. Once having arrived in academia, however, my behavior became very strategic to ensure I could stay in that career should I desire it. I thought very carefully about what I would have to do to achieve tenure. My years as a graduate student hanging around the chairman's office had given me some valuable insights into the process and dynamics of tenure decisions. It was obvious to me that one's relationship with colleagues, how those colleagues perceived a candidate's contribution to the school and collegial life, and whether or not one was "liked" are important subjective criteria that influence decisions.

Research and teaching obviously are important, but I had seen many borderline tenure cases determined on the basis of other subjective aspects. For the most part, tenure decisions are a collective assessment of a candidate's potential: the potential to be a productive scholar and teacher, but also the potential to be a compatible colleague. No matter how brilliant the scholar, members of the collective still have to decide if the candidate is someone they can live with for the rest of their professional lives. Unlike personal relationships, divorce usually is not possible.

Although I had no intention or expectation of being perceived as a "borderline" candidate, when the time came for tenure, I was determined to influence the process as much as I could. One of my strategies was to ensure that I was perceived as a very desirable colleague. This was somewhat problematic for me for three reasons. The first was that I was a one-person department. No one else in the faculty was in the same discipline (strategic management). Any courses in the discipline that had been offered prior to my recruitment had been taught by sessional instructors and, unlike other business schools, my institution at that time did not have business policy/strategic management courses in the core undergraduate curriculum. Therefore, my expertise was peripheral to the main foci of the primary program, and I did not have a natural set of colleagues.

Second, at my institution tenure and promotion decisions are made by a faculty-wide committee. When my tenure decision was made, I would be evaluated by people who represented the traditional functional business disciplines. I would not have a departmental colleague to champion my cause. Since strategic management in the mid-1980s was a discipline that was still evolving, there was a danger I would be perceived as "different" and peripheral to the research foci, just as I was to the teaching foci. I realized that I would have to establish a faculty-wide base of support.

Third, I was aware that potentially my gender could be a factor. No women had been given tenure in the faculty. While I was not expecting gender to influence my colleagues' conscious decisions, I was willing to admit the possibility that being a female equaled "different" on an unconscious level. Since, there were already a number of factors on which I differed from the rest of the collective, I believed that success would depend on my ability to demonstrate commonalties and minimize perceived differences.

I have observed over the years that as a route to tenure assistant professors adopt a strategy of first focusing almost exclusively on their research, and secondarily on their teaching. There is a tendency to minimize or avoid committee and service work, to limit the number of teaching preparations, and generally to opt out of any activity they perceive as tangential to their main purpose. I decided to adopt a different strategy: to seek out committee work, involve myself as much as possible in the activities of the school, develop the ability to teach a number of courses in different functional areas, and to involve myself as much as possible in day-to-day academic life. My objective was to minimize any perceived differences between me and my colleagues and to establish myself as a valuable and contributing member of the school.

I had the good fortune of working at a very democratic institution that, by policy, mandated assistant, associate, and full professor membership on all tenure and promotion committees. During my first few weeks as a new faculty member, I was asked to serve on the faculty tenure committee. Although it was a lot of work, this assignment proved to be a very valuable experience; I gained a lot of insight into the evaluation process. More importantly, it gave me exposure to some of my senior colleagues in the faculty with whom I served, and allowed me to start building working relationships with them.

I also implemented my strategy of "involvement" on the teaching side. Although I was hired to teach business strategy, and it would have been possible to teach only that, I offered my services on a half-time basis to the human resources management group during my first year. Since I had no natural colleagues, I felt it was very important to establish a home base in some group. I taught two organizational theory courses that first year, as well as strategy courses. While this entailed extra course preparations, I felt that the benefits outweighed the costs. I was able to demonstrate the ability to teach courses in a number of areas (valuable in a young, growing school), and I had an additional opportunity to develop a network of colleagues who (presumably) were comfortable with me.

The third element of my strategy was to seek out every member of the faculty, introduce myself, and learn something about them: the focus of their research, what they taught, background, etc. It was important that I knew everyone and also that they knew me on more than just a superficial basis. Now, all of this takes time, but I believe that it was time well spent. I am rather amazed that there are faculty members in my school (both junior and senior) who freely admit that they don't know half of their colleagues. Quite clearly, they have a different belief about the value of relationships than I do. I was following a strategy of networking, which I believe has paid off for me; and, in many ways, this strategy probably formed the foundation for my successful move into administration.

As I reflect on this early strategy, it seems fairly clear that I built a foundation that enabled me to become an administrator. I developed a wide network of individuals with whom I worked on committees or interacted as a colleague. People were comfortable with me, and they trusted my competence. I also became an information conduit. Since I had a wide range of contacts and was active on various committees, I was a good source of information, which I shared freely. These are traits that continue to serve me well.

During my first year in a tenure-track position, I probably spent about ten hours a week on committee work and collegial interactions. I don't consider that excessive, nor did I resent spending the time, since I'm one of those rare persons who actually enjoys committee work. The rest of my time was divided almost equally between teaching and research. I taught one night a week, but apart from that night, I generally followed my habit of not working evenings or on weekends. While I may not put in the same long hours as some of my colleagues, nor be as productive as them, I have maintained a balance in life between work and leisure activities. I pursue many other non-work activities that I regard as equally important in my life as my work. No one will ever accuse me of being a workaholic!

My pre-tenure research strategy was simply to continue what I had done in graduate school; that was, to collaborate with a group of colleagues and be rather eclectic in the work I pursued. Some may see this as a potentially risky strategy, and I, too, had seen colleagues criticized for producing too much jointly written work and for being unfocused. My research strategy, however, had been successful in the past, and I saw no reason to change. More importantly, I decided early on that I was going to conduct research in areas that interested me, or I wasn't going to do it at all. I also have very little taste for solitary work and preferred to work collaboratively.

I also differed from other junior colleagues on a key dimension: I wasn't worried about job security. Since I was ambivalent about my academic career, I was quite prepared to return to the private sector and develop a new career should tenure not be forthcoming. Although, admittedly, I would have been extremely miffed about "failing," if leaving the institution was not my choice but one forced on me by others.

My pre-tenure strategies were successful. I was granted tenure and promoted to associate professor at the start of my fourth year at the university. Normally, tenure decisions for assistant professors at my institution are made during the sixth year. Currently, early tenure consideration is permitted with the dean's approval. When I applied for tenure, a system was in place that permitted candidates two attempts. Everyone had to be considered for tenure in the sixth year, but they could also apply in the third year. If people failed, they were reconsidered in the sixth year. It was a comfortable system, which unfortunately has been eliminated.

I felt sufficiently confident of my progress at the end of three years that I decided to seek early tenure consideration and apply for promotion at the same time. I had established a very good publication record, my teaching evaluations were above average, and my service and committee work were well above average. I did not view seeking early tenure as a particularly risky strategy since, if I failed, I would have a "second chance" in the mandatory review during the sixth year.

The downside of my decision was that I could create considerable ill will among both colleagues and external referees if they had to review me twice. In the past, there had been some successful applications for early tenure. The tenure decision aside, my request to be considered for early promotion was riskier; there were no successful precedents within the faculty. Also, there were no tenured female faculty members nor any above the rank of assistant professor within the faculty at this time. I did not know, however, what impact, if any, this situation would have on my case.

My decision to seek early tenure was not taken rashly, however. I sought advice from a wide variety of senior colleagues. I did this to gain the benefit of their advice but also to float the idea of early tenure consideration well before the event, so people would have the opportunity to think about it and to become comfortable with it. The advice that I received was unanimous that I should proceed. While everyone pointed out the downside risks that I had identified, most considered these to be minimal.

Consistent with my academic training and personal inclination, I try to control my environment as much as possible. Although letters and evaluations from external referees and faculty colleagues were critical inputs to tenure decisions, I also knew that the best person to explain the focus and relevance of my research, teaching, and service was me. I took the opportunity to write a detailed five-page personal statement that made my case to the tenure committee. This document was submitted along with my publications and working papers.

Statements from the candidate are mandatory in tenure decisions at some schools, optional at others. I am convinced that candidates can help themselves enormously by writing a careful and thoughtful assessment of their contributions and potential. The chair of the evaluation committee told me informally that the document I submitted was very useful in helping assess the focus and relevance of my research and teaching. He went on to say that it was regrettable more candidates did not engage in the same exercise. This was particularly true for those faculty working in emerging disciplines or conducting interdisciplinary research where it was often more difficult for committees to make an assessment. My experience supported my initial instincts: we all have to sell ourselves, no one else can or will do it for us (at least, not as well), and one cannot assume that one's record will speak for itself!

The letter I received from the chair of the tenure committee supported my belief that my strategy of involving myself in committee work and developing a strong collegial network was successful. The committee was very positive about the quality of my scholarship and teaching. In addition, they singled out my above average committee work and the fact "that [I] have been a most congenial colleague." I was told informally that I was perceived to be far more active and prominent in faculty activities than would normally be the case for someone of junior status and short time in rank. I also was told that my case and the resulting decision was perceived to be an easy one, in part, because the committee members believed they knew me well, knew my work, and could assess my potential with a high degree of confidence.

I was promoted and granted tenure at the start of my fourth year of employment (the first female tenured faculty member). Naively, I thought that I would feel a great sense of relief at being able to get on with the rest of my life. I passed those first great hurdles, and then I crashed! I began to ask myself, "Is that all there is?" The entire year following my tenure decision was a disaster in terms of motivation and productivity.

I lost all interest in my research. I abandoned the area of inquiry that formed the basis for my dissertation and early publications. There was more to be done on the topic, but I lost interest. What was worse, I couldn't generate any enthusiasm for initiating new work; I simply wasn't interested in anything. I still put in my hours at work, but I wasn't very productive. I spent a lot of time gazing out of the window and reading the popular business press. I also became much more accessible to my students and spent more time with them. Since I felt guilty about not doing much on the research side, I spent a lot of time reworking my teaching notes and revamping courses.

More senior colleagues called my state "post-tenure depression" and said it was a common condition that would eventually pass. Many related their own experiences with the phenomenon, which seemed to vary in duration (in my sample) from a few weeks to eight months. I seemed to develop a particularly bad case, however, and numerous times over the next few months I contemplated leaving academia and going back into the private sector. I simply had lost all interest in my job. There were numerous offers from colleagues to join them in collaborative research but nothing tempted me out of my funk. I knew that I wanted (needed) a change.

The opportunity that set me off on a new path eventually came about through a change of deans. A new dean had been appointed just at the start of my post-tenure depression. He was an external appointee whose previous post had been dean of business at an Eastern university. He was unfamiliar with the faculty, the university, and the local community. During the spring of his first year in office, the dean was required to start a search for someone to fill the position of undergraduate program director, since the current director would be stepping down in the summer.

If the previous dean (who had a long tenure with the university) had still been in office, it is quite likely that he would have approached a number of senior professors whom he knew well as potential candidates. The new dean did not know any faculty members very well and started asking various people who they thought might be a potential director. My name was suggested by a number of different people in rather diverse areas of the faculty. I can only assume that the fact he was hearing the same suggestion from a number of sources must have impressed him, since he offered me the position of undergraduate program director.

## A FIRST STEP ON THE ADMINISTRATION PATH

The position of undergraduate program director is one of the four senior administrative positions (excluding the dean) in my faculty. A reader might assume that given my perceived need for a change of pace, I might have eagerly seized the opportunity being offered. In fact, I thought the offer was ludicrous and didn't hesitate to tell the dean so. In my eyes, a newly tenured associate professor, who had been with the institution for a mere five years, was hardly an appropriate candidate for a senior administrative position. This was particularly so, if the person knew virtually nothing about the undergraduate program per se and had never even read the university calendar! I also was acutely aware of the difficulties faced by the typical university administrator trying to "manage" a professional bureaucracy. I had learned a lot by being the "fly on the wall" during my student years.

The Dean assured me he was well aware of my junior status but that his research told him that I would have the support of the faculty. He appealed to my higher sense of duty to "God, Country and the University" and said this was a significant opportunity for me. Various senior colleagues and friends also urged me to accept the position, and eventually I was persuaded.

I took up my first university administrative position with a great deal of anticipation and trepidation. On the negative side, I had never chaired a faculty committee, I was unknown outside of my faculty, knew none of the people in the university bureaucracy or other faculties with whom

I would interact, and was almost ignorant about the program for which I was responsible. On the positive side, I had been a successful middle manager in the private sector, knew quite a lot about university politics, had very strong interpersonal skills, and seemed to have the support of key people within the faculty.

I adapted to my new job very quickly, and it proved to be just the antidote to jolt me out of the state of ennui in which I had wallowed for almost a year. I learned very quickly that I enjoyed administration. Those aspects of the academic life which troubled me—the solitude and pressure to produce research for its own sake rather than for significant or lasting impact—became irrelevant issues. Although administrators are quite often viewed with derision or contempt by many faculty members, I was happy in a job that I thought was important: providing a service to both students and faculty. I know at heart that essentially I am a "doer" rather than a "thinker." I like to be involved; I like people; I like to have some control over shaping my own destiny. My first administrative job let me play to my strengths.

A program director's job is an eleven month one. I was responsible for the day-to-day management of an undergraduate program with approximately 1,200 full-time equivalent students. Since my school operates on a trimester system, there really isn't any down time, although enrollments are lighter in the May-August semester. Undergraduate program staff are responsible for student admission and advising, scheduling classes, booking orders, hearing student appeals, and anything else pertaining to the undergraduate student experience. As director, I supervised a staff of three persons and was responsible for developing and monitoring the curriculum, chairing the faculty undergraduate curriculum committee, and developing policies and procedures pertaining to the teaching function (e.g., levels of teaching support, class size, etc.). I was also the faculty liaison with other university undergraduate programs; a large portion of my time was spent at meetings of various senate undergraduate committees. As one of the three senior administrators within my faculty, I also was a member of the management committee that supported the dean.

On average, I spent between thirty and thirty-five hours a week on program and faculty business. Teaching responsibilities took about fifteen hours a week and, if I had any time or energy, research came third. Although I was working more hours than I had previously done as a regular faculty member, I was very careful to take time for myself and keep up with exercise, meditation, and leisure activities that are critical for a balanced life. I made the conscious decision that if any activity had to be given up, it would be research. The implicit contract I made with myself was that I could afford a two-year break from research if necessary to do a good job as an administrator.

Although my tenure as undergraduate director was enriching and successful, it also was tumultuous. There were major stresses in my personal life: the prolonged illness and death of one parent and the illness and depression of the other. At work, things were also difficult. Part way through my first year as director, the dean abruptly resigned and a new (internal) dean was appointed. As a consequence, some major adjustments on my part were required.

The new dean's style was very different from his predecessor: He was much more "hands on" and directly involved in day-to-day administration. He also had different expectations for the three administrators who reported to him, in that he was directive rather than consultative. His management style was more like that found in the corporate sector rather than in the university. I had been used to running a relatively independent program, one in which the dean did not get involved in operational decisions. I very much resented and resisted the new dean's attempts to tell me what to do. Consequently, the second year of my appointment was very frustrating and fraught with acrimonious arguments with the dean over policy issues.

At the end of my two-year administrative appointment, I was worn out, physically ill, and ready for a break. Two years in a demanding administrative role during a time of great personal stress, following closely on the heels of a major career change and a push for tenure, had exacted a significant toll in terms of my health. All my life I have been prone to stress-induced illnesses, such as migraines and chronic back pain, and these conditions returned with a vengeance.

At my institution, program directors and department chairs are paid a small yearly stipend in addition to their salary. Appointments are nominally half time; that is, one is expected to devote half one's working time to administrative matters and the other half to teaching and research. Administrators usually carry half the normal faculty teaching load. At the end of their term (usually two or three years), they are entitled to eight months of paid leave.

When my appointment expired, I went on administrative leave and took my eight months to catch up on my reading, retool my teaching, and start up some new research. I learned very early in my administrative term that the idea of a "half-time" administrative appointment is fictional. When you hold a major administrative position, it is almost impossible to keep a successful research program going—not if you are serious about doing a good job and still want to have a personal life. Teaching obligations have to be met, so it usually is research that receives short shrift. I know of very few colleagues who have managed to maintain active research portfolios while in major administrative roles.

I was not unduly troubled, however, by "losing" two years to administrative duties, two years in which my research output was minimal.

My tenure and promotion to associate professor had been achieved very early, so any extra time I might take before promotion to full professor would not be a problem. (The average expected time in rank between associate and full professor at my institution is nine years.) When I stepped down as program director, I thought that I would take my administrative leave and return to faculty ranks. I had enjoyed my experience in administration and believed I had been an effective administrator, but I could not immediately see any further opportunities. I did speak with the dean, however, and told him that sometime in the future I might be interested in another administrative job.

I had decided that I liked administration, and my particular background, experiences, and skills were well-suited for a career as a university administrator. Also, I had learned over the previous two years that I enjoyed university life much more when I was active in its management and doing something that I believed was important and necessary. Those factors which faculty typically value most about academic life, such as the ability to be left alone and pursue solitary reflection and research, were the things that I liked the least. Many times, colleagues had expressed the sentiment to me that they just wanted to be left alone! I, on the other hand, wanted to be involved; I need contact and interaction with other people. I also relish the opportunity to achieve some concrete results and solutions to real problems, whether it is improving the working environment of faculty or developing and implementing new courses and programs. Constructing elegant theoretical models does not much interest me any longer; applying those models to real problems does.

I decided that I would pursue administrative opportunities in the future. Since I had been well socialized into the academic life, however, I perceived that before I could consider a more senior administrative position, I first had to get myself promoted to full professor. Most senior administrators at my institution are full professors, although there are and have been vice-presidents and deans who were associate professors. I did not see this as an option for me, however, in part because the values and culture of my faculty have been too well inculcated in me. Rank does count in my faculty, irrespective of one's other achievements, even if distinctions between ranks are made only in subtle ways. Colleagues who have failed to achieve professorial rank are perceived as "failures," and there are strong peer pressures and expectations to focus one's activities on achieving promotion. In the past, this could be achieved only through research and publications. There is also a strong economic incentive at play in that separate salary scales are in place for associate and full professors.

The future, however, turned out to be much closer than I thought it would be. When I finished my administrative leave, the dean offered me a special assignment as planning director for the faculty. This was a one-year appointment, working with him to coordinate and facilitate a major strategic planning initiative and to prepare the faculty for its first comprehensive external review. I did not even think twice about accepting this job, since strategic planning was my field of expertise and interest. It was easy to rationalize that another year of reduced research productivity wasn't really a problem and, after all, it was a terrific opportunity.

## ESCALATING THE COMMITMENT

For me, becoming an academic administrator was like being sucked into quicksand: I was drawn in a little at a time. When I finished my year as planning director, the next opportunity followed immediately. I was offered the position of director of graduate programs, which I declined. I told the dean that I had already been a program director (of a much larger program), and I didn't think that repeating the experience would contribute in any way to my professional development. His immediate response was to offer me the position of associate dean. At this point, I realized that I had reached a major milestone and that some serious rethinking about my career was required.

If I accepted the offer to become associate dean, it would be for a term of not less than three years. I would have "lost" a total of approximately six years in productive research time, which in turn would significantly delay any possibility of promotion. In fact, it was quite likely that I would irreparably damage my ability to ever get a research program back on track and, consequently, to achieve promotion. I also knew that if my tenure as associate dean was successful, there would be other opportunities for more senior positions. My real decision was whether or not to make a major career change, since I would be "leaving the academy" in the sense that my primary concerns would no longer be those of a typical faculty member, namely research and teaching.

I knew I was a good administrator—I enjoyed administration and wanted to continue in an administration capacity. Yet, the opportunities had come too soon and too quickly. I was quite certain, however, that by choosing the administrative path I would have to accept the fact I never would become a full professor. At my institution, one gets promoted to full professor on the basis of scholarship and teaching ability, not on the basis of one's administrative contributions. One of the official criteria explicitly states that a candidate for full professor shall have established an "international reputation" for scholarship. I saw the decision to become an administrator essentially as a decision to forgo promotion, since my previous experiences had demonstrated the futility of trying to maintain a research portfolio at the same time.

The whole issue of rank troubled me greatly, since I didn't want to be perceived by my colleagues as a second-class citizen if I remained forever as an associate. On the other hand, I knew I would be unhappy giving up administrative work to devote my time to research in order to achieve promotion. I calculated that I would need to put in four to five years to achieve this objective. There was a distinct possibility that I would very much resent having to do this and thus lose interest, fail in my objective, and be no better off than if I had stayed on the administrative path.

My colleagues did not help much. While most thought I would be a very good career administrator, they also thought that I would be wasting my talents for research. The notion that I might pursue an administrative career and choose to remain an associate professor, rather than seek promotion at some point, was almost incomprehensible to most people. The decision was extremely difficult, given that I had accepted the academic value system almost without thinking. I also believed there were potential administrative positions from which I might be precluded if I were not a full professor.

The difficulty was compounded by the fact that monetary issues would be involved. Since there are separate salary scales for each rank at my institution, a choice to pursue administrative opportunities, and thereby most probably remain an associate professor, was also a choice to accept a limit on my salary after a certain point. This would occur in about four years when I reached the top of the associate professor scale. At that time, I would receive only across-the-board salary increases to the scale but no merit increases until I was promoted and moved onto the salary scale for professors.

I made myself and all my friends miserable as I wrestled with my decision. In the end, I reviewed the underlying criteria that have guided every career and personal decision I've made: to do what I want to do (not what anybody else thinks I should do) and believe that everything will work out somehow! (Like Scarlet O'Hara, I believe that tomorrow is another day.) Naive perhaps, but it's been a successful strategy for me. Once I "rediscovered" this guiding principle, the rank, the potential salary limitations, the move away from "mainstream" academic life, all became relatively unimportant, and I simply did what I really wanted to do. I accepted the offer to become associate dean.

## WHAT DOES THE FUTURE HOLD?

It was a good decision. I have enjoyed my tenure the past three-and-a-half years and have had the opportunity for tremendous personal and professional growth. I have a very different view of the faculty and university from where I now sit than I had before. I believe that I am making a valuable contribution to the university, and this is perhaps the best use for my particular talents. There are many colleagues in the faculty who are fine scholars and teachers. There are far fewer of us who have the ability to be good managers. I am convinced the need for good governance is as critical in a public institution as in a private one. Certainly, the need for accountability is greater.

I have committed myself to a career in university administration but, as always, have decided that this commitment will be on my terms. There have been a number of opportunities for advancement that I have let pass. I have been approached twice by headhunters seeking candidates for deanships at Eastern universities. I am not interested in changing cities, however, and my locational preferences are as strong as ever.

At my own institution, I was asked to be a candidate for the position of associate vice-president academic. I declined, since I perceived the job to have many negative aspects and few positive ones that would further my professional growth. For the same reasons, I declined to be a candidate for a special staff position in the president's office.

I may have arrived where I am through a series of ad hoc choices and pure good luck, but my career decisions at this point are fairly strategic. I selectively choose university-level committees and special assignments that I think will add new skills and experiences, broaden my network of colleagues, or pique my interest. I am undertaking further career development in two areas: increased experience with university financial management policies and procedures and greater external exposure in business and government communities.

I can say with quiet confidence that I have evolved into an able administrator. Since I also am a woman who is (was) a successful academic, there are many opportunities available, as my institution actively seeks out female candidates to fill administrative positions. Where do I go from here? When an interesting position, perhaps as dean, becomes available at one of the universities in my area, I most likely will be a candidate. I also have considered positions at the local colleges. Strangely enough, I also am revisiting the idea of a return to the private sector. As I gain more experience and become better known in the business community, opportunities seem to fall in my lap.

As I said at the start of this narrative: opportunity and personal whim have shaped my choices. I don't know what I will do next, but I'll know it when I see it. My metamorphosis is not yet complete, and it's uncertain whether I shall emerge as a butterfly or a moth. The end result is almost immaterial to me. Change and the opportunity for growth and adaptation is the important thing in my life; I need these to prevent boredom and depression. I've also learned the hard way that it is important for me to maintain a balance in my life between work and play and to manage stress well. I'm trying very hard to live by two axioms: (1) don't sweat the little things, and (2) almost all things in life are little things. As long as my world is in a constant state of flux, I'll be happy. Unlike most people, I love complexity and discontinuity. A simple, stable professional life is beyond my comprehension and certainly not to my taste.

# 8

# Mid-Career Women: Trial by Fire

*Never measure the height of a mountain until you have reached the top. Then you will see how low it was.*

—Dag Hammarskjold

In the three preceding chapters, we heard the stories of three mid-career academics. Two have just been recently tenured and the other has decided to accept a second term as associate dean. Their stories give us a clear picture of the hazards of the tenure process, the trade-offs in fulfilling family and professional demands, and the difficulties inherent in administrative roles. Although each woman is pursuing a unique path forward, there are commonalities in their stories that are explored in the sections below. First, a brief snapshot of our contributors.

## CONTRIBUTOR SNAPSHOTS

### Cynthia M. Beath

An associate professor in information systems, Cynthia has just received tenure at Southern Methodist University (SMU) and completed her first sabbatical year. Along the way, she has worked at two universities in which her discipline was not well respected. At SMU, she feels that she finally "belongs," being in a school that both expects and needs her leadership skills. Her research strategy is eclectic, opportunistic, and field-based, and she uses partners and grants to push her to completion on difficult projects. She is making a difference within the information systems research community with her detailed and supportive reviews and her willingness to organize conferences and special interest groups. She has "integrated" her work and private life, rather than trying to "balance" them, finding that colleagues can be both research and teaching collaborators, as well as good friends.

### Sheila M. Puffer

Sheila has just been granted tenure at Northeastern University, after spending a total of nine years as an assistant professor at two U.S. universities. She has combined her love of languages, organizational behavior research, and drive to achieve into a niche role as a leading expert on Russian management. Her strategy of following her own interests in research, rather than focusing exclusively on top journals and "hot" topics, has kept her interest high and life exciting. Significant support from her husband and his sharing of her interest in Russian culture has allowed her to combine a rich family life with a fascinating intellectual journey.

### Carolyne F. Smart

After attaining tenure early in her career, Carolyne was offered several administrative portfolios in quick succession. For the past four years, she has been associate dean of Business Administration. Her abilities as an administrator are creating many opportunities for service to the university, but she has had to resign herself to the fact that she may never attain the rank of professor. She is now working to achieve the qualities and skills necessary for advancement to more senior administrative ranks. Throughout her career, she has maintained a clear separation between work and non-work life, concentrating on meditation, yoga, and activities with her husband.

## CAREER THEMES

Most of the themes identified for the early-career women are also present in this group. Additionally, the new theme of serendipity plays a role in these more mature careers. Through their stories, we can see that personal mastery was practiced by all of the women and that each has a unique but effective way of balancing work and family life. From these themes, we derive valuable lessons to pass on to others who are facing the "trial by fire" called tenure, and who are fashioning a productive, scholarly life.

## Serendipity

When we read the stories, several of the events seem random in nature and are interpreted that way by the writer. For example, many seemingly serendipitous events occurred to Carolyne Smart, who was offered one opportunity after another during her career—first, the job offer at the only possible university in her chosen location and then several assignments in administration. Although one might feel that Carolyne was "lucky," she seems to have been well-positioned for all these happenings. As a strategic management graduate, it was no surprise that her skills were appreciated in her early academic appointments. As a capable manager in her previous career, it is more than a coincidence that her enjoyment of administration would lead to significant advancement.

Sheila was also on the receiving end of fortuitous happenings when she made the move from SUNY to Northeastern and was hired into a contract position on a prestigious U.S.-Soviet research team at Harvard. Although the timing was chance, the candidate herself embodied more than a bright young researcher. Speaking fluent Russian and having spent a year in a management course in Russia, must have made her a very appealing hire. Here again we see luck, a rich set of skills, and a willingness to accept risk culminating in excellent opportunities for advancement.

The lesson we draw from these instances is that opportunities exist in the academic environment—jobs, research, and support. However, they often seem to "happen" to those who have been proactive, taken some risks, developed a wide range of skills, and done high-quality work. In other words, luck happens to those who have prepared for it.

## Personal Mastery

All three women are addicted to achievement and excellence, and made strategic choices about obtaining the skills and knowledge to advance. One area that most of our contributors have had to master is teaching. Both Cynthia and Carolyne report being totally unprepared for the classroom. Carolyne, who admits being "addicted to perfection," spent four months with a speech therapist to develop a teaching voice. As she says: "I've never regretted the investment. I don't know whether anyone even noticed a difference, but I gained a measure of control and felt much better prepared to teach my first courses." In working on her teaching, Cynthia has videotaped herself, sat in on others' classes, invited peer review of her own teaching, and done some research on adult education.

Both Cynthia and Carolyne were very proactive concerning tenure. Cynthia created an MIS group at the Academy of Management so she could get to know the researchers who would publish in her field. When she saw another deserving colleague denied tenure, she searched for a university that valued her research area. She honed her tenure package by obtaining advice from peers and senior colleagues and, through this effort, knew that she was finally in the right school "by the support I received as I put my tenure package together, not the decision by the board of trustees."

When realizing that her colleagues would sit in judgment of her at tenure time, Carolyne "followed a strategy of networking" in which she "sought out every member of the faculty, introduced myself, and learned something about them: the focus of their research, what they taught, background, etc. It was important that I knew everyone and they knew me on more than just a superficial basis."

Sheila must be honest when she says "sleep is not a priority." She always seems to be simultaneously involved in several important undertakings. She coupled her part-time M.B.A. with a full-time government job, consulting, and teaching at the university. In Russia, she took an executive management course while acting as a representative for a Canadian trading company. She is still broadening her perspectives, most recently by attending an M.B.A. course in strategic management. She "invests in her own career" by stretching the research money into as many conference opportunities as possible in order to disseminate her research.

## The Female Dilemma

Cynthia and Sheila provide us with humorous glimpses of women trying to secure a foothold in a field populated and controlled mostly by men.

Eight months pregnant, Sheila interviews for her first academic job, believing that her condition would indicate her seriousness and dedication to her career. However, the reality is that her condition made her femaleness even more obvious than it would have been otherwise, and she had to accept an offer from the faculty that showed the most support, rather than being able to choose from the best schools in the country. When she traveled to Russia with the Harvard research team, she was again pregnant, but this time had to downplay it with uncomfortable Russian colleagues.

Cynthia took her soon-to-be ex-husband along to interviews, where he acted the devoted spouse in order to help her "appear normal." As she reports: "He patiently sat through all dinners and lunches, asked appropriate questions, and indicated his sincere interest in moving to Minnesota, Boston, New York, or Austin." This strategy worked in that she got an offer from a prestigious school, but backfired to some extent since the school she chose had few single or junior faculty. As a result, she found it difficult to make friends and contribute to the governance of the school.

Cynthia also reports a double-sided expectation in the classroom. Using Deborah Tannen's language, she has had to "one-up" her male students in order to establish her credibility in a technical field. In addition, Cynthia remarks, "My students expect me to be more flexible, understanding, sympathetic, fair, and available to help them outside of class than my male colleagues."

Carolyne became the first tenured woman in the faculty on the strength of her publications and service record, but her intensive networking with peers ensured that she was known to all and left little to chance.

### Support Systems

The support systems created by all three women are different in nature but exceedingly strong. Cynthia has created a peer network through organizing the junior faculty camp and conferences and by giving generously of her time to review papers from colleagues. She has not relied much on senior colleagues for personal support since the beginning of her career.

Sheila's major support system is a husband who "shoulders many of the family responsibilities," has taken a job that doesn't require travel or much overtime, and who genuinely shares her interest in Russian culture, having a Ph.D. in Russian literature himself. This is truly an integration of work and family that, coupled with his interest in her career advancement, has allowed her to be very productive and successful. An ideal situation, this allows an academic the maximum flexibility possible to travel for data collection and research dissemination. Another of Sheila's strategies to augment her research productivity is the development of partnerships with senior colleagues in addition to working with students and junior faculty.

Carolyne has had several mentors, most notably the two men who brought her into the academic field. The influence of her Ph.D. supervisor, particularly his insistence on publications and diverse research efforts before graduation, extended past her first job and well into her preparation for tenure.

### Periods of Stress

Points of stress for mid-career women are different than those of women in other career stages. As one would expect, they revolve around the tenure process and the choice of roles to play as a tenured faculty member.

Carolyne has faced several difficult times in her academic career. After successfully achieving early tenure: "I passed those first great hurdles, and then I crashed! I began to ask myself, 'is that all there is?' The entire year following my tenure decision was a disaster in terms of motivation and productivity." In hindsight, perhaps Carolyne's distress was a result of a deep antipathy for the singlemindedness needed to be truly successful as an academic. She had other talents and needed to find a way to express them, which she eventually did. However, the road she chose was not an easy one, since it, too, brought a painful realization: "I was quite certain that by choosing the administrative path I would have to accept the fact that I never would become a full professor. . . . The whole issue of rank troubled me greatly since I didn't want to be perceived by my colleagues as a second-class citizen if I remained forever as an associate." Fortunately, she was able to resolve these conflicts and chart a path based on her own priorities.

Cynthia's stress periods also revolved around tenure, although it was the tribulations of others that caused her the most concern and influenced her to leave her first job and move to another school. "While at UCLA, I saw a colleague get chewed up and spit out by the tenure process. It was a miserable experience for me. . . . Back at Minnesota, it was deja vue all over again as another favorite colleague went through the same experience, no-holds-barred ego battery by a tenure committee. . . . By spring, I was ready to throw in the towel and go back to consulting."

However, the real problem for Cynthia, apart from difficult tenure processes, was enduring disrespect for her field of expertise, information systems. "School politics—mostly the animosity of non-IS faculty and administration for the IS faculty, the IS program, the IS doctoral students—dominated every conversation. . . . Even if I got tenure . . . I would be part of a disrespected team. I would never be an insider, an institution builder. Life looked glum." Her solution was to move to a school with more respect for her research area.

## Achieving Balance

All our women scholars have wrestled with the competing spheres of work and home, and the wide variety of contributions one is expected to make as an academic.

Cynthia rejects the notion that one must separate home and work and find a "balance" between them. As she says, "My life is more characterized by integration than balance . . . my social life is intertwined with my academic life, and so my private life is my academic life. . . . Almost all my friends in Dallas are people I know from SMU. . . . For me, one of the primary advantages of academic life is that I do so enjoy the people with whom I work."

Alternately, Carolyne maintains a strict separation of work and home and refuses weekend and night work, in order to create an oasis of peace at home. As she says, "nobody can accuse me of being a workaholic." To some extent, Sheila's considerable travel to conferences and research sites detracts from time with her family. She strives to achieve balance by minimizing the outside commitments of contract teaching, consulting, and professional associations.

## LESSONS TO OTHERS

The stories of our contributors enable us to extract some lessons that may reduce the dangers of this middle period of one's career and improve one's productivity and enjoyment.

1. Commit to your goal. Early in her career, a colleague warned Sheila that she would have to make a choice between being a producer or a consumer of research. She decided to be a producer and has developed a number of strategies to achieve this goal. She sets short-term goals and commits herself to targets that will need significant effort. To maximize her use of time, she "resists the temptation to read rather than to write." She is clearly a focused and determined researcher. When she mentions having a "sense of urgency," we know these words translate into personal deadlines, internally generated pressure, and a willingness to do what it takes to succeed.

2. Work with others. Although many of our institutions profess a liking for single-authored works, many academics work better when they have a partner to challenge views, push a project to completion, and polish articles for publication. Sheila and her research partner "sit at the computer together, each making our contributions to the research . . . we even use just an hour if that is all the time available on a day we schedule for our writing."

3. Take risks. Although the advice from department chairs and senior faculty is often to concentrate narrowly on one topical area of research, we see a very different strategy employed by our contributors. Sheila has actively created new combinations of research interests—by following her love of languages and cultures and by being inclusive rather than exclusive in her learning. Sheila notes that "my plan was to be adventurous . . . my idea of adventure in research was to be eclectic, as well as to do interdisciplinary research." Carolyne echoes this sentiment, saying, "I never feared being fired, of not getting tenure, offending people. . . . I've usually done what interested me at any given time. . . . I do expect change." Taking calculated risks and following their intuition has paid off well for these women.

4. Create a personal vision or set of values. Only one of our contributors has articulated a personal vision in her chapter. Nonetheless, it is obvious that

a stated goal such as Sheila's "to become known as the leading Western scholar on Russian management" acts as a powerful focusing mechanism. Another way to achieve some coherence and direction is to identify a set of personal values through which one filters opportunities. As Cynthia says: "I have no trouble making choices, and those choices must be guided by something . . . not a vision, not a sense of where I'm going, but a strong sense of who I am and what I'm about." Focusing one's efforts in these ways provides both direction and courage in the face of difficult tasks.

# III

# Leaders in Their Field

# 9

# "Going with the Flow"

## Janice M. Beyer

*Know the true value of time; snatch, seize, and enjoy every moment of it.*
—Lord Chesterfield

It wasn't until I was asked to participate in a doctoral consortium at the 1981 Academy of Management meetings that I realized how much I deviated from the conventional wisdom in the way I had thought about and managed my academic career. By that time, I had earned tenure and been a professor for eight years. All of the faculty of the consortium were asked to give an account, for the benefit of those about to become academics, of the overall career strategies and research goals we had pursued in our careers. I'd never thought about my academic career in that way before. As I listened to the other presenters, I felt very inadequate. They sounded so rational, as well as successful. I suddenly realized that I had never been properly socialized in the norms that everyone else there seemed to have known and followed. Perhaps I had missed this crucial part of my socialization, because I was a married woman with children while in graduate school and did not have time free to hang around with "the boys." Or perhaps, because I was a faculty wife, I had unconsciously assumed I already knew it all and had therefore missed signals that were being sent to me about what was expected. In any case, here I was—with nothing that seemed suitable to say.

I decided that the best thing I could do was to tell the truth: I had just worked hard, followed my interests and opportunities as they arose, had faith that the academic system would reward me if I was worthy, and then let things happen. I said something to that effect, but didn't feel very comfortable about it. I don't remember any of the Ph.D. students coming up to thank me for my honesty either. They were probably un-impressed. I wasn't nearly as illustrious a figure as the other faculty in the consortium.

## FLEXIBLE PLANS

It wasn't that I had never made plans. As I was growing up, I had developed career goals, of a sort. But they were contingent goals. As a girl of my generation, I saw clearly that any career goals I made would have to adjust to whatever my husband-of-the-future was doing. I didn't see myself as a spinster. I expected and wanted to marry. It went without saying that my husband's career would come first. That was just the way it was. Somewhere along the line, I developed a conceit that I would be able to adjust and find ways to satisfy my aspirations to some degree, as I actively supported his.

When I was a young girl, my career aspirations had centered on be-coming a journalist. I had seen various movies that made newspaper work seem like a socially important and exciting career in which women worked alongside men as equals. In addition, my most glamorous rela-tive—one of my mother's sisters—was a journalist. Her life looked very exciting and important compared to that of my other working-class rel-atives. I thus became editor of my high school paper, worked as a copy girl at a local newspaper, joined the editorial staff of the college news-paper, and took all the journalism courses I could fit in while in college. For good measure, I included courses in radio and television. This part of my life formed a pretty rational, goal-oriented path to a known career.

It wasn't that simple, though. My parents felt that they had made substantial investments in my music education and wanted me to con-tinue it. They saw teaching music at some level as a good career for a woman. I wasn't so sure. I had tried private piano teaching and didn't enjoy it that much. Nor did I like the idea of teaching music in grade or high school. I didn't want to spend my life trying to keep high school troublemakers or younger squirming kids in line during orchestra or chorus practices. But I went with the flow—if my parents wanted me to study music, I would study music and turn it into an advantage by becoming a newspaper music critic or perhaps by teaching music at the college level. The latter aspiration was ill-formed, for I did not know any professors and had only the vaguest ideas about college teaching.

Combining the fields of journalism and music seemed possible until my romantic life took a serious turn. At the end of my sophomore year, I started dating my first husband, Tom: We were married before we began our senior year; I was expecting our first child by the time I grad-uated. He had very definite career plans; he wanted to earn a Ph.D. in psychology and become a researcher and academic. His enthusiasm and certainty began to make an academic career seem more attractive and achievable for me, as well. When we found out I was pregnant, our plans to go to graduate school together seemed impossible to achieve. We never thought of loans from parents or the government. As we saw it, there was only one choice to be made and it centered on his career: would he get a job now or go on to graduate school? When job interviewers advised him to go on for his Ph.D., the choices again seemed clear. He would go to graduate school and I would work. And that's what I did. I began full-time work five weeks after Claire was born.

My search for a job in journalism had begun when she was only three weeks old, but with such a small baby and no full-time experience, the best job I could find was as a bookkeeper at a radio and television station. I didn't mind too much. Tom was racing through his Ph.D. program in psychology at Berkeley, and my turn would be next. As I observed Tom's activities and we hung around with other graduate students in his program, studying people began to seem very attractive and exciting. Gradually, I decided I wanted to change my field of study. I'd never felt I had outstanding musical talents anyway. However, when Tom graduated and I broached the idea of studying sociology, he responded with a line I will never forget: "That's sick, you're just trying to compete with me." This was the era in which penis envy was still a respectable theory of the psychology of women; I had no comparable intellectual ammunition with which to fight back. I didn't agree with the attribution, but I gave in anyway. It didn't occur to me to wonder what his reaction meant in terms of his feelings for me. I adjusted my aspirations again because my marriage was more important to me than any career.

So I began graduate school in musicology instead. I would return to the idea of teaching music at the college level. I was successful in my studies because of my general analytical abilities, but I felt like a fake. I knew I had no outstanding musical abilities and that music was not my life's central interest, as it was for my professors and the students around me. It was easy to slip into the decision to have another child and take a leave of absence from graduate school. I wanted another child; the only question was when.

## CHOOSING TO ENTER ACADEMIA

My decision to enter academia was gradual and highly responsive to my other life experiences—a fleeting notion while I was in high school and as an undergraduate that developed by osmosis into a serious aspiration during my husband's graduate education. Although twice deferred, once the aspiration formed, it never left me. When the children were in school, I would get another chance—it would be my turn.

Fortunately, before my next attempt at graduate school, the women's liberation movement had begun. Most personally important for me was Betty Friedan's book *The Feminine Mystique*. I felt the book literally saved my life, for I had been dogged with depression at various levels of severity after my second daughter Andrea's birth. Until I read Friedan's book, I had no accepted outlet for my frustrations and disappointments except to turn my negative feelings inward. Before reading it I felt deficient and guilty, because I did not feel totally fulfilled by my wife and mother roles. I *should* be happy; I had every reason to be, according to the cultural ethos of the time. It was an unbelievable relief to realize that other women felt as I did. It was not abnormal to want to realize my abilities in some kind of meaningful work. Now I could begin to plan to go back to graduate school with greater assurance that I was not "sick" for wanting to do so.

Of course, that didn't make my entrance assured by any means. As I learned later from friends on the Cornell faculty, where Tom was then teaching, my application encountered several hurdles I had not anticipated. The first I probably created myself. I decided to apply for the master's rather than the Ph.D. program. I didn't understand, and Tom didn't bother to explain, that this would not be viewed favorably by the faculty reviewing my application. As I know now, when slots in a Ph.D. program are limited, faculty want to admit students who are ambitious to become professors at other leading universities. Instead, my application said modestly that I wanted to assist others in their research. In my attempt to be practical, I had arrived at another compromise.

Again, I was going with the flow. Cornell had a nepotism rule, Tom had tenure at Cornell, and we liked living in Ithaca. I did not want to be a professor at a predominantly teaching institution, and that's all there was around Ithaca. Besides, I wasn't sure, after all of the self-doubt that the intervening years had generated, that I had the ability to do Ph.D.-level work. I knew I was organized, logical, and good at helping others, though.

The second hurdle to my application was that, because of a national oversupply of new Ph.D.'s in some fields, the Cornell administration had just imposed a quota on all departments saying that it could not admit more Ph.D. students than it graduated. I initially applied to the department of rural sociology and was put on a waiting list. When all of the admitted candidates accepted, the school offered to admit me mid-year or the following year. I was too eager to get back to school to wait that long. I decided to make a late application to the School of Industrial and Labor Relations (ILR), which had a much larger Ph.D. program, and where I had really wanted to go all along, but felt I should not apply because many of the faculty there were close friends.

As I discovered, a good friend on the admissions committee argued my case, although his influence was limited. The best he could do was to admit me as a noncandidate in the program. He explained to me that I would have to prove myself with straight A's for a full load of courses before I could become a regular degree candidate. I would also have to pay tuition and fees.

I accepted the conditions imposed and registered for four courses, including the first statistics course I had ever taken. I didn't find the course work especially hard and could keep up without much difficulty. I was well-organized, and I enjoyed every minute of my assignments. Tom had always been helpful with cooking and other housework. Our daughters were very self-reliant and got along well together; Ithaca provided a relatively safe and supportive environment for children. As the semester progressed, I could feel myself beginning to grow intellectually and personally, but I was still not entirely confident that I would do as well as needed on all of my final exams. When Tom announced that he wanted to go on a ski vacation during the final exam period and leave me alone with the children, I was angry, hurt, and puzzled. I had supported him every minute he was in graduate school. Couldn't he see that I needed his support now? After I protested he didn't go. I did manage to earn A's in all my courses and was rewarded with regular status and what all of the other Ph.D. students had—a half-time research assistantship.

I was assigned to a new professor, Gerald Gordon. Gerry's egalitarian approach and entrepreneurial inclinations were just what I needed. He did not try to shape my interests and was very supportive. I decided to study the topic of science in universities for two reasons: first, I felt both science and higher education were institutions of crucial social importance, and second, there was little prior organizational research on universities or the interface between them. In my second year of graduate work, I began discussing the existing literature on universities with Gerry. He soon encouraged me to jump right in and design my own research project. Furthermore, he urged me to design a project on what I thought the field should know about universities and not to worry about the money or other resources required. When I did that to his satisfaction, he got me the funding I needed to survey all of the faculty in eighty university departments and to get computer programs written for the analyses that went into my master's thesis. It was a very ambitious thesis, for I then viewed it as my terminal degree effort. When I succeeded in getting a paper from my thesis accepted in the *American Sociological Review (ASR)*, my faculty friends began to urge me to continue for a Ph.D. degree.

By this time, I had gained much more confidence in my abilities; also, Tom had been influenced by the women's liberation movement, and he was being encouraging. I could now visualize getting my own research grants rather than working on other people's, and I embarked on Ph.D. work.

Cornell had a very flexible Ph.D. program with few required courses. My program of study was pretty much up to me and my committee. This flexibility made it possible to manage my studies and home life at the same time. I never enrolled in late afternoon classes or stayed for late afternoon colloquia. Andrea was attending an alternate school and needed to be picked up and driven home. If I couldn't fit my assignments into the relatively short time I was at the university during the day, I worked after the children were in bed. Years later, reflecting on the many things I kept going while I was in graduate school, I would say, "I did my graduate work with my left hand on Tuesdays."

What I meant was that throughout those years, I tried to manage my studies so they would interfere minimally with my accustomed role in the family. I shopped, entertained, sewed costumes, cooked the meals, did the laundry, and kept in touch with our extended families. I took the girls to music lessons, to doctor appointments, and to ride their horses, and watched them perform at horse shows for long hours. I didn't feel like superwoman, either. I had good cleaning help once a week, and both my children and Tom were very helpful and resourceful. In our family, everyone pitched in as needed. We enjoyed doing almost everything together. I thought we were a very happy and fortunate family.

Two years after beginning Ph.D. work, I took and passed my comprehensive exams. During that time, I continued to analyze my university data, wrote papers, and submitted them to various journals. I was beginning to feel competent and accomplished, but passed my comprehensive exams in April of 1972 under great emotional stress. By that time, there were various signs that my marriage was in trouble. I hoped that once my exams were over, everything would be back to normal. It wasn't to be. Tom left the marriage in July.

## CHOOSING THE FIRST ACADEMIC POSITION

There was no question about what to do next. I would finish my Ph.D. and get a professorial position. I didn't see any other good alternative. Thus, with great sorrow and a sense of futility about the value of plans, I continued my research. I separated out a set of hypotheses and results on power issues already obtained from my large data set on universities, vowed to finish my dissertation that year, and looked for an academic position.

I wasn't very savvy about the job market in business schools, never having attended an Academy of Management meeting. The ILR faculty was not very helpful. In particular, Gerry was writing rather equivocal recommendation letters. I had unwisely told him that if I didn't get a job I wanted, I would stay at Cornell for another year to write a book with him. He probably thought it was in both our interests that I stay. Although others, notably the sociologist Richard Hall, were recommending me for various positions, I received only one invitation for an interview. It came through the efforts of Larry Williams, a member of my committee and a good friend. The position was at the management school of the State University of New York at Buffalo. I went for the interview, was offered the job, and accepted. The position met my minimum requirements: a Ph.D. program and a teaching load light enough to allow me to seriously pursue my research interests. By that time, I was grateful that someone was willing to hire me, for as one faculty member had unkindly put it, I couldn't expect a good job—I was a middle-aged woman. I was thirty-nine.

Later that spring, the higher education department at Berkeley invited me for an interview, but I felt committed to the Buffalo job. In typical fashion, I had gone along with the first reasonable opportunity that came along.

## DEVELOPING A POST-PH.D. RESEARCH AGENDA

Sometime in December, before I started writing my dissertation, I had begun helping another ILR faculty member, Harry Trice, with his research. He had just won a large grant to study alcoholism programs, in work organizations and hired me to help in designing measures of organizational structure. The new intellectual challenges involved were just what I needed. Writing my dissertation had become a painful prospect, because it was associated in my mind with the loss of my marriage.

Harry not only provided me with lots of room to exercise my methodological and conceptual abilities in helping design his study, he also provided me with affirmation of my abilities and worth as a person. Our professional relationship soon became more personal, for he too, had just experienced the end of a long marriage. It seemed inevitable that we would discuss the emotionally disturbing contacts we were each having with our lawyers, children, and former spouses. It was only after I experienced his emotional support that I was able to actually begin writing my dissertation. Harry had arranged for lots of speaking engagements and other professional travel to fill up his days and buttress his finances. He'd teach in the early part of the week and travel toward the end of the week. We usually had lunch together on Mondays. By the weekend when he got back into town, I'd have a chapter written.

At the same time, we were making great progress in designing the study of alcoholism programs. It was this project that provided me with much of my post-Ph.D. research agenda. I was enjoying working with

Harry and his crew of assistants. The way he ran this project matched my ideals of what social science research should be like. In addition, he was giving me lots of opportunity to use my ideas, and he had the funding to collect an important data set. Equally attractive was that his research was on a topic that mattered. If workplaces could make effective interventions into the lives of employees with drinking problems, and we could document how this was done, society would benefit. I therefore did the natural and obvious thing—I continued my involvement with the project after I left Cornell.

A year after I joined the SUNY at Buffalo faculty, Harry and I married. Our close and deeply satisfying intellectual collaboration had deepened into affection and then love. We worked and played together very harmoniously. We both respected each other's ideas; we had complementary skills and knowledge of the literature. We co-authored many publications from the data set, including my first book, which surely helped me earn tenure. We wrote for various audiences, with the first priority given to scholarly journals. Many of our papers, however, were written specifically for publications read by practitioners concerned with managing alcoholism programs, including medical doctors. We also reported our findings at numerous meetings of professional groups working with alcoholism problems. It was another thing I admired in Harry and wanted to do myself—share findings that mattered with the people who could put them to use.

While working with Harry, I did not entirely abandon my interest in universities nor the data set I had generated. I continued to work on papers begun during graduate school and a paper based on my dissertation. I also extended some of my findings from that research with a study of scientific journals.

When I got that single job interview and offer in 1973, there were very few women faculty in business schools. I was one of the first two women hired into tenure-track positions in the School of Management at SUNY-Buffalo that year. I had been around academia all my adult life, and it seemed obvious to me that I would have to prove that I could do research on my own if I expected to win tenure. That meant I needed some publications without Harry's name on them. My data set on universities was strong enough to gain me serious consideration, so I continued to work on it. Perhaps because of my prior writing experience, I had a pretty good track record in gaining acceptances. I did plenty of revisions and not all of my papers were accepted, but I kept writing and submitting, and eventually my efforts usually paid off.

## TEACHING IN THE PRE-TENURE YEARS

Because I had planned a research career, I had done only one stint as a teaching assistant while in graduate school. I was painfully aware that I had never taken or sat in on a business school class, never mind taught one before. As the first day of my first class loomed, I was scared stiff to go into the classroom. With Harry's moral support and presence in Buffalo, I managed it. I wasn't a great success and didn't expect to be— my priorities were elsewhere. My interests were in research, and I felt sure that research would be the main criterion by which my tenure was decided. If not, a good research record could earn me a job elsewhere.

I was conscientious enough to want to do a professional job as a teacher, but I had been such an eager student myself that I was probably insensitive to the motivational aspects of teaching. I think I gained the reputation of being tough but fair and of teaching to the top students in the class.

My main teaching assignments were to lead the required courses in organizational behavior at the undergraduate and M.B.A. levels. I also taught research methods at the Ph.D. level and developed electives on power, women in management, and organizations and the environment. At the end of two years, I had taught eight classes with seven different preparations. I was eager to impart knowledge that I felt was exciting and important for aspiring managers, but I most enjoyed teaching the Ph.D. students and working with them on their or my research. I felt most competent and appreciated in that teaching role. It seemed to come naturally.

As it turned out, being one of the first women professors in the school presented special teaching challenges. I still remember vividly the time during my first semester of teaching when a student in an undergraduate class raised his hand and asked a question meant to harass me. He prefaced his question by innocently saying that he wanted to ask about something that wasn't exactly relevant to what we had been discussing but that he had been reading about in the library the night before. He went on to say he had come across a study published in a psychology journal that concluded that men between the ages of eighteen and twenty-two had a sexual fantasy every ten minutes. He then pointed out that since there were thirty-six men in the class and I had been lecturing for forty minutes, 144 sexual fantasies had occurred in that classroom since I began my lecture. He ended with his question: What did I think of that?

I was silent for a few moments. And then, to my surprise, I blurted out an honest reaction based on my experience that sexual innuendoes often intruded at times when they were unwanted and inappropriate. I found myself saying, "In men my age, it's more like once a minute."

The class laughed, the student sat down, and I never got another question like that again.

## CHOOSING OTHER PROFESSIONAL ACTIVITIES

Becoming active in services related to my profession wasn't difficult. The first requests came from the *Administrative Science Quarterly (ASQ)* before I was even out of graduate school. I was occasionally asked to review papers, usually on science or higher education. After I graduated the ad hoc reviewing continued, and within a year or two after graduation I accepted a position on the editorial board of *ASQ.* Other journals also began to ask me to review papers in which my publications were cited.

The only professional organization in which I was active at that point was the American Sociological Association (ASA). I attended both the national and regional meetings. I remember meeting Jeff Pfeffer at one of the national meetings, probably about a year after I graduated. He sought me out because he was familiar with my *ASR* paper on the effects of paradigm development on the functioning of graduate departments in the sciences. He invited me to have lunch, and we discussed his ideas for extending that line of research as well as obtaining research funding for the project. Thus began a friendship and sponsorship that has lasted over the years. Jeff was one of the persons who wrote letters for both of my promotions and later asked me whether I wanted to run for president of the Academy. He has appreciated and built upon my research, including his recent award winning and controversial paper in the *Academy of Management Review (AMR)* on research in management. Over the years, I suspect he has supported and sponsored me in ways I don't even know.

I found the management school at Buffalo to be very collegial in the best sense of that word. All faculty served on one or another committee of the school. I began on the library committee—not a very active group—but soon graduated to the M.B.A. program committee, which handled the M.B.A. curriculum and admissions. It wasn't long before I was serving on a search committee for a new dean for the school and another for an undergraduate school dean. I was also elected a representative to the faculty senate and a member of the policy committee of the school. I enjoyed being part of the governance of the management school and university and felt it was an important part of my professional role. But I was careful not to overdo it. Most importantly, I left enough time for my research.

## BALANCING IT ALL

I didn't really feel overburdened in the years before tenure. I expected to work hard and did. Much of my research work was with Harry or with graduate students I enjoyed. The routine did not seem onerous. My expectations of myself were high; I always assigned term papers and gave essay exams, which I graded myself. One year, I remember, I had over 150 term papers as well as essay exams to grade just before Christmas. I had waited a long time to be a professor, and I enjoyed almost every part of it to some degree.

One circumstance that made my life easier in one sense was that my younger daughter, who was only thirteen when I began teaching in Buffalo, decided a year later to go and live with her father in Ithaca, where she had grown up. She missed the way of life there, and never really adjusted to living in Buffalo. Tom lived on a farm where she could have her horse with her. Her much-beloved older sister was attending Cornell as an undergraduate. I just couldn't compete with all of that. I was devastated by her leaving and, to deal with the grief, threw myself into my work.

For twelve of the thirteen years I taught at Buffalo, I was in a commuting marriage. Harry continued to work at Cornell, so during the school year we usually only saw one another on weekends, except for holidays, vacations, or when we had some mutual professional meeting or business. It was about a three-hour drive from Ithaca to Buffalo, and Harry made it many more times than I did, especially in the winter. When we got together, we often worked on our research much of the time. We also played tennis and went to parties, concerts and out to dinner, but we were not big socializers. Our main release from work was when we took vacations to the Caribbean and other resort-like locations. To my surprise, the people I met socially seemed to view our commuting marriage as glamorous and romantic. I never saw it that way and would have preferred to be able to live together on a daily basis. Harry accepted frequent separations more willingly than I, and after awhile, I realized and accepted that he would not leave Cornell until his retirement. The connections he had built there were too important to his work and ultimately to his professional identity to give them up. I, in turn, was unwilling to take a much inferior job to be near Ithaca. Commuting was our only solution.

While I considered our living arrangement a less than ideal solution, we were able to make it work for as long as we did because of a variety of circumstances. Harry was a full professor with a good income. I had enough salary and assets from my prior marriage to support a comfortable separate home in Buffalo. His children were grown and out of college soon after we married, so we were relatively free of family obligations and could spend our time on our own interests. During the summers, we spent longer stretches of time together, either working with and supervising our research crews collecting data, analyzing data, and writing proposals and papers, or doing other tasks connected with our research.

During those years, we also attended lots of professional meetings together. In August, we usually went to the meetings of ASA, the Academy of Management, and the Society for the Study of Social Problems. We also frequently attended the annual meetings of either the Eastern Sociological Association or the Eastern Academy of Management. We usually gave one or more joint papers at every meeting we attended and took turns presenting. There were no real questions raised by either of us about doing all of this. It was what Harry had always done in his career. I took it for granted that it was what I was supposed to do.

Looking back, I can see that I opened the way for many other opportunities by attending and presenting papers so regularly at these meetings. People in the field began to know who I was and what I did. Another bonus was that I met and became good friends over time with Carolyn Dexter. Carolyn sort of adopted me, as she has so many other women, and has urged me on throughout my career. She was the first to suggest I think about taking on a position as officer in the Academy and then campaigned for me with her wide circle of contacts when I became a candidate. Over the years, I've turned to Carolyn many times for practical advice and collegial support.

## THE TENURE PROCESS

Because I had been so focused on research from the beginning of my graduate work, and because I had succeeded early in having articles accepted for publication, I wasn't really worried about getting tenure. I thought I deserved to be brought up for tenure early, but didn't ask. I didn't expect to be considered until the year after a colleague in the department, who had his degree a year longer, made tenure. By then it was my fifth year and clearly my turn, I felt. I don't remember asking to be brought up; it was expected in the school and in the department and just seemed to happen. I'm sure someone formally asked me if I agreed, but I don't remember the occasion. By that time, I had seventeen articles published and a book with Harry on our research findings about to be published.

I remember having doubts earlier about whether I had been wise to work so extensively with Harry, especially when it looked like a research proposal we had struggled over for one whole summer would not be funded. I was concerned that writing the proposal had delayed finishing our book. But my worries were unnecessary. The book did get written in time for the tenure review, and the research grant was later funded.

Getting tenure was, of course, a big relief. The end of my first marriage had left me feeling financially insecure. Everything I had counted on for my future security was suddenly gone. While I had married again, I did not want to ever again have to count on anyone but myself for financial security. Winning tenure gave me that sense of security.


## STAYING ACTIVE

Having tenure did not lead me to consciously change my professional routines in any way. I had always spoken my mind in departmental and school matters; I continued to do so. I was as busy as ever with research. My teaching responsibilities and activities did not change.

About that time, however, I began to get more involved in professional activities. Even before tenure, I had been asked to join a grant proposal review committee for the National Institutes for Education. Karl Weick chaired the committee; committee members included Karlene Roberts, Bill Starbuck, and Gerry Salancik from the field of organizations, as well as sociologists, anthropologists, psychologists, education scholars, and public policy researchers. Going over the proposals with these people was a very broadening experience for me. I also became good friends with the other scholars in the field of organizational behavior. In particular, I became better acquainted with Bill Starbuck, whom I had known when he taught at Cornell. He was co-editing the two volume *Handbook of Organizational Design* at the time and, when I learned he was still looking for contributors, I volunteered to write a chapter. We quickly agreed on a topic. It was difficult to fit in writing that chapter, but I managed. When it turned out that Bill really liked it, he became one of my sponsors and mentors.

At about the same time, Tom Mahoney asked me to join the editorial board of the *Academy of Management Journal (AMJ).* After some hesitation I agreed. I was still on *ASQ*'s editorial board and didn't want to overburden myself. I continued on the *ASQ* board until I became editor of *AMJ* three years later. I was to rejoin the *ASQ* board again when my involvement with Academy affairs lessened.

I had not been socialized into attending meetings of the Academy of Management while in graduate school, but two years after I joined the Buffalo faculty, someone suggested to me that I should go. From that time on, I made a point of submitting papers for presentation and attending the annual meetings regularly whether or not my papers had been accepted. While there, I made a point of going to the business meetings of the organizational management theory (OMT) and organizational behavior divisions of the Academy. I'd sign up to review papers and, in that way, began to get known in the divisions. Suddenly, just as I felt I would never have a chance to participate at a higher level, I was called and asked to run for program chair elect of the OMT division. I lost the election, but was asked the next year to run again. I did, and this time I won. My ascent up the ladder of offices in the Academy had begun.

I found being an officer in the OMT division very rewarding. The other officers were stimulating and fun to work with. The division was very innovative, and I was gratified to be participating in its activities. I felt I was making a difference. As I became better known through my activities and publications, I found myself being asked to do too many different things. I had to begin making choices, where before I had been pretty much able to accept all of the opportunities that came my way. Sometimes, it was easy to refuse because I simply didn't feel qualified. Often I decided by asking myself—would it make a difference to the field? To society? I felt fortunate to be doing research on alcoholism with Harry Trice—a topic that I thought could conceivably make a difference in people's lives. I wanted to do the same in my teaching and professional service.

## MOVING AROUND

By the time I was at Buffalo for about ten years, I had been a full professor for several years and was growing restless. I had been, for most of my stay, the only "macro" person in the organizational behavior (OB) and human resources (HR) department. The other faculty were either micro HR or micro OB, except for two collective bargainers, and I could not persuade enough of my colleagues or the dean that we should hire other macro faculty. I was deeply disappointed that some of my colleagues did not support me on this issue, because I had always used my influence to support their interests. I felt stymied from making the contributions I wanted to make to the school and department without colleagues in my area. I also felt increasingly isolated from researchers who were working in my primary areas of interest—organizational structure and organization-environment relations. Harry and I shared a sociological perspective, but his prime interests were elsewhere, so I quietly began looking for a new job. Unfortunately, most of the places that approached me were also weak on the macro side of the field.

After a couple years of more or less discreet looking, Bill Starbuck asked if I would consider coming to New York University (NYU), where he had recently moved. I was hesitant because I did not think I'd enjoy living or working in New York, but Bill and people like Jeff Pfeffer assured me that it was a great place for an energetic woman like myself. So I went for an interview and was very favorably impressed by the fit between my interests and those of the faculty. When they offered me a job and assured me good support for my editorial duties on the *Journal* (I was then in the middle of my term as editor of *AMJ*), I decided to move. I spent a very professionally rewarding two years at NYU. There was indeed an excellent fit between my interests and values and those of the other faculty. I felt I made a difference and, as chair of the recruiting committee, attracted some good people to join the faculty. However, I found the commute between New Jersey, where I had chosen to live (because it was relatively close to Ithaca) and New York onerous. Plus, just being in New York was exhausting.

After I had been at NYU for only a year, Bill Glick approached me at the Academy meetings about whether I would be interested in moving to the University of Texas in Austin. Bill was someone I had tried to hire at Buffalo, and I respected him greatly for his work as a member of the *AMJ* editorial board when I was editor. I told Bill I was not interested, but he persisted and got me to agree to come for a visit. I put off the visit until late in the fall. When I went, I was pleasantly surprised by the atmosphere of the department and the attractiveness of Austin. Nothing fit my stereotyped ideas about Texas, and moving there began to look more attractive. The department included strong macro researchers like George Huber and Sim Sitkin. I had met Sim at culture conferences and been very impressed by his grasp of the field and by what a nice guy he was. George was in the middle of an impressive, large-scale study of organizational change.

It was a hard decision, because I still liked my colleagues and everything else about NYU except being in the New York City area. After much thought, I realized that because of the demands of being *AMJ* editor, I hadn't really started a research stream at NYU and it was therefore a good time to move. With regrets, especially in consideration of Bill Starbuck who had been so very supportive, I decided to pursue the offer and accepted a job at the University of Texas after another visit to Austin. Later, I learned that Jeff Pfeffer had again been in the wings, recommending me to the UT faculty as just the person for them.

Once more my decision had an unexpected price—the end of my second marriage. Harry did not feel ready to retire and didn't see how we could commute such a long distance. As it turned out, after a period of separation, we worked together very productively again and completed the book on organizational cultures we had begun several years before. After his retirement he bought a home in Austin, where he spent part of the year. Until his recent death, we remained very close friends.

## HITTING THE BIG TIME

The first professional request I received that really gave me pause was when Karl Weick asked me to edit a special issue for *ASQ* on the utilization of organizational research. His request followed a symposium I had organized on the topic at the Eastern Academy meetings. At first I refused, but after talking it over with Bill Starbuck, decided to accept.

I hesitated because I didn't feel ready to take on such a big responsibility, but Bill reassured me that I was up to it. Karl worked closely with me on the issue, and we seemed to agree readily on what to accept for the issue, and why. This experience greatly increased my confidence in my judgment.

The next big challenge and opportunity came when I was asked to be editor of *AMJ*. I had only been on the editorial board for one term and was totally flabbergasted that I would be asked. I hesitated for several weeks before accepting. Since this story has been told elsewhere (Beyer, 1995), I won't go into more detail here. Being editor of *AMJ* turned out to be the most gratifying experience thus far of my professional life. I felt I was really making a positive difference in the field and in individual careers. I am still grateful that the opportunity came my way.

The next challenge was not as unexpected, but still gave me cause for deliberation. I was asked to run for election as program chair of the Academy, and was torn by conflicting emotions. I had already interrupted the book on culture I was writing with Harry to be editor of *AMJ*. Did I want to continue that interruption even further? The book was important to me, because I hoped it could accomplish something I thought mattered—to integrate the cultural perspective into mainstream organizational studies. After I had taken stock of where the Academy was and where I thought it could be going, I decided that I could perhaps make a difference in the Academy as well. Perhaps Harry could finish the book with another co-author. If not, I'd try to find time to work on it. I thus accepted the nomination and was elected the second time I ran.

The most exciting and satisfying time for me in the sequence of Academy offices was when I was vice-president and program chair. I chose the theme of the social consequences of management for the Academy of Management annual meeting, and with the help of people like Jeff Sonnenfeld, Carolyn Dexter, and Peter Frost, we put together a sterling set of All-Academy sessions on such topics as managing diversity, the work/family interface, and corporate impacts on the environment.

As it turned out, being president of the Academy two years later wasn't nearly as satisfying. The role was more political than I expected, and, in the end, I was unsure I had made a positive difference. The high point for me in this role was giving the presidential address, because I could talk to the Academy membership about things that I thought mattered in our profession but were rarely confronted. My remarks on professionalism provoked very mixed reactions, but I've since been asked to repeat that speech a couple of times to other audiences. If I didn't reach everyone, I had apparently made a difference to some.

The final challenge that I didn't expect came when I was sent by the board of governors to represent the Academy at the founding conference in Frankfurt of an international federation of professional societies like the Academy. I was uncomfortable in the role because international management was not my area of expertise, and I did not speak any foreign languages. I made sure that the other representative was one who compensated for my deficiencies. We chose Hans Schollhammer, who was German-born and educated, had been active on the Academy's international committee, and was an expert in international management. Hans' presence and counsel helped to give me the confidence to push for changes that the Academy board wanted in the proposed statutes of the new federation. I was unsure about how my suggestions would be received. I knew that the writer of the statutes, Horst Albach, was an extremely prestigious German scholar. Would he and the others be willing to entertain changes? In chairing the meeting, Professor Albach was both cordial and statesmanlike; he and the other delegates readily agreed to the changes I proposed on behalf of the U.S. Academy. To my amazement, before the meeting was over, not only had all of the my suggested changes to the statutes been accepted by the assembled delegates, but I had been selected to be president-elect of the group, now called the International Federation of Scholarly Associations in Management. The name was awkward but conveyed our identity clearly, and it made a pronounceable acronym—IFSAM.

Of all the jobs I had taken on in the past, this one seemed most daunting to me. But I applied my usual criterion—could I make a difference? That depended to a large extent on whether IFSAM as an organization could make a difference. As I thought about it, it seemed to me that promoting communication among academics in similar professional associations from other countries through an umbrella organization could potentially improve the quality of management research and its utilization worldwide. The existence and activities of IFSAM could help to broaden the knowledge base, facilitate cross-national research efforts, and increase the visibility and legitimacy of management research in general. The next question was: could I make a meaningful contribution to those efforts? I decided I could, not because of my expertise in management studies or my cross-cultural sensitivity and knowledge, but because I am a pretty good organizer. And so it happened. During my four-years as IFSAM president-elect and then president I worked hard to set precedents for the future and to organize activities in a way that would work with our far-flung set of officers and council members. As past-president, my job will be to attract strong nominees and run the election for the new officers. The six years spent working for IFSAM have been another growth experience and opportunity and a chance to make new academic friends.

## LOOKING AHEAD

The transition from my heavy involvement in Academy activities to a more typical academic role has not been easy. In particular, it's been hard to hit my stride again in doing and publishing research. While I continued to try to do some research during the years I was holding offices in the Academy and IFSAM, it seemed impossible to bring projects to fruition. The experience of being editor made me very critical of my own potential contributions. In addition, I was trying my hand at doing qualitative research for the first time. It wasn't until after I was out of the Academy presidency that I found time to make much progress. Even so, it took years to put together and polish the accounts of two projects. Other things kept intervening. Also, the structural conditions to support research didn't seem nearly as favorable as they had been when I was an assistant professor. The clamor of demands on faculty in business schools has grown.

As my term as IFSAM president was waning, I began to think about what was left to do. Where else could I make a difference by my efforts? I still haven't decided. I am not attracted to governance positions in universities, although I know they can make a difference. I hope instead to continue to do research that makes a difference. I have sought funding to do research on the cultural aspects of implementing total quality management, which I see as potentially revolutionary for the practice of management. I hope to finish some research I started on media-conveyed images of child care for working mothers. I am participating in various research projects documenting what has happened at SEMATECH, the consortium in the semiconductor industry, because I think it is an important social experiment in interorganizational cooperation. I've got more than enough to do for years to come and will have to resist some of the opportunities that keep coming my way.

This chapter is an example. I didn't resist because I thought telling my story might assist other women academics. I don't know exactly how, but I only have to think it's a possibility to feel the effort is worthwhile. I'm still going with the flow and am not sure that a more planned course will work for me, even as I now contemplate trying it.

Going with the flow has, after all, worked pretty well for me in career terms—perhaps because I was lucky, perhaps because the times were different than they are now. I know one thing for sure—going with the flow brought me many happy and satisfying experiences. When I made plans, they never seemed to work out. When I stopped making plans, I didn't too often get disappointed, because I had no definite set of expectations and no fixed timetable to miss. I see graduate students these days being instilled with what I feel are overly ambitious sets of expectations by their faculty mentors, and, in reflection, am glad that didn't happen to me. It's much nicer to find yourself pleasantly surprised by the successes that come your way, than to be disappointed by the failure to reach lofty goals that only a few are destined to attain.

I now see the rationally planned career in which the protagonist controls his destiny as part of a heroic male myth that is rarely realized by anyone. The myth places work and career progressions as the central self-defining objective of people's lives. Those who waiver or fall off the chosen path are somehow deficient. It is a myth that treats the kinds of adjustments I made to accommodate my husbands and family as a weakness, or at least unfortunate, but practical barriers to realizing rationally derived plans often arise, especially for family-oriented women or men. Thus, my more opportunist stance toward a career may prove to be a more realistic and comfortable way to climb the ivory tower. Perhaps I didn't get as high as some who followed the heroic myth more closely, but I got high enough to look back with satisfaction and contentment.

## NOTE

The author wishes to acknowledge the support of the Tuck School, Dartmouth College, where she served as The David T. McLauglin Visiting Professor during the writing of this chapter. Shortly after this chapter was written, Harry Trice died in an accident. I dedicate this chapter to him in memory of all I learned from him about being a scientist, a professor, and a woman.

## REFERENCE

Beyer, Janice M. 1995. "Becoming a journal editor." Forthcoming in Peter Frost and Susan Taylor (eds.), *Rhythms of Academic Lives*. Newbury Park, CA: Sage Publications.

# 10

# "A Nonlinear Life"

## Karlene H. Roberts

*A little kingdom I possess,*
*Where thoughts and feelings dwell;*
*And very hard the task I find,*
*Of governing it well.*

—Louisa May Alcott

In some ways, my career reflects the development of my field (organizational behavior). In some ways, it reflects societal trends. It has been a journey across rocks and crags, many interesting seashores, and a few pastoral valleys. It is probably less a story of decision points and more a story of serendipity. It is a story of the professional requirement for a high tolerance for ambiguity.

Several of my college friends and I recently ruminated about our current places in life. None of us could have guessed at the time of our graduation from Stanford where we would be today. Those of us chatting grew up in California and went to peaceful high schools and then to college. I had no intention of being on a major U.S. business school faculty, teaching, and researching about organizations. In fact, at the time I graduated from college, the appropriate future paths for women were to get married and have children, or teach at the kindergarten through twelfth-grade level, be a nurse or social worker—before getting married and having children. In fact, I tried a year of social work education, but it didn't work for me. My life is a series of fortuitous events, surprises, and major challenges, which often came in the form of people. At least earlier in my career, very few of my opportunities involved any real choice points. Once the superordinate goal of getting into and staying in academe was decided, any opportunity that would enhance that goal was seized upon, because there were very few academic opportunities for women when I completed my Ph.D.

I am professor of business administration at the Walter A. Haas School of Business at the University of California at Berkeley. Long ago, I left the editorial boards of the major journals in my field. Long ago, I completed my administrative duties in the School of Business. And long ago, I received tenure; long enough ago that I have expunged from memory most of the very negative aspects of that process. Not so long ago, I watched my only child leave home for his college experience.

In recent years, my research has focused on the design and management of organizations and systems of organizations in which error can have catastrophic consequences, such as the loss of the organization, damage to surrounding environments, and even loss of future generations. Most organizational researchers are simply not allowed in such organizations, and part of my story is about learning to hold my own in highly sophisticated, technologically advanced organizations that are "macho" in orientation, where women are scarce, and where outsiders are kept out.

## COLLEGE AND THE PH.D.

A nurturing family and a father who could send his only child (a daughter at that) to Stanford provided a base for all that was to come. My father struggled considerably to do that. Life at Stanford for women was characterized by the expectation that college was primarily for finding a husband, and parents wanted to make sure their daughters were armed with that husband by graduation day. I was not.

I went from Stanford to Columbia to complete a Master's of Social Work, that job being more preferable to me than a job in nursing or teaching, until I married and started a family. It didn't work. I was miserable, and as I looked around at what other recent Stanford graduates were doing, it seemed to me the men were having all the fun, going to law school, beginning careers, etc., while the women were by this time either married or biding their time until they got married. In particular, it was clear that if I were going to engage in any career I would have to underwrite additional education to do so.

Meandering to the University of California's psychology department turned out to have life-long consequences. A young faculty member in that department convinced me to enter the Ph.D. program, which I did, and I immediately focused on personality psychology. I came to my senses a year later and switched to industrial psychology. The department was enormously nurturing and offered me a place to grow intellectually. I was also married in those years, which provided me with a stable environment (and soothed my parents' anxieties).

About a year before I intended to take my oral examination, several members of the industrial psychology faculty announced they were leaving Berkeley the next fall either temporarily or permanently. That moved my orals up a full six months. During that same time, I had been the department's lead teaching assistant, and the combination of doing that and getting ready for an early oral left me exhausted. I should have taken this as an indicator of things to come, because my career has always followed a stressful route. My husband was a Ph.D. student at Stanford, and we were truly exhausted, starving students.

Along the way, one of the faculty members suggested my husband and I do a summer student "digs" trip to Europe, which we did learning a vast amount as we went. Because of the stature of the Berkeley faculty in industrial psychology at that time, I was offered wonderful opportunities to engage in management education British-style. I heartily recommend a "breather" somewhere in the Ph.D. program.

Completing our Ph.D.'s was a major challenge for both my husband and myself. For the most part, he commuted from Berkeley to Stanford to complete his degree, and we lived on a poverty-level income.

## A JOB

When I completed my Ph.D., it was understood by my faculty that I would follow my husband to his job and perhaps get a job in a local community college. My husband completed his Ph.D. the next year and had many good job offers in the United States in his field. I had none. He decided to stay at Stanford, and my challenge was to find work. We didn't talk about this because there was nothing to talk about. He had to make a choice in a world in which there were no choices for me to make.

There were no permanent jobs in northern California for a woman with a Ph.D. in industrial psychology. To make matters worse, by this time, I had been socialized by Berkeley's psychology department to feel that the only appropriate job for a Berkeley graduate was a research-teaching job. In an effort to make my resume look as much like a resume of a person with a permanent job as I could, I simultaneously took three positions. I worked as a lecturer in psychology at Berkeley, as a research associate at the Graduate School of Business at Stanford, and as a researcher at Stanford Research Institute (now SRI International). While I could get the teaching and research experience I needed, I could not write research grant proposals, because one had to be a regular faculty member to do so. The situation did allow me to venture into cross-national management research (which I stayed in for a number of years).

Three years after I completed my Ph.D., the Business School at Berkeley hired me in a tenure-track position, and we moved back to the East Bay. I did not go into a job market as new Ph.D.'s do today. Whatever job openings occurred around the United States were unknown to me. I have no idea why Berkeley hired me. The competitors for my job were strong candidates and are well known in the field today.

When I joined the Berkeley faculty, no university in the nation was under much pressure to hire women. The race toward tenure was run in a world in which the Civil Rights movement was still rather new, women's rights were not discussed, and the Vietnam War engendered almost constant campus turmoil for a number of years.

## RESEARCH AND TEACHING BEFORE TENURE

There was not much time for research and teaching before tenure, because I was tenured three years after I was hired into the faculty. The University of California's tenure time clock begins the date the Ph.D. is awarded. That meant that what I had been able to do in the setting of three temporary jobs was heavily weighed.

Early in my career, I enjoyed teaching undergraduates. I was sufficiently close to their age to find their college experiences familiar and enjoyable. I taught psychology students for the first two years after my degree. Psychology classes were then, and are now, filled with a mix of students. My first thought about my early business school class was, "gee whiz, all white males." It goes without saying, that has changed over the years. As I matured, I came to enjoy the Ph.D. students more and have always worked relatively closely with them. I think one's student preferences probably change over the course of a career.

Before tenure, virtually all of my publications were serendipitous in nature. While I was interested in and chose to work in organizational communication, research methodology, and cross-national management research, the rest of my work was done because I was invited along on a project. This was the only way I could build a resume. For example soon after I was hired in a tenure-track position, I was asked to co-author an organizational handbook chapter on organizational communication by a leading researcher in my field. I was delighted with the honor, and writing the chapter was among the first activities in a lengthy research program in organizational communication that followed.

It took two years after I was hired into the faculty at Berkeley to find external funding opportunities so I could be more independent in my work. Obtaining that funding was extremely important, because it allowed me to hire research assistants and pay for field research that is always expensive. The nature of the research also provided a springboard to some of the most exciting research adventures I've had and am having later in my career. For example, we were funded to work on a major organizational communication project directed toward understanding how good communication develops among maintenance and flight crews on the U.S. Navy's then newest fighter aircraft, the F-14.

## PROFESSIONAL ACTIVITIES PRIOR TO TENURE

I had few opportunities for professional activities prior to tenure, and engaging in many of them would have been a bad idea. In those years, Berkeley heavily weighted research productivity in its faculty evaluation, particularly for junior faculty, and service activities were ranked as secondary. In pre-tenure times, when deciding on which activities to engage, scholars necessarily need to consider the activities rewarded or punished by their departments.

## A CHILD

The third year after joining the Berkeley faculty was a banner year. Not only were research grants beginning to materialize and my tenure case had gone forward, but a son also came into my life. Brett was adopted when he was five weeks old. During the interval between the adoption and the tenure decision, I recall many times thinking that if I didn't get tenure, I could never look back and blame it on being absorbed by my family. Not very comforting—one of my colleagues commented at the time that he was sure had I looked pregnant I would not have gotten tenure.

There never has been a balance between a career and a family, rather it was a surge from one to the other. I was back in the classroom, carrying a full teaching-research load two weeks after my son's arrival. At that time, good child care was quite scarce. Thus, Brett was with me as much as possible. I suppose one thing most academic women with children learn is how to take a baby to the pediatrician while grading papers. Further, my research required frequent travel. Fortunately, my parents often helped out and, when possible, I booked flights through Orange County, California, where I would jump off the plane and hand the baby over the fence to his waiting grandparents.

During Brett's growing up, I became a single parent. Thus, my adult life has been comprised of two stages: first, by a traditional marriage in which I could work if I completed the usual homemaking requirements, and second, a full-time involvement in single parenting and my career. The challenge of maintaining a research-teaching career in a major university, while paying sufficient attention to the needs of a small child, was great. Parents in communities in which I've lived were expected to contribute time on a weekly basis to their children's classrooms, soccer leagues, and other extracurricular activities. Failure to be active in the community as a parent resulted in less attention given the child by both other parents and the school system. There are obviously other kinds of contributions parents make to their children on an ongoing basis, and being the only parent making these contributions for Brett made an inherently difficult situation all the more difficult—for both parent and child.

When I became a single parent, I decided to be as close to Brett as possible while maintaining an intense research-teaching career, and, at the same time, expose him to as many foreign environments as I could. My reasoning was that academicians don't make a great deal of money, but they often have more overseas opportunities than people in other lines of work. The least I could do was to help Brett understand a little about cultural differences. I think my intentions proved fruitful, and as an adult, Brett makes plans that continue to expose him to yet new international adventures.

As a caveat, faculty members at Berkeley often better their positions at Berkeley or elsewhere by going into the national job market. During my early years at Berkeley, I was unable to do that because my husband wanted to stay at Stanford. Later, I couldn't market myself nationally because, given California's divorce laws, I would have lost custody of Brett. That was too large a price to pay for a salary increase!

## POST-TENURE TEACHING AND RESEARCH

While I enjoyed teaching undergraduates, the core course, which is our primary offering at the undergraduate level, became tedious after years and years. I have enjoyed more advanced students and topics because both offer opportunities to think about the newer developments in my field. As for being a female teacher, I feel students expect more of me in terms of interaction and listening to their problems than they do of my male colleagues. Evidence of this is that my office is always filled with students during my office hours. I've seen many male colleagues holding office hours who seldom seem deluged with students; I would bet that I am also asked to write more letters of recommendation. However, from Berkeley's pool of students, I have developed a number of close friends over the years, and feel fortunate to be at a university with absolutely superb students.

At about the time I received tenure, I decided to co-author a book on research methodology. That was truly a learning experience that fostered re-thinking the research enterprise and led me to think more closely about issues of aggregation in my field. I've found it useful to have a methodological as well as a content focus, because I feel it makes my research richer.

When I began my career, most of my work was fairly micro, including work on leadership and job satisfaction. A decade later, there was considerably more macro activity in the field, partly because for some years sociologists had been joining psychologists in the ranks of business school organizational scholars. Most scholars continue in their careers along much the same streams or tributaries of those rivers in which they originally began, but I changed entirely. In fact, I recall my colleague and friend, Karl Weick, saying some years ago that it was very uncertain and frightening when he switched his career focus from being an experimental social psychologist to the much more uncertain arena in which he operates today. I thought about this remark when a fortuitous event happened a decade after I received tenure.

During the summer, I was in conversation with some colleagues from different disciplines at Berkeley about organizations that could do great harm to themselves, their environments, and unsuspecting publics (environmentalism was becoming a hot topic in society at large). We had potential entrance to several such systems and decided to meet with their managers to elicit information about their major managerial challenges, in hopes of developing a research agenda.

At about this time I had the opportunity to talk with Charles Perrow about his new book, *Normal Accidents,* which became very important to my later development as a scholar. In the book, he talked about the disaster at Three Mile Island and stated that we would see future disasters of this scope within the decade. Of course, the accident at the Chernobyl power plant in 1986 proved him correct. Perrow also explained marine transport as "an error inducing system," where safety goals and efficient operations are far from assured, and that technological improvements increase output as well as accidents. Since little work existed in which organizational catastrophes were examined from an organizational perspective, few insights were available to individuals who found themselves struggling to manage such systems.

More specifically, my interests led to involvement in a research program with the U.S. Navy to sail aboard one of her aircraft carriers during a normal deployment. A carrier flight deck is arguably the most dangerous five acres of property in the world. Decks are characterized by the interaction of highly advanced aircraft technologies, mixed with enormous amounts of jet fuel and human enterprise and surrounded by ordnance that may be nuclear as well as conventional. People can, and do, get sucked into aircraft jet engines when they don't do exactly as they are supposed to do. By congressional act, women weren't allowed duty aboard America's fighting ships at that time.

I saw this as a real challenge for a number of reasons, not least among them that there was a law that might prevent me from being a part of this research team. Additionally, the world of Navy aviation is macho and doesn't include many women. I have never been as frightened in my life as I was during this initial project in high reliability organization research. Despite the fact that I had a skilled escort, being among jet aircraft landing and departing at forty-eight- to sixty-second intervals in a very confined space (and in an environment of potentially explosive jet fuel and live munitions) was a major challenge—not to mention trying to learn the ropes and working up to twenty-three hours a day at the same time.

Another part of my fear was the knowledge that I was doing something no other woman had done (I sailed aboard the carriers for five years, while simultaneously carrying a full teaching load, being a single parent, and serving as an administrator in the School of Business), and I might do it wrong. If I failed, I increased the probability no other woman would do something like this in the future. I've been off the carriers for several years and still meet Navy officers who were either aboard the carriers when I was and remember me or who heard stories about me going to sea.

It took a year to be comfortable in this situation. People unite in such stressful situations, and officers allowed me to bond with them as I tried to overcome my fear of the situation. The Navy's training of this "flight deck trekkie" was superb. Officers and enlisted men were careful to explain everything that went on, so when I left the ships years later, I had a thorough knowledge of how they knitted themselves and their air wings together. Of course, I paid my dues by doing deck work during night flight operations (inherently more dangerous than daytime flight operations) very early in my tenure at sea. I am also thoroughly checked out with simulation knowledge about the F-14D Tomcat—fighter-interceptor aircraft and the E-2C Hawkeye—early warning airborne system. Paying ones dues is everything in such sensitive organizations.

In this research, we put ourselves outside the paradigm of "normal" organizational studies where researchers don't go into organizations at all but rather theorize about them from afar, dash in and out of places with their questionnaires, or don't go near organizations that require security clearances. These factors combined to produce a situation that didn't allow graduate students, because we couldn't get them clearances in any of the organizations. Also, managers in these organizations want to keep outsiders out because they might become part of the problem or say something potentially explosive about the organizations. The organizations are enormously sensitive to the political whims of a vocal public. Thus, we struggled with the development of long-term trust and confidence.

We therefore knew it would take longer to publish the research because of the lengthy process of building trust and confidence in the organizations, the lack of graduate students to do the research, and the paradigm shift. This is not the kind of research one does prior to tenure. Despite these barriers, I maintained the normal publication rate by publishing material from past research.

One research step can lead to the next. Because of my work with the Navy, several of Berkeley's engineering school faculty came to know about me. One of them invited me to join his studies on human and organizational error in offshore drilling and the movement of oil, illustrating the fact that most of the research in this area targets the engineering aspects of navigation safety and oil spill prevention. Little attention is given to human issues, even though investigations of major accidents often conclude that the problem was due to "human error." I would have the opportunity to study the very industry Perrow labels "error inducing." My previous experience of convincing engineers that social scientists can offer something to their organizations was about to be put to the test.

To address a variety of human and organizational problems in the oil industry, my engineering colleague and I put together a sizable team of graduate students. Our aim was to conduct cross-disciplinary research (e.g., merging sociological, psychological, and political science perspectives). This broader-based approach made grant proposal writing difficult, because (in this case) funders were used to hearing an engineering story. And, from a professional standpoint, my credentials were less acceptable in the industry than those of an engineer. However, I engaged in this form of research activity for the same reasons I studied other high-risk organizations that have the potential to result in environmental harm: they are exciting, face major challenges, and are politically sensitive. I also enjoy opening new frontiers.

## POST-TENURE PROFESSIONAL ACTIVITIES

Opportunities to make professional contributions opened up for me after tenure. I've always enjoyed the professional activities in which I've engaged but didn't seek them out. To my surprise, I became a fellow in the American Psychological Association (APA) very early in my career. When I was appointed fellow in the Academy of Management, I was the third woman fellow of the Academy and the first fellow from Berkeley. I was overjoyed to serve on the Academy's board of governors and to be chair of its organizational behavior division.

Shortly after the tenure decision, I received requests to serve on journal editorial boards. While I don't presently serve on any, I have served on the editorial boards of most of the major journals in my field. In particular, I have always enjoyed assessing the logical consistency of argument and the logical consistency of argument with research design.

One of the most enjoyable experiences I have ever had is the four years

I served on the research review board for the School Capacity for Problem Solving Group of the National Institute of Education. That board evaluated and funded research proposals on schools as organizations. It was interdisciplinary and included political scientists, psychologists, sociologists, and faculty from city and regional planning. We were allowed a great deal of flexibility and had the opportunity over the years to treat ourselves to a day—or even a whole conference—with scholars of our choosing whose work intrigued us. Our small group of scholars feasted at the table of research and theoretical development conducted by top social scientists from around the nation. The activity fed my desire to work at an interdisciplinary level.

I chaired the organizational behavior and industrial relations group in the School of Business for seven years. That was an extremely good experience, because we recruited several fine scholars and much of my job required managing a faculty group that was, by and large, older than me. Just after returning from my first trip with the Navy project, I took over as associate dean of the undergraduate school of business, for two years.

More recently, I served a three-year appointment on the National Academy of Science's marine board committee on advances in piloting and navigation. The marine industry is a small and powerful industry world wide, which provides me with an opportunity to get to know people representing its various segments—from oil shippers to marine pilots and from tug and barge operators to the U.S. Coast Guard. This experience has been important both to my current research and the practical understanding I have gained of the industry and its people.

## A WRAP-UP

Professional women probably experience more role conflict than their male counterparts. Some of this comes from intra-role conflicts—between being a spouse and a professional or being a mother and a professional. One example of this latter role conflict is particularly vivid in my mind. One Saturday evening, I was in the middle of preparing supper for a group of research colleagues when the phone rang. The Navy was calling to see if I wanted to immediately join a carrier at sea that was in the final phases of readiness training. The challenge for me was to cover my classes and administrative duties, find care for my son, and cover my community duties as "soccer mom" and "classroom helper," while completing the dinner preparation and cleanup and making travel arrangements to a distant Navy location. All of this happened about 10:00 P.M. I knew that whether I went along or not, the men on the team would be going. If I couldn't go, my research opportunities would be less than theirs. During the party, I began phoning other moms to ask if they could

fill in for me "just this once." They had trouble understanding my pre-
dicament and were sceptical about its value—role conflict at its best!
However, I was determined to be part of the project group and managed
to climb aboard the carrier with the other researchers at the appointed
time.

# 11

# "My Academic Life: A Metamorphosis in Three Stages"

## Mary Ann Von Glinow

*Life is tough, but it's tougher when you're stupid*
or
*It's a small field and a long life.*

—Bob House, circa 1975

Someone recently noted that I'm at the top of my field right now, and, being such a good friend, reminded me that it's downhill from here. Chilling thought, since I don't process my career linearly. My career is not independent of context: everything, and nothing. It's filled with time-warped images, family, happiness and sadness, successes and failures—basically a highly subjective interpretation except for the documents that line all our lives in some archival sense.

To give this some life and color, I'm not going to treat this chapter chronologically but somewhat kaleidoscopic. Chronology is an artifact of historians who reduce us to days and dates that anchor us in things that are mostly inconsequential. A kaleidoscopic view is shuffled, un-shuffled, and in real time. The collective past is available, documented, and can be presented as an academic resume of achievements. Since it is so public, it is ironic that it is also so private. We each have our in-terpretations of our past, and all of it is filled with very different realities. This I learned a long time ago, when I was a child.

I'm the product of an Air Force family—reared on air force bases all over the world, three-year stints at a time. This constant movement gave me a sense of worldliness, even as a child. Living in France, speaking a different language, and always being on the move molded my view of the world. I was always interested in things international. As a high school student, I was a delegate to the Model United Nations, as an undergraduate student, I studied at the U.N. I subordinated this in my Ph.D. program but have later come back to it with a vengeance.

I never thought about entering academia. It just happened. When I was in the master's program at Ohio State studying for my degree in public administration, I discovered that public sector work seemed to have a thankless component to it and that those I knew in such jobs had very little real impact on real-world events. I decided I'd rather do something else. Hesitating only slightly, I then moved on to the doctoral program there. That was when I met some of the most important and influential people in my life, including Steve Kerr, my future husband. Ohio State was a superb preparation for my first job, which was at the University of Southern California (USC). I remember interviewing in California during a winter of terrible oil shortages and freezing weather. I walked out of the airport, saw the palm trees decked out in their Christmas garb, experienced warm, balmy weather, and knew I had reached nirvana.

When I went to USC with my new Ph.D., I must have entered some sort of lunar cycle that disentangled me from the web of "domestic" emphasis and vaulted me back into the international arena. I met Roy Herberger, then an associate dean, who tried to get me involved in a Japanese research project. He is now president of the American graduate school of international studies at Thunderbird, located in Arizona. His path and mine have criss-crossed periodically over the years.

I started some comparative and cross-cultural research in the early 1980s in Los Angeles, itself an amalgam of cultures that was stimulating enough to keep my interest for the next decade. Six years later, I became the first woman at USC's School of Business to become tenured. Six years after that, I became the first, and only, woman to be promoted to full professor—a lot of firsts. When I left USC, I was still the only full professor who was female, and as of this writing, that still continues to be true. I had catapulted through the ceiling into some rather strange experience. Being a "first" or a "solo" carries with it unspoken responsibility. I was trotted out by the administration on regular occasions to address many different constituencies. I received much attention from the board of trustees (see, we *do* have a woman full professor), local businesses via executive education programs, and the media. At USC, I had a lot of media exposure, which was a heady experience for a "solo" and someone without mentor or guidance for such activities. I remember my three-year review with my department chairman. He gently told me that I seemed to be on the right trajectory, but it would be very helpful if I could get more involved in, say, the Academy of Management to illustrate leadership.

At the time, I had no idea what I had to do and queried him on what steps I might take to achieve such a position. The answer was vague, not through any omission on his part, but because these things are unknown to most people. Mentors, for women, are hard to come by and even harder to keep. Aside from my husband, who was my most important mentor (in life as well), I relied on my networks of female counterparts and academic cohorts for advice. We are now a strong group of women, because those experiences of early academic life shaped and molded us into what we are. You will hear about several of these important women in this book.

Now, I am a professor of management and international business at my second place of academic employment: Florida International University in Miami, another ethnically rich city. This is my second academic job, having spent the first fourteen years at USC. I teach a doctoral seminar on international human resource management and am ensconced in many research projects—all international in scope.

I travel a lot, am involved in a number of exciting research and consulting projects, and have five or six dogs (depending on who is being fostered), three cats, and a husband who shares my passion for animals and animal welfare and the crazy life we lead. I've lived/worked/vacationed in forty-four countries. When I was working as a secretary/clerk typist at Ohio State back in the early 1970s and completing my master's in public administration, I never fantasized about being where I am now, yet I never doubted it. For me, each year has been better than the one preceding it, despite losses, deaths, and endless commuting.

Several themes seem worthwhile enough to discuss. These repeat themselves in cyclic fashion: achieving mastery, achieving balance, and animals. Against that backdrop are people, places, and for want of a better word—cosmic forces.

## ACHIEVING MASTERY

I have always needed/wanted challenge in my work life and my personal life. I'm an Aries. Things that were too easily gained, seemed less important. Getting a Ph.D., and then a job, and then tenure, and then becoming a full professor all seemed part of a natural swing in gaining mastery of this profession. Each of these events isn't isolated but part of a whole process. This process hasn't been easy, but it hasn't really been difficult either. The tenure process, for example, was a gut-wrenching process, not because of what event occurred, but because it was the first time someone else had the option of saying that I might not have achieved mastery at something. My mother always used to accuse me of not having a "clean room," so I resented that someone had to poke around in "my room" and pass judgment. She died the year that I got tenure, and since she was probably my best friend at the time, tenure didn't seem that hard in retrospect. Of course, tenure was significantly less important than who had been the dominant female force in my life and who had always known how to look at me and make me shiver with guilt for unknown crimes committed. However, when my mother died, I gained perspective on tenure and other worldly things that I had previously seemed to lack. I reached the conclusion that if things were not going well personally, nothing was going that well, regardless of the successes in the workplace. Thus, when I gauge the impact that the process of tenure had in my life overall, I remember a comment Ralph Stogdill made to me as a doctoral student: "All tenure does is allow you to continue doing your work."

The tenure process must be taken in context. Very little is important when your family is at stake. I still feel that way. I place a high premium on my personal life and its satisfaction, and treasure the life my husband and I have created. I know that personal life satisfaction is not an "event" but something that must be carefully tended, like a garden. And, once achieved, it must constantly be reachieved again and again. Such is achieving mastery.

Gaining mastery over the things that I do as a professor has always meant being current and good at what I do: knowing when to push students; knowing things that had their genesis in my early childhood experiences and being able to parlay them into meaning today; and knowing how to be "real" in the sense of *The Velveteen Rabbit*. I have taken considerable guidance from Carl Rogers' work on being genuine and authentic in everyday communication. However, I used to think that I had to be something I wasn't in order to succeed. There's something about our field that has to break you down, in order to build you up. I have only recently found that I didn't have to try to be something that I wasn't. As my husband has always maintained, "be careful about what you wish for . . . you may just get it."

Age has played a role here, too. Turning forty was a major event for me, like all decades are, I guess. However, I realized that forty isn't just an extension of one's thirties, but a chance to really make a mark. After all, men were talking about their peers who hadn't moved on to senior ranks by age forty as though they were some sort of failure. Before, I was too worried about other things like getting tenure, being published in the right journals, and acquiring grants or this or that—quite materialistic. I thus took a candid look and realized that I had chosen to play the game, but I had a choice: I could start all over again or move on to another arena. I'm struggling with this now. Years ago, when I was an assistant professor and my department chairman asked me what I wanted as my career goal, I said spontaneously, to be the president of the Academy of Management. ("Be careful what you wish for . . .") I hadn't really thought about it, but it seemed a reasonable goal, maybe even a stretch goal. I am now asked what my new goals are, and I haven't gelled them as yet. I know the general sense of where I want to go, but the specifics elude me. Not that I ever have the time to actually sit and think about this, mind you, as I am always on the move.

Successes and failures in my academic career are shared with my network of female friends who meet at least once a year, generally at the Academy of Management meetings. These women are the ones who have helped give considerable texture to this experience that is uniquely my own. Two have significantly impacted my successes: Janet Fulk and Joanne Martin. Janet Fulk is my life-long best friend, who helped craft my metamorphosis by being friend, guide, teacher, protegee, and shopping partner. Janet, and now Joanne, both span issues of mastery and force me into discussion of my second topic: achieving balance.

## ACHIEVING BALANCE

Balance is a state of mind. I find balance, even in the midst of turmoil, if my personal life is aligned with my professional life; or, if I can manage to balance the demands of the job and not become overloaded. The quickest way to feeling overwhelmed and out-of-whack is for the tasks to pile up, with no time to accomplish them, so, I have learned to work in great spurts of energy, for short to medium periods of time. Generally, that means weekends for me. I have learned to compartmentalize the tasks that need doing and am generally able to manage my time accordingly. When I find that I am unable to balance the demands on my time properly, I have a tendency to bag it all and sleep or shop. It is like when the diet has been broken, what is one more treat anyway? I run on high speed most of the time and find that most of my colleagues are amazed at how much I accomplish. I attribute it to great colleagues and doctoral students but also to a keen willingness to delegate authority/responsibility. Also, time management is important.

Balance also is a personal thing; the balance one achieves among family, work, and friends. I have always had a close relationship with my family. My father died this year, making my brother and me orphans. I feel a strong sense of imbalance with the loss of my parents. I also lost two of my dogs recently, which has been another imbalancing factor. However, perhaps the most difficult part of my life is that my husband and I have long been involved in a commuting relationship. This began in 1989, when his job shifted to the East Coast and mine remained on the West Coast; For a number of reasons, we elected to move our home from California to Florida in late 1991. I still had my job in Los Angeles, so I commuted for one year, and then started at Florida International. In retrospect it seems dreadful, but I'm of the opinion that you can do anything as long as the parameters are known. I knew it was only for the school year, so it became another loss associated with professional/ personal/career balance. Now, Steve works in New York, and I in Florida. We have two homes, although our center is in Miami.

Commuting, of course, exacerbates achieving balance, and we have had to manage this well. It has not been easy. Steve has his own balancing act, but his position at General Electric is the right mix of challenges for him. Sometimes being on the road is very difficult to manage, but by and large, we have evolved a manageable commute. This arrangement gives us both a lot of time, generally, during the week to do the "work" part of the balancing equation, and that leaves weekends to get reacquainted. We tend to guard the weekends jealously simply because this is our only time for our family. The difficulty is that I am often on the road, with consulting, teaching, or conference and Academy concerns, which eats into these valued weekends.

Family, to me, is my husband, my dogs, and my cats. I don't have any children, although I think about adoption periodically. My mother was forty-five when I was born and forty-eight when my brother was born; I thought that I would wait until forty to make this choice. Ironically, I seem not to have had much say in this decision, since my husband's son, who is now twenty-three, lived a short time with us in Los Angeles when he was sixteen; it was difficult for all of us. My stepson and I have now moved through the difficult stage, but there were times when I would cheerfully have strangled him, and I'm sure he me. However, something about time and distance helps to cure all things. This situation has also influenced who I am and how I have learned to cope with difficulty.

The balancing act has been difficult. I used to wear my emotions on my sleeve, and people could easily read my mood. Nowadays that is rarely true. I have had too much work in Asia, and too much appreciation for hiding one's emotions, to give away that card. I have learned to smile a lot, which also stems from years in Asia, and also to juggle a full schedule of family, friends, and work. I suspect the juggling act won't stop, and, in fact, will intensify. Each year it seems so, at least. I juxtapose the concept of balance with the concept of mastery, because it is very difficult to do international research without being in the international culture and away from family. This challenge presents no easy solution. I have thought about taking a visiting professorship in Hong Kong or France but will not sacrifice my family life for my professional life. Instead, I try to get to Asia at least once a year, though generally more, and now Latin America is seeping into the picture. Thus, I will continue to suffer the constant jet lag with ill humor, knowing this is the choice I have made.

Balance is also a question now in whether to spend my time on academic or consulting concerns. I recently had the opportunity to consult to a number of multinational corporations and found it a fascinating process. I've tried to incorporate the key learning I've gained in the consulting arena into the work that I do in academe, knowing full well that this must be balanced wisely. Yet, I find that I have been stretched much more in my profession through my consulting opportunities. Generally speaking, it's important that my work have practical applicability; nothing else makes sense for me. For example, I have had most success talking with managers about how our enterprises—and human resources/ management practices—can become more internationalized.

## MY ANIMALS

I have no idea why I am as impassioned as I am around animals, but I am. I have supported almost all the animal welfare/rights groups around. I have marched in protest against fur-wearing, hunting, vivisection, and the like. Most recently, I have supported a large number of dogs that were displaced from their kennel. I suspect that my next avocational activity will be running a kennel and placing animals who have been strays or abandoned. I mention this simply because the editors asked for the forces that shaped our lives, in achieving what we view as our own unique path.

All of the components—achieving mastery, balance, and my animals— have helped shape who I am and what I find important in my life. This strategy did not come to me overnight; rather it was something that evolved over time. I may have been hypocritical with some of my students when asking them to create a career path that encompassed work and family timeliness. I haven't done this, nor would my current career resemble the one I would have created in the 1970s. And, most likely, the path that will emerge for me in the next twenty years will be unlike any I would have chosen—except that the same three themes will dominate; I would always like to have mastery, balance, and my animals as the center of a whole number of Venn diagrams that variously come and go.

My life, so far, has had a very kaleidoscopic tint. I see no reason for that to change. What I do see are the development of some new skills in managing change plus a tolerance for change and an ability to relish it. I daresay, most of us have no choice. Has my gender helped? Hindered? I don't know. It seems to me that this is a one-tailed test, in that I've no way of knowing what I could have achieved as a male. I have gained entry into some venues simply because I was female. However, I've also had my share of off-color remarks and difficulties related to gender. On balance, however, I've navigated the path well, since I now teach in some of the most prestigious executive education programs in the world, consult to some of the largest multinationals, teach some of the most impressive doctoral students, have entry to some important opinion leaders in this and other countries, and enjoy great colleagues. In addition, I have a wonderful family and am involved in many animal programs. I suspect that the next decade will have even more challenges, and even more opportunities. I live my life by the thought of the "road not taken," so tend to be more risk taking than most, in areas that don't compromise my value set or family. I know I will continue with my international agendas, hopefully building my institution's presence in those arenas. I will also continue with my consulting and animal welfare work and perhaps adopt a child. Wouldn't that add complexity? What-ever path emerges, I suspect I will build on the foundations already created rather than forge an alien direction.

# 12

# Leaders in Their Field: Making a Difference

*Our obligation is to give meaning to life and in doing so to overcome the passive, indifferent life.*
—Elie Wiesel

The senior academic women described in the preceding three chapters have led the way in developing the field of business as we know it. When they began their careers in faculties of business an average of twenty years ago, men held most of the positions and all of the power. Each overcame the hurdle of tenure to create new avenues in research and, more specifically, in theory development. Janice Beyer, Karlene Roberts, and Mary Ann Von Glinow each has a unique story to tell, and yet there is also a commonality in the themes that underlie their accomplishments. In the following sections, a brief summary of each contributor is presented, along with an analysis of the common career themes.

## CONTRIBUTOR SNAPSHOTS

### Janice M. Beyer

Janice had to struggle against the norm that a young woman would marry, have children, and adjust her desires to fit with her husband's career. Although she initially subordinated her career interests, once her children were in school and with support from ideas generated by the women's liberation movement, she began pursuit of a Ph.D. at Cornell in the mid 1960s. She completed comprehensive exams at the same time as the end of her first marriage and then, following graduation, was offered a position at the State University of New York at Buffalo. Much of her ensuing research work was in collaboration with Harry Trice, who she later married. Janice's academic choices have been strongly driven by whether or not the project or activity would "make a difference" to the field. In addition to a full research agenda, she has undertaken a wide spectrum of professional service activities. She feels her opportunities have been greatly enhanced through strong personal and professional relationships.

### Karlene H. Roberts

Also fighting against society's expectations for women, Karlene obtained her Ph.D. and then deferred her academic climb so her husband could succeed in his. Rather than seek the first best position possible, she took on three jobs simultaneously in an effort to build her resume to look equivalent to a permanent job placement. Three years after completing the Ph.D. and developing her credentials, Karlene was offered a tenure-track position at Berkeley. Three years later, she adopted a child and then became primary care provider when she and her husband divorced. Trying to balance career and family was a major challenge and necessitated remaining in California rather than exploring the national job market. Interested in the sensitive and politically charged research area of institutional accidents (e.g., Chernobyl), she began research aboard U.S. aircraft carriers. The research agenda has meant working in a traditionally "macho" environment and setting a precedent that women can excel on "uncommon ground."

### Mary Ann Von Glinow

The product of a U.S. Air Force family, Mary Ann has combined her international interests with a research career. Although she had no early intentions to enter academia, she completed a Ph.D. at Ohio State before taking her first position at the University of Southern California. Mary Ann feels strongly that her professional activities are set in the broader context of life interests and obligations. She has a strong network of friends, a long-term and supportive relationship with her husband, and a love of animals and concern for animal welfare. Mary Ann's multiple interests mean certain trade-offs of time and energy between husband and career, and between consulting and research. For years, she has managed a commuting relationship that at times spanned the continent. She maintains a very heavy agenda, exacerbated by her duties as the current president of the Academy of Management.

## CAREER THEMES

### Serendipity

Although the idea that our present and future can be controlled has appeal, the stories of these three leaders in the field tell a tale of chance events and, to some extent, good fortune. Karlene Roberts notes, "it is probably less a story of decision points and more a story of serendipity." Although it is perhaps a misleading synopsis to suggest that accomplishments are the result of a "lucky" combination of circumstances, like our mid-career women, these senior contributors describe their professional histories in terms of following opportunities and fortuitous events. They also recount tales based on rational and planned action. As Janice Beyer describes,

Going with the flow has, after all, worked pretty well for me in career terms— perhaps because I was lucky; perhaps because the times were different than they are now. I know one thing for sure—going with the flow brought me many happy and satisfying experiences. When I made plans, they never seemed to work out. When I stopped making plans, I didn't too often get disappointed, because I had no definite set of expectations and no fixed timetable to miss.

Hard work was part of the "unplanned" set of actions. Janice further suggests, "I just worked hard, followed my interests and opportunities as they arose, had faith that the academic system would reward me if I was worthy, and then let things happen." This description not only documents expectations that the system is fair and will reward hard work but also indicates an ability to be flexible. Whether academic systems are truly fair is questionable. Whether flexibility is required is most likely a truism, especially in a system where seizing opportunities is important to optimizing career development.

In a similar vein, Mary Ann Von Glinow writes, "I never thought about entering academia. It just happened." According to her, there existed no set plan and no systematic agenda of goals to mark the path. At the same time, the ability to take risks and perhaps to tread the path less traveled was important.

Neither was their choice of research orientation always planned or systematic. Karlene offers, "Before tenure, virtually all of my publications were serendipitous in nature." While she had some specific research interests that were pursued, "the rest of my work was done because I was invited along on a project." Key events, including the development of a research stream, occurred through random circumstances such as meeting certain people. Karlene adds, "My life is a series of fortuitous events, surprises, and major challenges, which often came in the form of people." A meeting with Charles Perrow was instrumental in her choice of research topics and development as a scholar. Janice was also greatly influenced in her research interests through chance meetings—first through the assignment to a professor early in her career and later through her association with Harry Trice. In the latter case, Janice and Harry Trice created a long-term research program together.

### Personal Mastery

If the road was not clearly demarcated from the start, it is evident that these women have the personal tenacity to succeed, regardless of their exact chosen profession. They are all well organized, persistent, flexible, and able to tolerate ambiguity. They possess very high personal expectations. These women have kept writing and submitting, not stopping despite rejections by journal reviewers. To some degree, the difficult challenges have been desirable. Mary Ann describes, "I have always needed/wanted challenge in my work life and my personal life." As overachievers, these women accomplish one task, and quickly go on the next.

In addition, "making a difference" in their fields became increasingly important. In many ways, the balancing act for the senior women is more complex than for women at other career stages. Now, given greater options, these leaders in the field are challenged to make choices as to the most worthwhile avenues to follow, knowingly turning down excellent opportunities. Janice Beyer summarizes her feelings about making a difference in the following way,

I felt I was making a difference. As I became better known through my activities and publications, I found myself being asked to do too many different things. I had to begin making choices, where before I had been pretty much able to accept all of the opportunities that came my way. Sometimes, it was easy to refuse because I simply didn't feel qualified. Often I decided by asking myself—would it make a difference to the field? To society?

One of the reasons Janice agreed to accept the presidency of the Academy of Management was because she could make some meaningful changes there as well. However, to take charge and create change, one must have the power to do so. As Janice reflected, the role was not as satisfying as she had hoped, due to the presence of a political dimension.

Being women in business faculties in the 1970s and early 1980s meant breaking new ground. Karlene describes her research activities on a U.S. aircraft carrier and the trepidation she felt about failing. If this were to happen, future opportunities for other women could be lost. Janice accomplished a "first" when she became the first female editor of the *Academy of Management Journal* and the first woman president of the

International Federation of Scholarly Associations of Management. Mary Ann's achievements include being the first tenured woman at the school of business at the University of Southern California and later, the first female full professor. For all these women, being first in one's field entails special responsibilities as a role model.

## The Female Dilemma

Janice and Karlene both describe breaking through traditional roles and family expectations to pursue careers of their choice. As Karlene notes: "At the time I graduated from college, the appropriate future paths for women were to get married and have children, or teach at the kindergarten through twelfth-grade level, be a nurse or social worker—before getting married and having children."

Karlene mentions that "when I completed my Ph.D., it was understood by my faculty that I would follow my husband to his job and perhaps get a job in a local community college." When Karlene's husband completed his Ph.D. the year following her own, he made the choice where they would work, without joint consultation as to what might be best for Karlene. "We didn't talk about this (joint career decision) because there was nothing to talk about. He had to make a choice in a world in which there were no choices for me to make."

Janice writes, "As a girl of my generation, I saw clearly that any career goals I made would have to adjust to whatever my husband-of-the-future was doing. . . . It went without saying that my husband's career would come first." In reality, that is exactly what happened. Although they both wanted to do graduate work, Janice's husband went on to do a Ph.D., while she went back to full-time work five weeks after their daughter was born. At the time, Janice adhered to traditional roles for men and women and reflected, "I adjusted my aspirations again because my marriage was more important to me than any career."

As the women's liberation movement gained momentum, so did the legitimization of Janice's festering career ambitions. In addition, she had to overcome a lack of self-confidence resulting from years as the support person for her husband, while ignoring her own professional goals. Janice summarizes her dilemma at that time by saying, "I wasn't sure, after all of the self-doubt that the intervening years had generated, that I had the ability to do Ph.D.-level work. I knew I was organized, logical, and good at helping other people, though."

As with the other women who tell their stories in this book, the strains and responsibilities of an academic career can take a personal toll on relationships. Janice's first marriage dissolved just after she completed the comprehensive exams. We might speculate that earlier and more traditional expectations in the marriage had been stretched and reconfigured to the point where their relationship as a couple had fundamentally changed. The end of her second marriage resulted from a career move from New York University to the University of Texas. Although already in a commuting relationship, the distance was increased substantially. Janice recounts, "Once more my decision had an unexpected price—the end of my second marriage. Harry did not feel ready to retire and didn't see how we could commute such a long distance."

In contrast, Mary Ann has not seemed to endure the same career-related strains as Karlene and Janice. However, there are some significant personal differences in their stories. Mary Ann is without children and has not had to play the same balancing act between being mother and career woman. She feels she has had strong support for her career from her husband, in a long-term relationship where each partner is mutually respectful of the other's needs. They have been able to manage an extreme form of commuting relationship, first between Los Angeles and New York and more recently between Florida and New York. Mary Ann also travels extensively to do international research. Her boundaries are clear, however, and she notes that although she has thought about a visiting professorship outside of North America, this is unlikely because of an unwillingness to "sacrifice my family life for my professional life."

In some cases, role tension originates for women when they must be both academic expert and female nurturer—even in a professional setting. Karlene writes, "I feel students expect more of me in terms of interaction and listening to their problems than they do of my male colleagues." Unlike many male academics, additional time demands can be placed on women in business faculties, who may be perceived to interact differently with students or to provide more encompassing support. Alternately, women may be more challenged by students than their male colleagues surrounding their ability to remain in control. Janice cites the incident about the male student who tried to harass her by asking the question about sexual fantasies in the classroom. Remaining ultra-professional and firm while exhibiting a sense of humor are important requirements—for both men and women academics.

### Support Systems

The level of support received from others has had indirect implications for each woman's ability to excel. Such support has had two forms—personal and professional. In the stories these women tell, professional support was provided by mentors and networks of both male and female colleagues, who offered either explicit career assistance or a supportive shoulder when necessary. For example, at each point in her career, Janice consulted with and was helped by a network of senior professional colleagues. In today's even more competitive job market, active assistance from one's committee or advisor remains a critical component in landing the first job.

In the academic realm, support can be self-generated through various forums such as professional meetings. Janice generated opportunities to meet people who were later instrumental in her career through attendance and participation at the Academy of Management and other annual meetings. She recalls, "I can see that I opened the way for many other opportunities by attending and presenting papers so regularly at these meetings. People in the field began to know who I was and what I did."

Personal support was also received from family and friends. Mary Ann mentions that her husband is not only her mentor but her major supporter as well. Karlene talks about her parents, who were willing to assume child care responsibilities for her son when necessary. All women speak of a solid network of friends who provide emotional support and advice. As already mentioned by several of our contributors, Mary Ann notes how much she has relied on a strong group of women friends who collectively have helped to shape one another's career experiences. She adds, "These women . . . have helped give considerable texture to this experience that is uniquely my own." One friend in particular is cast in the multiple roles of "guide, teacher, protegee and shopping partner."

### Achieving Balance

Reflected throughout each story, and touched upon in the preceding sections, is a need to maintain balance in both personal and professional domains. It is a balancing act that is difficult to achieve. Karlene suggests, "There never has been a balance between a career and a family, rather it was a surge from one to the other." Whatever one decides, the very act of choosing never seems to end.

Married with children during the doctoral program, Janice describes a hectic schedule that included orchestrating activities on the home front (e.g., children's music lessons, doctor appointments, horse shows). She had cleaning help and tried to manage her studies to "interfere minimally with my accustomed role in the family." For Janice later on and Mary Ann now, this included the added complexity of commuting. Weekends or vacations are saved as a time to devote to one's partner.

Once in an academic position (especially post-tenure), the balancing act continues, but in a different way. Care must be taken to focus on research when administrative responsibilities beckon. Janice outlines how she became involved in one committee after another at her university, but within defined boundaries. She comments, "I enjoyed being part of the governance of the school and university and felt it was an important part of my professional role. However, I was careful not to overdo it." In some cases, a hiatus from research for the purpose of completing administrative duties can have disruptive consequences. Janice suggests, "The transition from my heavy involvement in Academy activities to a more typical academic role has not been easy. In particular, it's been hard to hit my stride again in doing and publishing research." Editorial work is likewise an expectation of senior academics and must be fitted into an already bulging schedule.

Mary Ann proposes that achieving balance "is a state of mind." It is an alignment of one's personal and professional life. She remarks, "I have learned to smile a lot. I have learned to juggle a full schedule of family, friends, and work. I suspect the juggling act won't stop, and in fact, will intensify." Mary Ann also feels the ability to delegate authority and responsibility to others is a critical component to lessening the load.

## LESSONS FOR OTHERS

Each of these women has led the field, challenged the traditional academic order in some way, and aimed to make a difference as a result of her professional pursuits. They all have been presented opportunities and overcome constraints in order to advance their respective fields. They represent role models for others who choose an academic path.

1. Maintain the vision. In the professional arena, women may induce change in their field if they pursue a focused agenda about which they have real conviction. For instance, although it may be tempting to conduct research that is either topical or likely to receive publication approval, these women leaders have tended to follow their hearts. Mary Ann has pursued international research based on an early love of travel, Karlene has tackled a difficult research topic aboard aircraft carriers, and Janice has conducted practical research that she believes "makes a difference."

2. Challenge tradition. The senior women presented here challenged several traditions—the most important of these being the narrow range of jobs that women were expected to fill. In nontraditional jobs, they did not shirk from the responsibilities and duties of changing roles, and they forged new firsts in their universities and associations. The consequences of these choices were often negative, such as living apart from spouses and children, or divorce. However, their ability to make a difference, create new theory, and lead the field has resulted in positive and long-lasting benefits for all women. Although no woman claims to be a hero, we can see that their lives constantly challenged them to reach higher. Their acceptance of these challenges is inspiring.

3. Develop broad skills. The ability to respond effectively to a fortuitous event was dependent on already possessing a wide range of skills from which to draw. For those of us who would like to excel, we would be well-advised to have a broad array of personal, technical, and political skills at our disposal.

Although Ph.D. programs provide technical competencies, essential process-related skills (e.g., how to navigate tenure or deal effectively with difficult students) are best learned from mentors or other professional associates. Building solid networks of supporters and associates is a precursor to success. Often this support comes from female friends or colleagues.

4. Juggle effectively. Moving beyond tenure, each woman began to devote more time to administrative or editorial duties, in addition to research and teaching. Making deliberate choices about which set of activities to emphasize at a given point in the career progression appeared important to leading the field. Setting clear priorities, effective time management, and the ability to delegate are prerequisites to managing an expansive workload. Once again, political support for one's activities from colleagues eases the transition from concept to reality.

# 13

# Conclusion: A Personal Quest

*Far away there in the sunshine are my highest aspirations. I may not reach them, but I can look up and see their beauty, believe in them and try to follow where they lead.*

—Louisa May Alcott

Although our women contributors have unique stories to tell and are at different stages of career development, they have much in common. They are extremely high achievers, with a personal mission to excel. There is an urgency in their steps, and they operate at a fast pace. Although the more senior contributors are identified as leading the field, the other women are also leaders in their own right.

All of the women have exceedingly heavy workloads. Some have created a lifestyle that integrates family and friends with their career; others have chosen to separate their work and home life. In all cases, these women have interesting and full lives. They know the value of hard work and seize opportunities as they are presented. From their stories, some overarching themes and lessons are elaborated in the following sections.

## CARPE DIEM

In the movie *Dead Poet's Society*, Robin Williams instills in his students the value of "carpe diem," informally translated as "seize the day." The importance of this phrase is not lost on the women in this book, who responded to events in order to maximize opportunities. These women have gone beyond the expected, set personal goals for excellence, and have not compromised cherished objectives. Underpinning their experiences is a sense of self-determination—a process of deciding who one really is and wants to be, and then creating the circumstances that support the realization of one's potential. Many of the goals set by these women run counter to the "male myth" of work achievement "at all costs." Instead, seizing the day has meant a rich combination of work and family, with an emphasis on doing what "makes a difference." Accomplishments are measured on a personally derived scale, transcending individual parameters to include what is best for the profession, students, or family.

As part of a formula for excellence, our contributors possess a wide range of personal, technical, and political skills. Their personal skill set includes excellent organizational capabilities, persistence, tolerance for ambiguity, and a willingness to take risks. These women are good at time management and *never* give up, although they may take detours along the way.

As part of a kitbag of technical skills, they all have Ph.D.'s from respected institutions. Each is a specialist in her chosen topic area, has excellent research skills, and is experienced to various degrees in the art of publication. Although most of the women have become proficient teachers, for many this did not come easily. Not typically part of a university program, teaching was often learned through a "trial by fire." Professional confidence has evolved based on a series of "small wins," to use Karl Weick's term.

It has been important for these women to operate effectively in a politically charged institutional environment. Political support was gained by learning from mentors and by networking with colleagues.

## OVERCOME THE EARLY OBSTACLES

For early-career women, choosing a dissertation topic about which one has passion is important. Effective completion of the thesis project requires staying power in the face of inevitable delays and other frustrations. In many ways, the dissertation is a test of endurance, like a long, hot bed of coals. Those who learn how to navigate the hot spots, who harden their feet, and manage to emerge with enthusiasm intact are well-prepared for the rigors of future scholarly activity.

Another issue of importance is to choose a thesis research methodology that suits not only the topic but one's skills and abilities. In some instances, a chosen methodology may be less accepted, or somewhat controversial, depending on institutional norms. Several of the women had to actively "sell" their committee on their concepts and accept and deal with objections in order to follow their own star.

When selecting a first job, several of the women had a narrow choice set due to decisions made by their spouses or for their family. Advisors may have suggested that they take work in a non-tenure track job or in a community college. Fortunately, none of our contributors took these routes, and they were able to eventually gain tenure-track positions in good univexrsities.

## CREATE A VISION

Each of the mid-career and senior women have shown us their current personal vision, comprised of unequal parts of research, teaching, administration, and professional service. It is important to note that these visions are temporary creations, designed to guide action but not to put one onto a single path forever. Attaining a vision tends to be done in time blocks of approximately five to seven years, with the first two being the Ph.D. and tenure. After tenure, one may choose to establish a new research program, take an active part in governance of the university or a professional association, or develop research and teaching relationships with practitioners. After a path has been explored, one may choose further involvement or a different direction. This freedom to choose and to change is, for most academics, the major payoff in a career that rarely brings wealth or fame and demands a high level of dedication and hard work to succeed.

One might speculate that with time and experience, the art of balancing work priorities, or work and nonwork activities, becomes easier. Based on the stories told in this book, this is not the case. The level of life intensity experienced by these women over time doesn't lessen, although to some extent it does change. For example, as children grow up and leave home, balancing work and family may become easier. At the same time, career opportunities shift and are broadened to present a wider range of exciting and challenging ways to contribute. For most women, managing a wide range of choices requires good time management skills and an ability to delegate.

The women profiled in this book want to succeed professionally, but not at the expense of personal friendships and family. As we have seen from these individual stories, there are several ways to balance one's life and to bring excellence to home and work tasks. One way is to strictly separate work and home life, allotting specific times to each. Another way is to develop synergies by working and playing with the same people, often an academic spouse or a network of local colleagues. A third solution is to integrate work and family life, perhaps by setting up a home office or by using the child care services at the university; work and home tasks are woven together on a daily basis. These are only three possibilities—there may be more. What seems important is to realize that balance and the creative deployment of workable solutions will be of concern throughout one's life.

## FORM PARTNERSHIPS

Perhaps different from models of achievement for men, women in this book have focused more on cooperation than on competition. They tend to form a community of colleagues with whom they share ideas and gather strength. They tend not to be loners, although they remain individualists.

Partnerships are formed at different stages of the career path. Early-career women gain necessary support from their thesis advisor and dissertation committee. A mentor, often in the form of a thesis advisor, provides information about the grey areas of institutional "sensemaking" and eases the transition from novice to early academic. Ideally, the mentor will share "insider" information about the institution, provide guidance about writing and publication, and offer introductions to key people in one's field. Attending conferences and presenting papers, either alone or in conjunction with a mentor, are good ways to increase visibility. One's mentor may also be a research collaborator with established funds for project development. Learning the ropes about how to apply for—and obtain—research funding is an additional bonus.

At the mid-career level, difficulties inherent in gaining tenure were eased by developing strong networks of support and forming coalitions with key gatekeepers. As part of a political process, getting tenure is dependent on determining institutional expectations, proving one's worth as a scholar and team player, and maintaining integrity along the way.

Our senior academics faced their own set of struggles for which they required assistance from others. In many ways, their set of challenges revolve around gaining support for initiatives that they believe could benefit their respective field. Developing new directions, trying to turn the tide in a discipline, and "making a difference" in various ways are based once again on support from others. At this level, getting key stakeholders "on board" is part of a successful strategy. Power is gained through having information, establishing centrality of one's positions, being able to provide support to others, and building coalitions.

## A NONLINEAR PATH

The path to success for our women contributors has broken the frame of the career models that emphasize success at any price or success through a narrow, focused channel of activities. Their careers have been part of a larger mosaic of carefully balanced priorities. They have operated in an environment where there are high levels of complexity—where children, life partners, and one's own career are all taken into account.

Of the nine women featured in this book, eight have academic lives that do not follow the expected progression of completing the undergraduate degree and then the graduate degrees, and finally moving on to a faculty position that results in tenure. Instead, these women have either had other careers prior to entry for a Ph.D. degree, chosen to work in business faculties while simultaneously consulting (a practice sometimes frowned upon for junior faculty), or moved at least once before tenure. For these women, a linear life format simply does not fit.

Another interesting component to these stories is that several of the women became members of business faculties at a later life stage than might be considered the norm. Knowledge accrued from a wide range of life experiences put them into a position to more quickly accelerate their careers and excel. These women were able to "hit their stride" quickly and surpass their own expectations for success.

These women have the capacity to be flexible in thought and action; they take detours without losing momentum. Although our contributors do not always have the luxury of following an ideal path, they have been able to create a successful route by capitalizing on opportunities. This may be the quintessential path for many people, not just women. As Janice Beyer remarks,

I now see that a rationally planned career, in which the protagonist controls his destiny, is part of a heroic male myth that is rarely realized by anyone. The myth places work and career progression as the central self-defining objective of people's lives. Those who waiver or fall off the chosen path are somehow deficient. It is a myth that treats the kinds of adjustments I made to accommodate my husbands and family as a weakness, or at least unfortunate, but practical barriers to realizing rationally derived plans often arise, especially for family-oriented women or men. Thus, my more opportunist stance toward a career may prove to be a more realistic and comfortable way to climb the ivory tower.

From these stories, we have been able to view each woman's personal quest for achievement. We couldn't have said it better. May the lessons learned guide us all onto a path that fulfills both personal and professional dreams.

# Index

# About the Contributors

CYNTHIA M. BEATH is an associate professor at the Edwin L. Cox School of Business, Southern Methodist University. In the eight years since the completion of her Ph.D., she has published extensively in academic journals such as *MIS Quarterly* and *Information Systems Research* and in practitioner journals such as the *Journal of the American Society for Information Science*, on topics that include information systems development, implementation, and maintenance. In 1993, she became a Fulbright scholar and spent six months at Thammasat University in Bangkok. Cynthia is associate editor of two of the top journals in the information systems field and was voted "Reviewer of the Year" by *Information Systems Research* in 1993. Recently, she and a colleague were awarded a large research grant from the decision risk and management sciences program of the National Science Foundation.

JANICE M. BEYER is currently both the Rebecca L. Gale regents professor in business and a professor of sociology at the University of Texas at Austin. Over the past two decades, her research has focused on alcoholism, educational institutions, research methodologies, ethics, organizational culture, and quality management. She has published extensively in both academic and applied journals, including *Administrative Science Quarterly, Organization Science,* and *Academy of Management Journal* and has numerous chapters in edited books. Her contribution to the academic profession includes a dozen years of leadership in the Academy of Management, culminating in a year as president, and five years of executive service with the International Federation of Scholarly Associations of Management, where she served as president. She has also been editor of the *Academy of Management Journal* and is currently a member of the editorial board of the *Administrative Science Quarterly*, the *Journal of Socio-Economics*, and the *Journal of Quality Management*.

YOLANDE E. CHAN is an assistant professor at Queen's University School of Business. She has degrees in electrical engineering (S.B. and S.M.) from the Massachusetts Institute of Technology, an M.Phil. from Oxford University, and a Ph.D. from the University of Western Ontario. Her research has focused on the alignment of business and information systems strategy and the business performance impact of information systems. Her publications have appeared in the *Journal of Strategic Information Systems, Business Quarterly,* and edited books. She has also written several teaching cases. She is the recipient of many awards, most notably the Rhodes Scholarship (1982), Marketing Science Institute Competition (1991), ICIS Doctoral Dissertation Competition (1993), and the Student Life Award, Queen's University (1994).

DIANNE CYR is an adjunct professor in the Faculty of Business Administration at Simon Fraser University. She has a Ph.D. from the University of British Columbia, an M.A. from the University of New Brunswick, and a B.A. from the University of Victoria. Her research has most recently focused on strategy and HRM in international joint ventures in the transition economies of Central/Eastern Europe. She is the author of *The Human Resource Challenge of International Joint Ventures* (Quorum Books, 1995) and has published in various journals including *Organization Studies* and *Human Resource Management*. She was the recipient of the Chateaubriand Fellowship to conduct research at INSEAD in France. In addition to academic pursuits, she is the president of Global Alliance Management, which specializes in the effective operation of joint ventures and strategic alliances.

JUNE N. P. FRANCIS is an assistant professor in marketing and international marketing in the faculty of business administration at Simon Fraser University. She received her degrees from the University of the West Indies (B.Sc., management studies), York University (M.B.A.), and the University of Washington (Ph.D.). Her academic interests have concentrated in the fields of cross-cultural marketing and exporting. Her major academic publications have appeared in the *International Journal of Business Studies*. Her current business involvement is as a partner in an international publishing enterprise. Prior to pursuing an academic career, June worked in product management for Procter & Gamble–Canada and Clorox Company. She currently consults with organizations on marketing and cross-cultural issues and with the Canadian government on export promotion issues.

MARLENE K. PUFFER is an assistant professor in the faculty of management, University of Toronto. Her degrees include a B.A. and M.A. (economics) from the University of Toronto and a Ph.D. from the University of Rochester. Marlene's research interests are international financial markets, international corporate finance, and empirical asset pricing. She has published in the *Journal of Banking and Finance*. Marlene is actively involved with AISEC.

SHEILA M. PUFFER is an associate professor in the college of business administration, Northeastern University. Her degrees include a B.A. (Slavic studies) and an M.B.A. from the University of Ottawa and a Ph.D. in business administration from the University of California, Berkeley. Her research interests include Russian management, comparative management, governance, and prosocial behavior. She has published six books and written many book chapters and articles in journals such as the *California Management Review, European Management Journal, Administrative Science Quarterly, Leadership Quarterly,* and *Human Relations.* Her professional service includes membership on the editorial board of the Academy of Management Executive. Sheila takes every opportunity to present her research and has made three dozen presentations at professional meetings and over two dozen presentations at universities, corporations, and community service organizations in the last decade.

BLAIZE HORNER REICH is an assistant professor of business administration at Simon Fraser University. Her degrees in economics (B.A.) and management information systems (M.Sc. and Ph.D.) are from the University of British Columbia. Blaize has spent almost two decades as a practitioner and management consultant in the field of data administration and information technology planning. Her current research interests are management of the information technology function, how organizations link their business and technology objectives, and methods of increasing the information technology competence of line managers. She has published articles in *Information Science Research* and the *Journal of Strategic Information Systems* and teaches in various executive programs.

KARLENE H. ROBERTS is a professor of business administration at the University of California at Berkeley. She is a fellow of the American Psychological Association and the Academy of Management. Her highly eclectic research has focused on organizational accidents, high reliability environments, and research methodologies. Her work has been published in many journals including *Management Science, Organization Science, California Management Review,* and *Organizational Dynamics.* She has edited five books and been the co-author of three more. She has served on the editorial board of academic and applied journals in management and psychology. Her administrative contributions include a seven-year term as chair of the organizational behavior and industrial relations group at Berkeley and two years as associate dean and director of the undergraduate school of business administration.

DENISE M. ROUSSEAU is a professor of organizational behavior at Carnegie Mellon University. Prior to her current position, she was at the Kellogg School of Management, Northwestern University. She received her B.A., M.A., and Ph.D. degrees from the University of California at Berkeley and is a fellow in the American Psychological Association and a member of the Society for Industrial/Organizational Psychology. Denise focuses her research on changing employment relations, psychological contracts in organizations, and human resource strategy, culture, and performance. The author or co-author of several books, her research has also appeared in such publications as the *Journal of Applied Psychology, Academy of Management Journal, Academy of Management Review,* and *Administrative Science Quarterly.* She is associate editor for the *Journal of Organizational Behavior* and on the editorial board of *Journal of Applied Psychology.*

CAROLYNE F. SMART is an associate professor and the associate dean, faculty of business administration, Simon Fraser University. Her undergraduate and graduate degrees are from the University of British Columbia. For the past five years, she has been active in the governance of the faculty and the university. Among other responsibilities, she has served as director of the undergraduate program, coordinator of an external review, and chair of the appointments committee. Her recent research has focused on the structures and processes necessary to promote internationalism in business faculties. Previous to that, her research centered on corporate responses to crises and decision-making under uncertainty. Her teaching encompasses undergraduate courses in business policy and organizational behavior and executive M.B.A. courses in strategic management.

MARY ANN VON GLINOW is a professor of management and international business at Florida International University. Prior to her current post, she was at the University of Southern California from 1977 to 1993. Her research is focused on mapping best practices in international human resource management, international technology transfer, and managing diversity. She has a Ph.D. in management science and an M.B.A. and M.P.A. from Ohio State University. She has authored numerous journal articles and several books including *International Management* (forthcoming) and *Learning Organizations, Culture Change and Competitiveness: How Managers Can Build Capability* (forthcoming). She serves on ten academic journal review boards. She is a president of the Academy of Management, and a fellow of that institution.

ISBN 0-275-95085-9

90000>

HARDCOVER BAR CODE